Landowners in Poland

1918–1939

Wojciech Roszkowski

EAST EUROPEAN MONOGRAPHS, BOULDER
DISTRIBUTED BY COLUMBIA UNIVERSITY PRESS, NEW YORK

1991

EAST EUROPEAN MONOGRAPHS, NO. CCXCIX

Contents

Chapter 1

INTRODUCTION

This book is an attempt to describe the economic, political, social, and cultural role of large landowners in Poland between the two world wars. So far there has been no complex monograph of this subject in English, although several works, covering some aspects of the landowners' activities, exist in Polish.[1] Apart from pure curiosity, the author was motivated by the necessity to rectify some stereotypes that exist in the historical literature on interwar Poland. Some Marxist authors seemed to believe that interwar Poland was a country ruled by "bourgeoisie" and "landowners," forgetting about he role of the "intelligentsia," the military, and the middle class.[2]

While analyzing the influence of large estate owners on the social, political, economic, and cultural life of interwar Poland, one must try to forget the post–1944 changes, which only make it more difficult to understand the interwar reality. Post–World War II Polish literature on this topic is full of "class" bias. Socialist political stereotypes and a priori judgments contributed to such misleading conclusions as those frequently repeated theses of the higher tax burden of peasant holdings as compared to large estates, or of "a total collapse of large–estate economy" that proved "apparently inefficient."[3] The social reality of interwar Poland was much more complicated than that.

Some authors stress the populism of Józef Piłsudski's rule while others tend to emphasize its authoritarianism. The controversy will probably continue, since the phenomenon of the *sanacja* rule in inter-war Poland was very complicated, just like the personality of Piłsudski himself. Anyway, he came from the circle of Polish landowners of the former Grand Duchy of Lithuania, and reflected the contradictory dimensions of Polish social life at the turn of the twentieth century.

The political, social, economic, and cultural life of the Polish Second
Republic was largely a result of the old noble tradition, the effects of
modernization under partitions, and the rise of populism in the early
twentieth century. Hence both the interwar Polish political democracy of the years 1918–1926, the authoritarian rule after the May 1926
coup d'état, as well as the economic, cultural life, and social changes
of Poland between the wars were quite a mixture of the old and the
new. It is in this sense that the description of the changing role of
the landowners in Polish life of the early twentieth century may cast
some new light on the legacy of interwar Polish independence.

Of course, historical theses largely depend on a chosen point of
view. While the author believes that political ideologies should be
kept as far as possible from the social sciences, his point of view
should be explained. It is not neutral when the ultimate criterion of
evaluation of a social phenomenon is social justice, equality, purely
economic rationality, or politics. The reason adopted in the present
study—a widely understood viability of the social system—makes it
necessary to analyze all the aspects of the subject under discussion.

After centuries of evolution of the aristocracy and landowners
as a social group in Poland, at the turn of the twentieth century the
group was quite diverse and its identity rather complicated. Landowners were basically the owners of land. As such they could be more
easily distinguished from other social groups on the principle of property rights and treated as a social class.[4] For an economic historian
this would be enough. It would even make things simple: it is easier to
examine a closed group that can be analyzed in statistical terms. But
for social history, especially if it deals with East Central Europe, it is
not sufficient to talk about property and income only. Equally important were and are such criteria as the noble tradition, the *connubium*
and *convivium*, access to power and place in the social hierarchy, and,
as Max Weber described it, the "way of life" that divided each society
into "estates."[5]

In a mixed society with strong feudal remnants, in which income
and property have never been absolute criteria, such as the Polish
society at the turn of the twentieth century, it is difficult to speak
about "classes."[6] After all, the Polish society of that time was still
deeply rooted in the noble tradition and, although the market economy and populist ideologies gradually changed social relations, such
criteria as social authority, the coat of arms, the family tradition, and
the Weberian way of life still played a very important role in social

divisions.

In Polish there is a distinction between the landowners *właściciele ziemscy* and the landed gentry *ziemiaństwo*, the latter term being in use until 1945. In interwar Poland large estates were available to people of various social origins. Although landed property can be treated as a distinctive feature of a social class this does not mean that all large estate owners belonged to the landed gentry, which was a sociocultural phenomenon rather than a political or economic term.

In the Polish–Lithuanian Commonwealth the term most widely used was nobility *szlachta*. The Polish–Lithuanian Commonwealth had a democratic system based on the legal equality of all the nobles. The mood of the nobility, the ruling class of Poland–Lithuania in its Golden Age of the sixteenth century, was affected not only by military victories, but also by material prosperity and religious tolerance. The average noble felt himself a real citizen of a free and successful state. When Polish King Zygmunt II August wanted to silence the criticism of his noble audience, a squire replied boldly "No servant am I, but a kingmaker and a deposer of tyrants."[7]

After the extinction of the Piast rulers, there were no Polish princely titles. Only in the Grand Duchy of Lithuania, where magnate paternalism survived, was the princely title of *kniaz* allowed by the 1569 Union of Lublin, but only in the case of a few families, such as the Ostrogskis, the Radziwiłł s, and the Sapiehas. Some of the most influential Polish families brought titles from abroad, mainly from Rome, but the use of titles was legally banned in the Commonwealth. Phrases implying that some nobles were "more equal" than others were erased from the record of the Sejm (Parliament). The nobility also recognized equality of the sexes, at least in the sphere of property rights. The basic denominator of the old Polish nobles, ethos was their principal belief in the value of an individual person: every noble was a *sobie pan* (a "lord unto himself").

Of course, this did not necessarily result in the practical equality of the nobles. In the Polish–Lithuanian Commonwealth, there had always been strong incentives for stratification within the nobility. First of all, some families enjoyed a more frequent access to high state offices. Membership in the Senate became the first generally accepted differentiation for the higher nobility. Second, because of holding high office, some magnate families were given leases on royal demesnes, which were sources of huge revenues greater than those from their family estates. The growth of many magnate families originated from the royal grants in the east. Some magnate families were so powerful that, during the seventeenth and eighteenth centuries, they could organize private armies and conduct their own foreign policies. The cases of the Russian "Dmitriad" of the Mniszech family in the early seventeenth century, the Moldavian policy of the Potockis, or the Radzwiłł ambitions to rule Lithuania in the mid-seventienth century may well illustrate this phenomenon. In 1764 some of the Polish magnates, such as the Poniatowskis, the Lubomirskis, the Massalskis, and the Ponińskis, received princely titles. This was contrary to the long tradition allowing only the titles specified in the Union of Lublin of 1569.[8]

The magnates showed extraordinary skills in self-consolidation of their group. The first entail in Poland was created in 1470. Later some other magnate latifundia, such as those of the Radziwiłłs (Nieśwież-Kleck-Ołyka in 1586), the Zamoyskis (Zamość in 1589), the Gonzagaa-Myszkowskis (Chroberz in 1601), and the Ostrogskis (Ostróg in 1609), became entails—not without strong opposition from other nobles.[9] But even without formal entail rights, the magnates tried to prevent division of their latifundia.

Magnate domination was pronouncedly regional. In the east, in the Ukraine, or the Grand Duchy of Lithuania, or even in Lesser Poland, the magnate latifundists played a dominating role, while in Mazovia and Podlasie there were hardly any magnate domains and nobility populated these areas in thousands. An average Mazovian noble had only about 6.6 hectares (sixteen acres). There were noble villages in which serfless noble families cultivated the land themselves, and there were even thousands of landless nobles (the *gołota*) who theoretically had the same rights as the magnates but, of course, in practice were frequently serving some powerful masters.[10] A village of the Dobrzyński petty nobles in the Nowogródek region at the beginning of the nineteenth century was evoked by Adam Mickiewicz in his towm *Pan Tadeusz.*[11]

From the seventeenth century on the political domination by the nobility in Poland–Lithuania was paralleled by deterioration of the economic situation. As long as the estate–corvée economy flourished the gentry gradually limited the peasant autonomy. Village self-government was abolished, tenants were required to work on landlords' estates, and the range of the corvée services was gradually increased. Finally the peasants were tied to the land. The collapse of Polish grain exports in the seventeenth century dealt a heavy blow to the estate–corvée economy. As a result the labor services were even extended, the peasants were forbidden to buy anything outside the estates, and the towns declined even further.

At the end of the seventeenth century the nobility may have seemed all powerful. They enjoyed all possible privileges and had but few obligations. However, the noble democracy had gradually declined into a noble anarchy. The traditional principle of unanimity in legislative diets began to be treated literally: Only one protest could now stop any measure from being voted by the Sejm. The *Liberum veto* gave the magnates the opportunity to manipulate noble deputies. The civil and martial virtues of the nobles, which had made the Commonwealth successful, were now corrupted. Christian moderation gave way to Eastern ostentation and lure of luxury. The all–too–easy victory by Catholicism over the Reformation also had a demoralizing effect: deprived of any intellectual challenge, Polish culture declined into passivity and challenge, Polish culture declined into passivity and ritualism. Even the religious toleerance began to disappear, since most of the Commonwealth's enemies were non–Catholics.

In the mid–eighteenth century Poland–Lithuania was still a country of formal noble equality, but was in fact only a loose federation of magnate domains. The magnates, frequently bribed by the neighboring courts of Russia, Prussia, and Austria, and buying noble votes in the Sejms, were leading the country to its ultimate ruin. Before the final dismemberment of the Polish–Lithuanian Commonwealth, the status of the nobility was changed by the Constitution of 3 May 1791. In an attempt to prevent further manipulations of the landless noble clients by the magnates, the patriotic faction managed to exclude petty and landless nobles from participation in the diets. The term "possessionati" was more and more frequently used to distinguish the landed gentry *ziemiaństwo* from the masses of petty and landless nobles. This was due to the constantly growing numbers in the lower stratum of the nobility. Numerous new grants of nobility to townspeople, merchants, and baptized Jews depreciated the noble coat–of–arms and deprived it of its earlier "Sarmatian" mythology. At the same time the *liberum veto* was abolished and a regular constitutional monarchy was introduced. However, the constitution did not come into force because of opposition by a group of magnates who, with the support of Russia, founded the Targowica Confederation against the reforms. The second, and soon the third, partition in the years 1793–95 put an end to the Polish–Lithuanian Commonwealth.[12]

The partitions even widened the gap between the landed gentry and the landless nobles. The legislation of the partitioning powers, which also ennobled new families, heightened the birth criterion among the landed gentry and checked its transformation from a closed estate to a more open class. The Constitution of the Duchy of Warsaw of 1807 gave the landed gentry the right to elect about 60 percent of the deputies of the Sejm. This situation did not change much after formation of the Kingdom of Poland under the Russian tsar. The Organic Statute of 1832, introduced after the defeat of the Polish November Rising, abolished national Sejm representation and the rest of noble privileges. Russia wanted to separate petty nobles from large and middle–size landowners in order to russify the former. Special Russian commissions separated those recognized as petty nobles and deprived them of the right to vote. Russian deportations of petty Polish nobles from the eastern territories of the Commonwealth, which started after the Bar Confederation in 1768, culminated with deportations of about 54,000 petty and landless nobles after the November Rising of 1830–31.[13]

The College of Heralds of the Kingdom of Poland (Heroldia Króestwa Polskiego) that operated in the years 1830–31, an institution unknown in old Poland–Lithuania, confirmed the nobility of only 52,000 persons, thus depriving about 250,000 people of noble rights.[14] Further new patents of nobility carried out by the partitioning courts only sharpened the criterion of birth, since the new nobles were not accepted by the old noble society. Rich nobility from senatorial families were frequently given Austrian, Russian, or German artistocratic titles. On the other hand the nationally and socially victimized petty nobility, who became the pioneers of the new intelligentsia, carried on the old noble ethos among the common people.

In the Prussian partition the Polish nobility was challenged by the agrarian laws introduced after 1807. The 1823 peasant emancipation law affecting the Great Duchy of Poznania was perceived by many nobles as a violation of their property rights. Soon, however, the most enlightened nobles reacted to the challenge of the Prussian emancipation laws of modernizing their economy. The example was set by General Dezydery Chłapowski of Turew, who had graduated from agricultural studies in England and was the first to introduce crop rotation, precise accounting and intensive animal husbandry.

In Austrian Galicia the Polish artistocracy and nobles were built into the "dominion system," in which their estates became the founda-

tion of the local administration and judiciary. Thus the emancipation
of the peasants was blocked and the feudal privileges of the nobility
were restored. This system was changed by the Austrian peasant
emancipation patent of 1848.

After the emancipation of the peasants, which was completed in
Austria in 1848, Prussia in 1850, Russia in 1861, and in the Kingdom
of Poland in 1964, the Polish nobility lost the remaining privileges,
but the term *szlachta* (nobility) or *ziemiaństwo* (landed gentry) were
still used to distinguish large landowners of noble origin. The emancipation of the peasants was a strong incentive to redefine the identity
of the nobles and the landed gentry in terms of ownership and income, and not of the family tradition and birth. However, under the
pressure of the peasant claims and the anti–Polish policies of the partitioning powers, the Polish landed gentry opposed this redefinition.
While defending their land ownership against German and Russian
policies, they frequently felt themselves the defenders ofthe national
weal. At the same time, while most of the landed gentry opposed
peasant claims to land, for national and religious reasons, they usually felt responsible for the social emancipation of the peasants. The
effect was a peculiar mixture of nationalism and paternalism of the
Polish landed gentry.

Although its use began at the end of the eighteenth century in
order to distinguish the *possessionati* from the landless nobility, at
the beginning of the twentieth century, the term *Ziemiaństwo* still
included, in the common udnerstanding, some of the traditional at-
tributes of a feudal estate. The remark by a landowenr that "not everywhere" was the distinction made in landed gentry manors between
"perfect gentry" and otehr people only confirms this interpretation.[15]
Neither in the nineteenth century nor in interwar Poland was it possible to enter the landed gentry society by simply buying land. Membership, at minimum, would require possession of land and a coat-of-
arms for several generations. Therefore the Polish landed gentry of
this period distinguished themselves by their Weberian "way of life"
rather than of their property as Marxian "means of production."[16]

Inthis study we shall deal with the role of waht were widely understood as large landowners *właściciele ziemscy*, no matter if they
were *ziemiańmstwo* or nouveaux riches, whenever more precise numerical data are required. This criterion is especially practical when the
economic role of the group is considered. However, whenever a social
or cultural role of the group is discussed, further distinctions will be

made and a group of *ziemiaństwo* or its inner circle, the aristocracy, will be distinguished.

Finally, there is the problem of what should be considered a "large landed estate" or, in other words, what are the criteria separating "large landowenrs" from smallholders. There havebeen many ways of dividing farms according to their size. In the Polish literature probably the most comprehensive approach to this question was suggested by Leon W. Biegeleisen, who distinguished five criteria: economic functions of the owenr, his social standing, the economic self–sufficiency, the size, and the gross return of the farm. By the economic functions of the owner he udnerstood the distinction between farms cultivated by the owner and those using hired labor (while the latifundia additionally required hiring of local management). By social standing he meant the owner's standard of livng, the social group to which he belonged, his education, and the general "way of life. According to the size, he divided farms into small holdings below 100 hectares, large estates above 100 hectares, and latifundia exceeding 5,000 hectares.

Chapter 2

COMPOSITION OF THE GROUP

Limitation of the group of large landowners to owners of estates over fifty or 100 hectares may seem a little artificial. In this way a number of large peasant farms are included, while many smaller farms belonging to gentry descendants are not. Such an approach also disregards considerable regional differences. Estates over fifty or 100 hectares in western Poland were productive, self–sufficient enterprises, while in the easternmost regions of Polesie or Nowogródek they could even be insufficient to make a living for the owners and his family. But if the number of large landowners is looked for, a precise numerical limit will be needed. The Polish statistical sources usually offer the limit of fifty hectares.

In the existing literature various estimates of the number of large landowners in interwar Poland may be found. Ludwik Landau estimated their number at 154,900 in 1921 and at 178,800 in 1927.[1] According to government sources, the number of the "landed gentry" in Poland was about 170,000.[2] It seems that these data were considerably overestimated. The problem was that the 1921 census showed 30,079 farms above fifty hectares and 18,916 farms above 100 hectares, while a later version of the census data lowered these data to 19,454 and 13,201 respectively. The difference was due to the fact that the census data were based on the category of "estates," while the processed data included information on the number of property units or owners, who could have had several estates.[3] Further on this distinction will be avoided, so that "estate" will usually mean the landed property.

Closer to the real number of large landowners were the estimates elaborated by the Supreme Council of Landowners' Organizations (Rada Naczelna Organizacji Ziemiańskich) for the National Exhibition in Poznań in 1929. The supreme body of the Polish landowners estimated their number at 0.36 percent of the population, or at about 110,000 people.[4] A little lower was the estimate presented by Mieczysław Mieszczankowski, who calculated the number of economically active and passive landowners in Poland at 100,000 in 1921, 90,000 in 1931, and 85,000 in 1938.[5] An interwar scholarly estimate claimed that the number of the landed gentry in 1938 was about 64,200 people,[6] while Janusz Żarnowski, the author of a study on the interwar Polish society, generally confirmed this figure on the grounds of the 1931 census and estimated their number at about 60,000.[7]

An attempt to establish the number of large landowners in interwar Poland should be based on a careful analysis of the available sources. The published results of the 1921 census were not too accurate. Relatively precise were the results referring to the Poznań, Pomerania, Warsaw, and Łódź provinces. On the other hand, Upper Silesia and western counties of Wilno province were not covered at all. The data referring to these areas were estimated later in the final version of the statistical report on the large landed property, published in 1925. The 1921 census covered 30,300,000 hectares out of 38,900,000 hectares of the territory of the Polish Second Republic. The toilsome task of filling the gaps was undertaken by Mieczysław Mieszczankowski, who estimated a further 7,600,000 hectares. Nevertheless, he changed the census data in relation to the land area only, leaving the number of farms and estates unchanged.[8] Thus the only foundation of the 1921 estimate may be the data published in 1925 as final results of the 1921 census in relation to large estates.

The 1931 census treated the large estates in a rather unclear way. Probably to prevent comparisons and criticism of the slow progress of the land reform, the census was based on the "economic units," or households, including at least one farmer owner or tenant. Moreover, the adopted limit of large estates was fifty hectares of agricultural land as compared to fifty hectares of the total area in 1921. The "economic units of fifty hectares of agricultural land or more" were, therefore, something different from owners of estates above fifty hectares of the total area. The number of these units—16,212—inlcuded not only owners, but also tenants, and eliminated those owners, whose estates had more than fifty hectares of the total area but less than fifty of agricultural area. The 1931 census showed 61,740 "economically active and passive members of economic units over fifty hectares of agricultural area," which means that each unit included, on average, 3.81 members.[9]

World War II broke out in 1939, too early to allow for the third population census in Poland. Also the agricultural census had not been completed by 1939. Some data collected in the course of this census can be found in the Archive of the Chief Census Bureau (*Główny Urząd Statystyczny*) in Warsaw. But their computation would require a lot of time, while the accuracy of the final results would not be too high because of gaps in the existing evidence. A statistical inquiry referring to large estates was, however, opened by the Supreme Council of Landowners' Organizations in 1939. Unfortunately, even these data were incomplete.[10] Additional computations, based on the 1939 inquiry of the council, were made by Stefan Stablewski.[11] All in all, even for the years 1931 and 1939, there are no precise data concerning the number of large landowners in Poland, and an estimate is therefore necessary. The available data are presented in Table 2.1.

Which of the figures quoted for 1939 were closer to the interwar reality? It seems that the data presented by Jan Stecki, as being a result of summing up of regional data, should be given a preferential treatment, although some of them are not entirely sure. The overall estimate does not differ much but some of the regional data are quite differentiated. For instance, the increase of the number of estates in western Poland, shown by Stecki, seems rather surprising.

Table 2.1 indicates that in the years 1921–1939 the overall number of owners of estates over fifty hectares has decreased by 9.30 percent and the number of owners of estates over 100 hectares has fallen by 13.60 percent. This decrease was most evident in central Poland, where the number of larger owners decreased by 25.90 percent, and that of owners of estates over fifty hectares by 22.60 percent. In the eastern and southern provinces this decrease was slightly slower, while in western Poland the number of large landowners even increased. In relation to the overall number of farm owners in Poland, which was 3,384,300 in 1921, 3,863,200 in 1931, and 4,511,600 in 1938/39, the share of large landowners fell from 0.57 percent in 1921 to 0.47 percent in 1931 and 0.39 percent in 1938/39.[12]

An estimate of the overall number of economically active and passive large landowners must be even more approximate, since it largely depends on the estimated average number of members of the owner's family. Ludwik Landau suggested that the average number of family members in Polish agriculture was 5.15, while the 1931 census indicated 3.81. It seems that the families of large estate owners were rather numerous and frequently included three generations, but

Table 2.1

The Number of Large Landowners in Interwar Poland

Province		1921	1931	1939	
Poland	Over 50 hectares	19,454	18,205	17,768	17,639
	Over 100 hectares	13,201	12,237	11,900	11,400
Warsaw	Over 50 hectares	8	(7)	(7)	(7)
City	Over 100 hectares	4	(4)	(3)	(3)
Warsaw	Over 50 hectares	2,661	(2,452)	(2,378)	1,938
	Over 100 hectares	1,884	(1,713)	(1,658)	1,278
Łódź	Over 50 hectates	946	(873)	(846)	858
	Over 100 hectares	790	(719)	(696)	(711)
Kielce	Over 50 hectares	846	(780)	(756)	711
	Over 100 hectares	717	(652)	(631)	603
	Over 100 hectares	717	(652)	(631)	603
Lublin	Over 50 hectares	911	(840)	(815)	611
	Over 100 hectares	732	(665)	(644)	524
Białystok	Over 50 hectares	672	(611)	(592)	439
	Over 100 hectares	672	(611)	(592)	439
Central	Over 50 hectares	6,337	(5,842)	(5,665)	4,906
Poland	Over 50 hectares	4,799	(4,364)	(4,224)	3,558
Wilno	Over 50 hectares	2,536	(2,295)	(2,212)	(2,555)
	Over 100 hectares	1,516	(1,351)	(1,297)	(1,221)
Nowo-	Over 50 hectares	1,245	(1,129)	(1,086)	(1,107)
gródek	Over100 hectares	858	(776)	(734)	(691)
Polesie	Over 50 hectares	856	(776)	(734)	(691)
	Over 100 hectares	676	(603)	(578)	447
Volynia	Over 50 hectares	852	(773)	(743)	817
	Over 100 hectares	720	(642)	(616)	577
Eastern	Over 50 hectares	5,589	(4,973)	(4,787)	(4,781)
Poland	Over 100 hectares	3,770	(3,372)	(3,225)	(2,936)
Poznań	Over 50 hectares	2,572	(2,500)	(2,475)	2,885
	Over 100 hectares	1,443	(1,393)	(1,379)	1,749

		1921 (a)	1931 (b)	1939 (c)	(d)
Pomerania	Over 50 hectares	2,355	(2,282)	(2,263)	(2,637)
	Over 100 hectares	903	(873)	(863)	(1,094)
Silesia	Over 50 hectares	115	(112)	(110)	(129)
	Over 100 hectares	95	(92)	(91)	(115)
Western Poland	Over 50 hectares	5,046	(4,894)	(4,848)	(5,651)
	Over 100 hectares	2,441	(2,358)	(2,333)	(2,959)
Cracow	Over 50 hectares	618	(597)	(591)	406
	Over 100 hectares	476	(457)	(452)	340

Province		1921 (a)	1931 (b)	1939 (c)	(d)
Lwow	Over 50 hectares	948	(916)	(906)	965
	Over 100 hectares	845	(812)	(801)	965
Stanisławów	Over 50 hectares	426	(412)	(408)	419
	Over 100 hectares	369	(355)	(350)	354
Tarnopol	Over 50 hectares	590	(570)	(564)	511
	Over 100 hectares	541	(519)	(514)	452
Southern Poland	Over 50 hectares	2,582	(2,495)	(2,469)	2,301
	Over 100 hectares	2,231	(2,143)	(2,117)	1,947

Source: (a) *Statystyka Polski*, t. V, "Wielka własność rolna" (*Statistics of Poland*, vol. 5, "Large Landed Ownership") Warsaw, 1925, pp. 1-2, table 1; (b) and (c) author's estimates based on the RNOZ data according to Stefan Stablewski, *Tezy uzasdniające koniecznoćć istnienia w Polsce gospodarstw wielkorolnych pozostających w prywatnym władaniu*, quoted after Szymon Rudnicki, *Pojęcie ziemiaństwa w II Rzeczypospolitej [The Concept of Landed Gentry in the Second Polish Republic]* manuscript, p. 4; (d) Jan Stecki, *Zestawienie ogólne ze statystyki większej własnośći ziemskiej na r. 1939 dokonane preze mnie na podstawie ankiety przeprowadzonej przez RNOZ [General Statement of Large Landed Estates for 1939 Made by Me Based on the RNOZ Inquiry]* Library of the Catholic Library of Lublin, File 537. In parentheses: data additionally estimated by the author. For details of the estimates: Wojciech Roszkowski, *Gospodarcza rola większej prywatnej własnośći ziemskiej w Polsce 1918-1939 [The Economic Role of Large Private Estates in Poland, 1918-1939]* Warsaw, 1986, pp. 31-32.

probably the number of children was smaller than in peasant families. Therefore, if an average of the two indices was rounded to 1:4.50 the number of economically active and passive large landowners in Poland would be 87,543 in 1921, 81,922 in 1931, and 79,375 in 1939. Such an estimate would be closest to that of Mieczysław Mieszczankowski.[13]

Stratification by Size of Land Ownership

The large landowners in interwar Poland were a strongly differentiated group. Its major part, the landed gentry, had its own way of life and other than economic criteria of stratification. In the landed gentry hierarchy, the most important criterion was the family tradition, while the income or owned land area planed a lesser role. An owner of several thousand acres of war–destroyed forests in Polesie was only theoretically a large landowner, while an estate of a few hundred acres of productive agricultural land in the Poznań region could be a source of much higher returns. From the landowners' point of view engagement in social work, such as landowners' societies or agricultural associations, was important since it bound people closer. Common religious practices and neighborly relations were also important. But it would be a mistake to entirely eliminate the economic criterion. As Róża Raczyńeka of Rogalin, a true "Polish matron of old times," said, "the basic principle of all aristrocracies was that the grandeur of the family could only be maintained on the basis of adequate property."[14]

On the other hand such criteria as the family tradition, *connubium* and *commensalitas*, are extremely difficult to measure; moreover, not all landowners belonged to the landed gentry. Economic criteria played an important role in a gradually modernizing Polish interwar society. However, the best of them—income—is very difficult to establish even in relation to a single landowner. At the present stage of our knowledge, a statement of the income stratification of interwar Polish landowners is simply impossible. All this encourages seeing a measurable criterion of landowner stratification in land ownership that is, in a determinant that was not too important but relatively easily calculated. Nevertheless, while looking at the landowner stratification according to the area of land possessed, one must realize that it does not show the hierarchy of value since the value of landed estates depended on the share of the agricultural area, the degree of war damage, indebtedness, the efficiency of management, and many other things.

The overall stratification of large estates in interwar Poland is shown in Table 2.2. The table clearly shows that a general decrease in the number of large estates was accompanied by an even more rapid decrease in the number of the largest of them, while the number of the medium–size and small estates declined much more slowly. Similar conclusions may be drawn about the progress of parcelling, which above all affected the largest latifundia. The most typical were large estates between 100 and 1,000 hectares. Because of the really huge concentration of land in the hands of the largest latifundists, it may be interesting to look at the statement of the largest landowners in Poland.[15] In 1922 as much as 40 percent of all the area of large estates in Poland belonged to 500 owners, while 95 of them had more than 10,000 hectares.

Table 2.2

**Stratification of Large Estates by Size of Land
Ownership in Poland, 1921–1939**

	50–100	100–500	500–1,000	Over 1,000	Total
1921					
Number	6,253	8,945	2,292	1,964	19,454
Percent	32.1	46.0	11.8	10.1	100.0
Area (a)	484.5	2,330.0	1,753.5	6,983.1	11,532.9
Percent	4.2	20.2	15.2	60.5	100.0
1939					
Number	6,079	8,566	1,730	1,264	17,639
Percent	34.5	48.6	9.8	7.2	100.0
Area (a)	442.2	2,413.9	1,538.6	4,818.5	9,213.2
Percent	4.8	26.2	16.7	52.3	100.0
1939:1921					
Number	97.2	95.8	75.5	64.4	90.7
Area	91.3	103.6	87.7	69.0	79.9

Source: Author's calculations according to *Statystyka Polski*, t. V, "Wielka własncść rolna" (*Statistics of Poland*, vol. 3, "Large Landed Ownership") Warsaw, 1925, pp. 1–2, Table 1; Jan Stecki *Zestowienie ogólne ze statystyski większej własncśći ziemskiej na r. 1939 dokonane przeze mnie na podstawie ankiety przeprowadzonej przes RNOZ* [General Statement of Large Estates for 1939 Made by Me Based on the RNOZ Inquiry] Library of the Catholic University of Lublin, File 537.

A special place among the large estates was taken by the entails, which generally could not be divided or sold without permission of the royal court or national legislature. The entail was the property of the heir entail (Polish *ordynat*, but was separated from the rest of his property. Because of the long Russian and Prussion rule in the Polish territories, there were also other forms of entail, *majorat* or *fideikomiss*. The largest of the Polish entails, the Zamość had belonged to the Zamoyski family since 1589. In 1918 its area covered almost 190,000 hectares, but in 1938 this area decreased to about 64,000 hectares of forests and farmland between Tomaszów, Krzeszów, Zamcść, and Kraśnik. Its heir in interwar Poland, Maurycy Zamoyski, was a man of political merit, a founder–member of the Polish National Committee (Komitet Narodowy Polski) in Paris in 1917, a candidate for the presidency in 1922, and ambassador to France.[16]

The second largest estate in interwar Poland, the Dawidnródek domain of the Radziwiłłs, was also an entail. Huge forests and marshes between the Polesian rivers Stwiga, Horyń, and Pripet had about 155,000 hectares and were the remains of the domain of David, the fourteenth–century Prince of Turów. Later the domain became the Radziwiłłentail of Kleck–Nieświeżk–Ołka, founded as a separate entail of Stanisław Radziwiłł. After his death in the Polish–Soviet war in 1920, it was inherited by his nephew Karol Radziwiłł.[17] The rest of the Nieśwież entail was inherited by Albrecht Radziwiłł in 1914. The part that was incorporated into Poland after 1921 covered about 80,000 hectares in the Stołpce and Nieśwież counties of the Nowogródek province, including about 65,000 hectares of forests and only 3,500 hectares of farmland.[18]

The Łańcut entail, founded in 1838, belonged in the interwar period to Alfred Polocki. It had about 30,000 hectares, while its owner, who had numerous other estates and shares in industry and banking, was one of the richest people in Poland.[19] Other large Polish entails included Volhynian Cłyka (about 30,000 hectares), which belonged to Ferdynand Radziwłł and then to his son Janusz, Sieniewa (10,730 hectares) of the Czartoryski family in Lwow Province, Przygodzice (15,000 hectares) of the Radziwiłł family in Poznań Province, Opinogóra of the Krasiński family in Warsaw Province, Chroberz of the Wielopski family in Kielce Province, and about two dozen others.[20]

There were also several Geman and Russian entails in the territory of interwar Poland. The German *fideikomisse* accounted for about 10 percent of the area of all entails. While the property rights of the German owners were respected on the condition that they adopted Polish citizenship, the institution of *fideikomisse* was gradually abolished. In the years 1922–1937 (42,000 hectares) of Prince Johann Heinrich von Pless–Pszczyński and Koszęcin (17,000 hectares) of Prince Karl Gottfried Hohenlohe–Ingelfingen. In 1939 seven more remained, including Świerklaniec (16,300 hectares) of Guido Karl Henckel Prince Donnersmarck. In Great Poland the "Jarocin principality" (7,300 hectares) of Prince Hans Hugo Radolin was also a *fideikomiss*. The owners stemmed from the Radoliński family (Leszczyc coat–of–arms), who were germanized and awarded with the German princely title for their service to the Prussian state.

In Galicia the largest *fideikomisse* included the Bohorodczany forests (5,600 hectares) of an Austrian Countess Maria Kristine Schoenborn. The *majorat* form of entailed property was recorded in the former Russian partition, where some of the Russian estates were *majorats*. Since most of them had been confiscated from their Polish owners and given to Russian officials for suppressing Polish national aspirations (so–called donations), the Polish law of 25 July 1919 provided for their gradual expropriation. One of them was the Puławy *majorat* (5,600 hectares) belonging to the descendants of Prince Ivan Paskevich–Erevanski, the commander of the Russian army that suppressed the Polish Rising of 1830–31.[21]

Entails raised ambivalent feelings in interwar Poland. On the one hand they were symbols of the old tradition and its continuity, not only in relation to the aristocratic families, but in a wider, national sense. On the other hand, they were an anachronism in a country affected by the land hunger of the landless peasants. On 28 March 1936 the government moved on the question of the family entails, suggesting that they tied up about 600,000 hectares necessary for reconstruction of the agrarian system in Poland. The defenders of the entails argued that these were mostly forest and wasteland not fit for parcelling, that they contributed considerable national revenue and that their distribution would give land in eastern Poland into non–Polish hands. Finally, on 13 July 1939, a law was passed abolishing entails at the request of the owners or local administration. Liquidation of entails established before the partitions or having a particular national significance was made subject to the additional consent of the government. The entailed estates would become regular property of the owners who would be held financially responsible for the entails' debts. Entails of special historic significance, mentioned in the law, included: Zamość. Nieśwież, Chroberz, Łańcut, Opinogóra, Czerniejewo, Przeworks, Gołuchów, Poturzyca, Sieniawa, and Roś.[22] The road to the liquidation of entails was open, but the process would probably take a long time.

Not all the largest estates in interwar Poland had the legal form of entails. The Rzepichów–Chotynicze estate (about 134,000 hectares), mostly forest and marsh, situated in the northern part of Łuniniec County in Polesie, belonged to the Sitkowiec line of the Potocki family: Jan and his son Jarosław Potocki. The Lenin–Czuczewicze estate (about 89,000 hectares) was also mostly forest and marsh in the eastern and northern parts of Łuniniec County just at the Soviet border. Until the early nineteenth century they had belonged to the Radziwiłłs. As the dowry of the only daughter of Dominik Radziwiłł they went to the Wittgensteins, later to the Hohenlohes, and finally were purchased by a Fyodor Ogarkov. In reborn Poland he was still the legal owner of this huge domain.[23]

Most of the largest estates in interwar Poland were eastern forests and marshes. This was the case of Worobin and Dąbrowica (about 60,000 hectares) in Sarny County, which belonged to Witold Broel-Plater. Bereźne (48,000 hectares) in Kostopol County in Volhynia, the possession of Emanuel Małyński, Telechany (36,000 hectares) in the Pińsk region, belonging to Karol Wojciech Pusłowski, and Woropajewo (31,000 hectares) in Postawy County of Wilno Province, the domain of Konstanty; Przeździecki.[24] A large part of the post–Radziwiłł Naliboki Forest (31,500 hectares) in Nowogródek Province had been purchased from the Hohenlohes by a Vladimir Falz–Fein, who carried on its rapacious exploitation in interwar Poland. Falz–Fein was a member of the international business elite, and was known for breeding sheep and kangaroos in the Ukraine and for having an ostrich farm at the foot of Mount Kilimanjaro.[25]

The largest estate in former Galicia belonged to Archduke Karol Stefan Habsburg, who retained his Żywiec domain (53,200 hectares) after having adopted Polish citizenship. His son, Karol Olbrecht, even served in the Polish army.[26] Huge Skole forests (44,800 hectares) belonged to Count Hermann Groedel in East Galicia. The largest estate in western Poland—Krotoszyn (27,000 hectares) in the Poznań region—belonged to the German Prince Albert Thurn and Taxis. In central Poland there were only few truly huge estates. The largest of them was Końskie (26,780 hectares) of Juliusz Tarnowski.

All this does not necessarily mean that the largest landowners in interwar Poland had only forests, marshes, sands, and wastelands in the eastern borderland. A huge economic potential was, for instance, in the hands of Alfred Potocki, who had not only his Łańcut entail, but also Stare Sioło in the Lwow Province, Hanaczówka in Podolia (altogether about 50,000 hectares), and many processing factories and industrial shares. He was a dedicated businessman and was probably much richer than the largest landowner in interwar Poland, Maurycy Zamoyski, whose Zamość entail was in financial trouble. One of the richest landowners was also Janusz Radziwiłł, who not only possessed Szparów in Volhynia and Nieborów near Warsaw, but in 1926 became the sixteenth heir of the Ołyka entail. He also had a lot of industrial and banking shares.[27] The question of nonagricultural activities of large landowners will be discussed in Chapter 4.

Geographic and Historical Differentiation

As a result of earlier history, the economic system of interwar Poland was regionally differentiated. The same applied to the large landed estates. Table 2.3 shows the share of estates of over fifty hectares in the total number and area of farms in Poland according to various regions. It is worth noting that some authors quote much higher figures to emphasize the domination of large estates in interwar Poland.

It is true that in 1921 large estates covered as much as 47.3 percent of the total area of Poland. But this share refers to all large estates, not only private, but also state–owned, communal, and church–owned ones. The 1921 census data indicate that of 14,202,800 hectares of large estates in Poland about 23.6 percent belonged to the state, 1.6 percent to churches, and 0.9 percent to other corporate bodies.[28] Moreover, the data shown in Table 2.3 refer to the total area. Since the large private estates had more forest, water, and wasteland than the Polish average, these data overestimate the domination of private estates. The land utilization structure will be discussed in Chapter 3.

Table 2.3

Territorial Distribution of Large Private Estates
in Poland, 1921–1939

Province	1921		1939	
	Percent of Number	Percent of Area	Percent of Number	Percent of Area
POLAND	0.57	30.4	0.39	24.3
Warsaw		30.4		22.2
Łódź		24.7		18.4
Kielce		25.3		18.4
Lublin		32.2		22.7
Biełystok		18.1		13.6
Central Poland	0.52	24.4	0.31	17.8
Wilno		32.0		26.3
Nowogródek		35.1		25.7
Polesie		50.8		36.0
Volynia		23.7		21.2
Eastern Poland	0.84	35.8	0.43	27.6
Poznań		40.3		37.3
Pomerania		19.7		18.1
Silesia		44.8		42.5
Western Poland	1.51	38.2	1.39	35.5
Cracow		21.9		16.9
Lwow		20.0		26.5
Stanisławów		22.7		21.5
Tarnopol		34.2		27.4
Southern Poland	0.22	27.5	0.16	23.5

Source: Author's calculations according to: *Mały Rocznik Statystyczny [Concise Statistical Yearbook]* 1939, p. 72, Table 4; Mieczysław Mieszczankowski. *Struktura agrarna Polski międzywojenne [Agrarian Structure of Interwar Poland]* Warsaw, 1960, p. 338, Table 148; *Statystyuka Polski,* t. 5, "Wielka własność rolna" (*Statistics of Poland,* vol. 5, "Large Landed Ownership") Warsaw, 1925, pp. 1–2, Table 1; Jan Stecki, *Zestawienie ogólne ze statyski większej własości ziemskiej na r. 1939 dokonane przeze mniena podstawie ankiety przeprowadzonej przez RNOZ [General Statement of Large Landed Estates for 1939 Made by Me Based on the the RNOZ Inquiry]*, Library of the Catholic University of Lublin, File 537.

The lowest share of the large private estates in relation to the total land area was recorded in central Poland in Białystok Province in particular, where lots of small and medium–size farms prevailed, both belonging to former nobles and peasants. While for the whole of Bisłystok Province the said share fell from 18.1 percent in 1921 to 13.6 percent in 1939, in 1921 it was the highest in Grondo County and the lowest in Suwałki (1.8 percent) and Augustów counties (5.9 percent). Also in Łódź Province the share of large private estates was lower than the Polish average. In Końskie County it was 33.7 percent, but in Będzin County it was a mere 11.1 percent. In the Kielce Province the maximum was recorded in Pińczów (28.6 percent) and Sandomierz counties (28.4 percent) and Częstochowa counties (11.1 percent).[29] In Warsaw Province the share of large private estates in the total area was equal to the Polish average in 1921 and fell a little below it in 1939. A relatively high share was found in Lublin Province, where the average was raised largely by the Zamość entail. In Zamość County the said share was 47.8 percent, but in the Siedice County it was only 10.3 percent, and in Biała Podlaska County 10.9 percent.[30]

The share of large private estates was relatively high in the to-tal area of the eastern provinces, and especially in Polesie, where in Łuniniec, Stolin, and Pińsk counties it exceeded 70 percent. But most of these estates included forests and marshes, while the share of farmland was the lowest in Poland.

Estates of up to 500 hectares were found in "agricultural" Pole-sie (Prużana and Breść counties), while in the eastern counties of Polish Polesie the large latifundia had only a marginal share of the farmland. The land ownership concentration was also quite differ-entiated in Volhynia, where the large estates had about 70 percent of land in Sarny County, but only about 14 percent in Krzemieniec County. This is why the Volhynian average was below the Polish av-erage. In Nowogródek Province the largest concentration of landed property was recorded in Baranowicze and Włożyn counties, while the lowest was in Lida County. Finally, Wilno Province had a higher concentration than the Polish average: the maximum was recorded in Dziena County (40.6 percent) and the minimum in Brasław County (15.8 percent).[31]

In the former Prussian partition the situation was equally differ-entiated. Poznań province had a relatively high concentration of land ownership: the maximum was recorded in Grodzisk and Śremcounties, while the minimum was in Międzychód and Czarków counties. In

Pomerania most of the large estates belonged to the state, so the share of the private estates in total area was not too high. In Upper Silesia this was entirely different. The five largest German latifundists had 94,50 hectares, while sixteen Polish landowners only 4,600 hectares. The land ownership concentration here was one of the highest in Poland, the maximum being recorded in Tarnowskie Góry (69.5 percent) and Lubliniec counties (58.1 percent), while the minimum was in Rybnik county (27.4 percent). Teschen Silesia had a rather low concentration of land ownership. After the incorporation of this area into Poland in 1939, the share of large private estates in the total area here was only 18.6 percent.[32]

In the southern provinces, which before World War I had belonged to Austria–Hungary, the share of large private estates in the total land area was similar to the Polish average. The minimum was recorded in Cracow Province, where small Polish peasant farms prevailed, and in Stanisławow Province, where the plots belonged mostly to Ukrainian peasants and where public estates had also a high share of land. The large private estates had relatively more land in the Lwow Province, especially in Tarnopol Province, where many Polish estates could be found. It is worth noting that in the provinces dominated by the Polish estates—such as Cracow and Tarnopol—the area distributed in the years 1921–1939 was the largest.[33]

This picture of the land ownership concentration in various parts of interwar Poland may be supplemented with data showing the average size of large private estates, as presented in Table 2.4. It is clear that the largest concentration of landed property was recorded in the eastern provinces and especially in Polesie. In Volhynia and Nowogródek Province they were much smaller, and in the Wilno region even smaller than the Polish average. In the western provinces the huge concentration of land in the small area of Upper Silesia did not counterbalance the relatively small estates of Poznań and Pomeranian provinces. Land ownership concentration was relatively low in central Poland, except for Lublin Province, while southern Poland had relatively big estates. Even in Cracow Province, where large estates accounted for the lowest share of the total area, they were relatively big. The average size of estates well illustrates the average types of estates: huge forest and marsh latifundia of Polesie and large German estates of Silesia, middle–size estates of East Galicia and Volhynia, and relatively small, but economically differentiated, estates of Poznań, Pomeranian, Wilno, Białystok, and Warsaw provinces.

Because of geographic and economic conditions, as well as the policies followed by the partitioning powers, specific features of large estates developed in various regions that merged with interwar Poland after 1918. In central Poland, which for some time had had the shape of the aotonomous Kingdom of Poland, landowners faced frequently changing economic and political conditions.

The industrialization and urbanization of the Kingdom was favorable for the modernization of agriculture, but the industrial development was not continuous and was mainly based on exports to Russia. Furthermore, the economic progress advocated by many Polish landowners faced various Russian bureaucratic obstacles. The desire of the Russian administration to maintain "easements" *serwituty*, or common use of private property, which stirred up social conflicts according to the divide–and–rule principle, and the overall lawlessness of the tsarist system were also serious barriers to modern economic development. A clear example of this may be found in the Russian ban on all social and cultural associations in the Russian partition until the revolution of 1905. It was as late as in 1907 that formerly semisecret "organic work" could proceed in many official societies, such as the Central Agricultural Association [Centralne Towarzystwo Rolnicze].[34]

The agriculture of the eastern borderland territories (kresy wschodnie) stagnated all through the nineteenth century. This was due to the competition of Russian grain exports and the economic discrimination policies of the Russian government. In Lithuania, Byelorussia, and the Ukraine, where, according to the Russian officials "istinnaya Matushka Rossiya" (true Mother Russia) began, the Poles were not allowed to purchase land. Hence the Polish landowners who were witnessing the birth or rebirth of the Lithuanian, Byelorussian, and Ukrainian nationality among their peasants, were stimulated to treat their land as a part of the Polish cultural heritage and not as an economic value.

World War I and the social revolution had wrought such damage that the easternmost regions of interwar Poland had only a shadow of their former prosperity. The complete absence of incentives for modernization had ossified the estate differentiation of the society. Relations between local peasantry and Polish landowners were precisely described by Melchior Wańkowicz, who said that the landlord was still like "the sun surrounded by a planetary system of several villages."[35] These relations deteriorated if the landlord did not fulfill his traditional duties, such as advising and assisting in the last weeks before the harvest. Where the landlords' failures were accompanied by religious or national conflicts, as in Volynia or Eastern Galicia, the hostilities frequently had a tragic end with the murders of Polish landolords in 1917–1920 and in 1939.

In the Prussian partition it was entirely different. Upper Silesia, with its domination of large German latifundia and advanced industry, was a separate socioeconomic unit. In Great Poland and Pomerania the size of German properties, although gradually growing, was not as big. The growing demand for food in Germany, the relatively low prices of agricultural machinery and tools, the dense transportation network, and the relatively liberal taxation, had produced extremely favorable conditions for the development of agriculture. On the other hand, the germanization policy, although sometimes taking brutal forms, had been usually kept within a legal framework created by the German authorities. Hence these Polish landowners had the only chance to defend their landed property in fierce economic competition with the Germans. Economic efficiency became a standard of patriotism, while the German pressure produced a unique cooperation between the Polish landowners and peasants.[36]

Galicia had been entirely isolated from external markets and overpopulated. Given the backwardness of the Galician economy, the Ausgleich of 1867 gave the Polish nobles an opportunity to enter the civil service. This double pressure had fossilized the old feudal concept that all activities, apart from diplomacy, politics, and the army, were not worthy of a noble. Large Polish estates in Galicia were frequently neglected, leased or sold, while the Polish nobles looked for careers in Vienna or Lwow.

Nationality Structure

The nationality issue as a criterion always makes a lot of trouble in social studies, because it is based on subjective feelings and can hardly be measured. In the case of Poland this criterion was also constantly evolving. In the old Polish–Lithuanian Commonwealth the nobility or magnates had been distinguished by the family tradition, the offices held, or the number of villages under their rule, while the languages used or the religion practiced were of secondary importance. After centuries of symbiosis, the noble class incorporated not only ethnic Poles, Lithuanians, and Ruthenians, but also many Germans, Italians, Swedes, Greeks, Hungarians, French, Tatars, and

Armenians. Jews could enter the nobility after adopting Christianity: this was the case of the followers of Jakob Frank, the Jeleńskis, the Poznańskis, and others ennobled by King Stanisław August Poniatowksi at the end of the eighteenth century, and there were even two cases of Jewish noble families. The Tatar nobles had usually retained their Islamic faith. According to Robert H. Lord, "Like the United States today, Poland was at that time the melting pot of Europe, the haven for the poor and the oppressed of all the neighboring countries."[37] The uniting force was the political system of the Polish–Lithuanian Commonwealth, but the common use of the Polish language led to a gradual polonization of the ethnic mosaic of the nobility in the seventeenth and eighteenth centuries.

The question of the nationality of the nobles sharpened under the partitions, when this ethnically differentiated, but more or less polonized, group faced the German, Russian, and Austrian policies and colonists, especially in the western and eastern borderlands. It was only then that the gap between the Polish and non–Polish nobility widened. This new national differentiation was not necessarily ethnic, but was due rather to the choice between the old Polish–Lithuanian tradition and culture or the "realistic" recognition of the invaders' expansion. Thus, for instance, the German Lossows chose the Polish side, while the Polish Radolińskis were germanized.

All this does not necessarily mean that the nationality of the landowners in interwar Poland was absolutely clear. First of all, there was the problem of landowners in the eastern borderlands. Many of them felt bound to the region as much as to the Polish culture. "Polish nationalists," wrote Edward Woyniłłowicz, "noticed my Byelorussian sympathies and claimed I was no Pole but a Byelorussian."[38] Many of the eastern borderland landowners in fact thought in terms of "gente Lithuani [or Rutheni], natione Poloni [Lithuanian or Ruthenian people of Polish nationality]." The cosmopolitanism of some aristocrats should also be mentioned. Although most of them were closely connected with Polish national life, there were among them some cases of national indifference and membership in an "aristocratic international."[39]

It is extremely difficult to bring various data concerning the nationality of large landowners in interwar Poland to a common ground. Table 2.5 includes an approximate regional nationality distribution of large landowners in Poland in 1921 and Table 2.6 presents this distribution according to the size of estates. The last column of Table 2.6

can be compared with the nationality composition of the 500 largest landowners in Poland in 1922. Within these 500 there were 80.6 percent Poles, 7.8 percent Germans, 5.2 percent Russians, 2.6 percent Jews, and 0.6 percent Ukrainians.[40] It should be noted, however that the data of both tables refer to the number of owners and not to the area they possessed.

In view of the lack of precise data for the last years of the Polish Second Republic, it is hard to say whether this nationality structure changed and in what way. The only evidence there is, Jan Stecki's calculations based on the RNOZ inquiry of 1939, show that the share of Polish owners in the total number of large estates owners in the Warsaw province was 94.0 percent, in Łódź Province 90.5 percent, in Kielce Province 85.4 percent, in Lublin Province 94.9 percent, and

Table 2.5

Nationality of Owners of Estates above Fifty Hectares by Province in Poland by Percent, 1921

Province	Poles	Germans	Ukrainians	Byelorussians	Russians	Jews	Others
POLAND	82.0	10.3	1.3	2.5	1.9	1.6	0.5
Warsaw City	83.3	–	–	–	–	16.7	–
Warsaw	97.8	0.6	–	–	0.4	1.1	0.1
Łódź	97.2	0.5	–	–	0.4	1.7	0.2
Kielce	95.9	0.2	–	–	0.2	3.7	–
Lublin	97.1	0.1	–	–	1.0	1.8	–
Białystok	93.3	0.1	–	2.4	3.0	0.9	–
Wilno	86.0	0.2	0.2	8.2	3.0	0.9	1.5
Nowogródek	87.4	0.2	–	8.2	2.8	0.8	0.6
Polesie	65.4	–	4.6	17.8	9.3	2.0	1.1
Volhynia	61.5	1.3	17.6	0.3	15.1	0.1	4.1
Poznań	58.6	40.9	–	–	–	0.1	0.1
Pomerania	67.6	32.2	–	–	–	0.1	0.1
Silesia	42.3	55.6	–	–	–	–	2.1
Cracow	94.9	1.0	0.5	–	–	2.6	1.0
Lwow	87.2	2.3	1.6	–	–	8.5	0.4
Stanisławów	84.8	0.9	6.0	–	–	5.7	2.6
Tarnopol	90.7	0.5	3.1	–	–	5.5	0.2

Source: *Statystyka Polski*, t. V, "Wielka własność rolna" (*Statistics of Poland*, vol. 5, "Large Landed Ownership") Warsaw, 1925, p. xi.

Table 2.6

Nationality of Owners of Large Private Estates of Various Size in Poland by Percent, 1921

Nationality	Total	50–100 Hectares	100–500 Hectares	500–1,000 Hectares	Over 1,000 Hectares
Polish	82.0	77.1	84.7	84.6	81.8
German	10.0	15.3	7.1	8.9	7.9
Ukrainian	1.3	1.2	1.4	1.2	1.6
Byelorussian	2.5	3.5	2.4	1.2	1.3
Jewish	1.6	1.3	2.0	1.0	1.5
Russian	1.9	0.9	1.7	2.7	4.8
Czech	0.2	0.3	0.2	0.1	0.3
Other	0.5	0.4	0.5	0.3	0.8

Source: *Statystyka Polski*, t. V, "Wielka własność rolna" (*Statistics of Poland*, vol. 5, "Large Landed Ownership") Warsaw, 1925, p. xi.

in Białystok Province 87.4 percent. For Polesie this share was 78.4 percent, Volhynia Province 73.4 percent, Poznań Province 62.5 percent, Cracow Province 90.3 percent, Lwow Province 77.0 percent, Stanisławów Province 42.0 percent, and Tarnopol Province 78.5 percent.[41]

These data mean that the land–parcelling process in interwar Poland diminished the share of the number of large estates in Polish hands everywhere, except for Polesie, Volynia, and Poznań provinces. This was connected with the transfer of large German and Russian estates into Polish hands. Elsewhere the land redistribution meant an incease of land ownership by Ukrainians, Byelorussians, and especially Jews. For instance, according to an inquiry of the Volhynian Landowners' Society, the land redistribution carried out in Równe and Kostopol counties in the years 1921–1935 decreased the share of the Russian owners by 88 percent, the Poles by 33 percent, and increased the share of the Jewish owners by 312 percent.[42] If the 1939 data are calculated according to the total area of large private estates, a 78.5 percent share of estates in Polish hands is the result. In other words, the share of the Poles in the total number of large private estates in interwar Poland decreased.

The Polish large estates dominated in central Poland, western Galicia, in Wilno and Nowogródek provinces, as well as in Podolia (Tarnopol Province). Most of these Polish owners belonged to the old nobility, but there were also many Polish nongentry owners, Polish families, such as the Krasińskis, the Polockis, the Stadnickis, the Tarnowskis, and the Zamoyskis, had estates all over Poland. But the majority of Polish owners in the eastern borderland area had Lithuanian or Ruthenian roots. These included the princely families of Czartoryski, Czetwertyński, Drucki, Giedroyć, Ogiński, Puzyna, Sanguszko, Świrski, and Woroniecki. The splendor of the Lubomirskis, the Olizars, the Radziwiłłs, the Sapiehas, and the Tyszkiewiczes came later. Numerous noble families from Lithuania and Ruthenia, such as the Domeykos, the Jundziłłs, the Mackiewiczes, the Meysztowiczes, the Olechnowiczes, the Tołłoczkos, and many others also had a long noble tradition. Polish families of German origin, having belonged to the German Baltic *Ritterschaft* and later polonized, included the Manteuffels, the Mohls, the Broel–Platers, the Plater–Zyberks, the Ropps, the Weyssenhoffs, and others. In the early twentieth century they were the pillars of the Polish Catholic culture in the east. Only the Keyserlingsks remained Germans, since they married Protestant Prussians.[43]

The Polish landed gentry of interwar Poland also had other national roots. There were families of Italian descent, such as the Scipio del Campos and the Badenis. Other families had come from France (Pourbaix), Sweden (Massonius, Reytan), Hungary (Marmarosz), Greece (Laskarys), Ireland (O'Rourke), and Norway (Moldenhawer). Some of them, such as the Agopsowiczes, the Krzeczunowiczes, the Krzysztofowiczes, and the Teodorowiczes, had Armenian roots. Quite a lot of Polish eastern borderland gentry had Tatar roots. These included the Tenikej–Emirza–Bazarewskis, the Emirz–Najman–Beg–Olesziewicz–Kryczńskis, the Aksak–Emirza–Skirmuntts, and the Hozm Emirza–Sulkiewiczes.[44] This whole variety of Polish eastern borderland gentry was sometimes called the "Lithuanian Poles." They were polonized natives of this area who "did not understand life outside of their family nest which remembered dozens of generations."[45] Since they spoke Polish and felt Polish, they could hardly come to terms with the Lithuanian and Byelorussian national consciousness reborn among the emancipated peasants.

The size of the large German estates gradually decreased, in both number and area. This was connected with the principle of Polish preemption introduced in interwar Poland, the abolition of the German anti–Polish legislation of 1880–1914, and with the sale of land by Germans who chose German citizenship after 1918. According to the Polish–German agreement of 30 August 1924, estates belonging to Germans who adopted Polish citizenship could not be forcibly redeemed, while in another Polish–German agreement of 31 October 1929 Poland gave up forcible redemption as well of estates of the Germans who opted for Germany. As a result most of the German estates in western Poland remained in German hands. These estates were only subject to the Polish land reform law, but its effects were rather slow. In some areas the German large estates prevailed over the Polish ones. For instance, in Pszczyna County in Upper Silesia fifty–six estates of over fifty hectares had about 50,000 hectares, of which about 40,000 hectares belonged to Johann Heinrich Prince von Pless–Pszczyński, and a further 7,800 to Thiele Winkler. Also in Pomerania the German estates were usually the largest: for instance, Heinrich von Keyserlingk had about 7,000 hectares in Wejherowo.[46]

The German owners of large estates were well organized. In Upper Silesia the German Schlesischer Landbund had 423 members and solid financial support, while the Polish Landowners' Society of Silesia (Zwiȥek Ziemian Województwa Śląskiego) was a branch of the Cracow Society and had only thirty members. Disposing of huge industrial capital, the German Silesian tycoons, such as Guido Karl Henckel, Prince von Donenrsmarck of Świerklaniec and Karl Gottfried, Prince Hohenlohe–Ingelfinger of Koszęcin, not only held large estates but also controlled wide sections of the Silesian economy. The sympathies of these industrial and agricultural magnates, formally Polish citizens, were on the German side. For example, in September 1939 Prince Donnersmarck ordered the inscription "Nie wieder Polnisch" ("No more Polish") to be placed over the gate of one of his mines. Also von Pless–Rszczyński, who spend most of the time in his German Lower Silesian castle of Fürstenstein (Ksiȧż, did not hide his German antipathy for the Polish state.[47] It is therefore no wonder that the Polish landowners only sporadically maintained relations with the German ones.

The Russian land ownership also gradually declined. Many of the Russian estates within interwar Poland had been granted by the tsars to Russian officials for suppressing the Poles. These "donations" were to be expropriated according to the Polish law of 25 July 1919, but the Polish authorities were rather slow to act. Most of the Russian estates were situated in Volhynia, Polesie, and Wilno, Nowogródek, and Białystok provinces. In Wilno Province one of the few Russians who simply bought his estate at Franopol in Grasław County (almost 15,000 hectares in 1918) was Nikolai Kharchenko. The estate of Jurowce in Białystok Province (615 hectares) belonged to the former tsarist foreign minister Sergei Sazonov, who lived in France and wrote anti–Polish articles for most of the interwar period. Elizaveta Shuvalov was the legal owner of the Pełcza forests in Volhynia (9,230 hectares). She also lived in Paris or on the French Riveria, where her administrators sent her profits from the exploitation of the forests. The Russian influence in the eastern borderland was extended by the Orthodox Church.[48] After the Bolshevik Revolution the Russian landowners in Poland did not have contacts with Russia, so their presence in Poland was not as dangerous as that of the Germans but, even so, there were only a few Russian owners who participated in the social life of the Polish landed gentry.

The range of Jewish land ownership grew. According to the Jewish press, in 1931 there were 700 large estates in Jewish hands, while the 1931 census showed 884 such estates.[49] The Jewish estates were concentrated in eastern Galicia, but were also found in the Warsaw, Kielce, Cracow, and Polesie provinces. In 1912 the area of Jewish large estates in Galicia was estimated at about 340,000 hectares. Polish nationalist sources claimed that all through interwar Poland this area had grown from about 500,000 to 2,000,000 hectares, also including other regions. This estimate is probably too high. On the other hand, the estimate by the Jewish press—336,000 hectares of Jewish large estates in Poland in 1931—seems to be far too low.[50] The largest Jewish landowners in interwar Poland included Hermann Groedel, who had huge Skole forests (about 44,800 hectares), David Lindenbaum of Kropiwnik in Drohobycz County (8,500 hectares), and Leon Lipszyc of Bielczaki in Kostopol County (7,250 hectares).

Jewish landowners had their Lesser Polish Society of Farmers [Związek Małopolskich Rolników] in Lwow chaired by Jan Gerstman of Połtew, and later by Karol Halpern of Wołczyniec. The society advocated the idea of "transformation" *przewarstwienie* of the Polish Jews through a change in their social structure. To solve the problem of Jewish overpopulation in Poland the society wanted the Polish Jews to colonize the countryside. In reply, the Polish landed gentry and nationalists accused the Jews of wanting to oust the Poles from their land. The concept of the *numerus clausus*, that is, the share in land ownership equal to the share of the total population, was raised by the nationalists. The idea was quite paradoxical, since the share of Jewish landowners was still lower than their share in the total population, while their share in the total area was only approaching the latter share.[51] Some of the most assimilated Jewish owners, such as Leopold Kronenberg of a family that had greatly contributed to Polish national life, were generally accepted in the Polish landed gentry society, but owners without such a tradition were not. The idea of a "Jewish landed gentry" *ziemiaństwo żydowskie* was ridiculed by some of the Polish landed gentry.

Some of the large estates in Volhynia and Stanisławów Province belonged to Ukrainians. For instance, Aleksander Tarashchenko had 5,600 hectares in Serchów of Sarny County. Byelorussians had some large estates in Polesie, Wilno, and Nowogródek provinces. Since their estates were usually smaller than average, their share in the total area was probably lower than that of the number of owners. About thirty Czech owners in Volhynia also had estates above fifty hectares.[52]

The nationality structure of large landowners in interwar Poland can be reconstructed with a margin for error. It seems that the number of Polish owners remained at the level of 82.0 percent, while their share in the total area of large estates probably diminished from about 82.0 percent in 1921 to about 78.5 percent in 1939. The number of German owners decreased from about 10.0 percent in 1921 to about 9.0 percent in 1939 and their share in the total area from about 7.9 percent to about 7.5 percent. The Russian owners accounted for about 1.9 percent in 1921. In 1939 this share was probably lower. Their estates covered about 5.3 percent of the total area in 1921 and about 4.5 percent in 1939. The share of the Jewish owners grew from about 1.6 percent in 1921 to about 2.0 percent in 1939, while their share in the total area grew from about 1.8 percent to about 2.5 percent. The number of Ukrainian owners probably grew above the 1.3 percent of 1921, and the number of Byelorussian owners rose above the 2.5 percent of 1921. The share of Ukrainian owners in the total area of large estates could have grown to about 2.0 percent and that of the Byelorussian owners to about 2.5 percent in 1939.[53]

Social Composition

One of the authors dealing with the landed gentry in interwar Poland, Karol S. Frycz, suggested a subdivision of the group of landowners into aristocracy, "one-and-a-half gentry" (*półtora szlach-*

ta)—that is families close to aristocracy but not so rich, old gentry families, new noble families (frequently of foreign origin), and nongentry owners of recent times.[54] If foreign owners, both aristocratic and nonaristocratic, are added, this division would be satisfactory. Nevertheless it is not too precise, since the basic criteria include not only the family tradition and wealth, but also the "ancestry" of the land ownership. One thing is clear: to become a landowner one had to have enough land. On the other hand, moving up the landowners' ladder was a very long process, so the social composition of the group could not change within twenty years of interwar Poland.

The first important distinction was made between the landed gentry and nongentry owners. The landed gentry included families with several generations of noble traditions, at least reaching back to the old Polish–Lithuanian Commonwealth, who lived on their estates and participated in the social life of their circle. Although the limits of the group were not too precise and its size was never measured, the landed gentry probably accounted for more than 60 percent of all the landowners, numbering about 10,000 families or about 50,000 people.[55] Some of this landed gentry lived outside their estates and availed themselves of hired management. A great majority of the landed gentry were Poles; non–Poles only sporadically participated in the life of the group.

From the perspective of land ownership, the top position was occupied by the aristocracy. Among the 500 largest landowners in Poland in 1922, 403 could be identified as Poles. In this number there were 12 Potockis, 12 Lubomirskis, 10 Radziwiłłs, 10 Zamoyskis, 8 Tarnowskis, 7 Tyszkiewiczes, 7 Czartoryskis, 6 Sapiehas, 5 Broel–Platers, 5 Czetwertyńskis, 5 Dzieduszyckis, and 5 Żółtowskis. The Drucki–Lubeckis, Raczyńskis, Kwileckis, and Czarneckis were represented by four owners, while the Baworowskis, Bnińskis, Chłapowskis, Dolańskis, Gołuchowskis, Krasickis, Ledóchowskis, Młodzianowskis, Mycielskis, Niezabytowskis, Ostrowskis, and Szeptyckis had three representatives. The first ten of the above specified families produced 82 owners who had about 1,400,000 hectares of land in 1922.[56]

The Polish interwar aristocracy numbered about twenty–five families, including also the Sanguszkos and the Krasińskis, who were not so numerous, and perhaps some others. It was a rather closed circle that intermarried within. Marriages outside the group, mainly with foreign aristocrats and business circles, usually Western European, but sometimes Jewish, were rather exceptional. Most of the top aristocratic families had titles of prince or count, but titles could be deceptive in measuring the rank of the family. They were used not only by the old families, but also by the families that grew in the nineteenth century. For instance, Roman Rzyszczewski stemmed from a petty noble Volhynian family but enjoyed the title of count because his father had made a fortune by marrying into the rich Warsaw banker family of the Epsteins, and had received the title in Vienna. Since titles had usually been given by foreign courts, they were not too appreciated by the average gentry. Both the old aristocracy and the rank–and–file gentry spoke ironically of the "Austrian counts." On the other hand, representative of some old princely families that declined in the eighteenth and nineteenth centuries could no longer be counted among the aristocracy. Such was the case of Michał Światopłk–Mirski, who could barely maintain his castle in Mir in Wilno Province and lived in the house of his land agent.[57]

The major part of the group of large landowners in interwar Poland was constituted by the "one–and–a–half" gentry and old gentry families. Many of them cultivated traditions reaching as far back as the fourteenth and fifteenth centuries. It was not extraordinary that the Bronikowski family of Żychlin in Łódź Province had possession of the estates for about 700 years. The interwar owner of Żychlin, Rafał Bronikowski, was the sixteenth known descendant of this family.[58] In Komierowo in Pomerania Province, Tomasz and Róża (née Zamoyska) Komierowski kept family records going back to the fifteenth century.[59] Altogether, probably about 50 percent of all the large landowners in interwar Poland could be rated as landed gentry with noble traditions reaching back to the Polish–Lithuanian Commonwealth. The Bacciarellis, whose ancestor was an Italian painter who had settled in Poland and had been ennobled at the end of the eighteenth century, were probably at the other end of the scale.

As a result of the division of estates among children or the sale of land in difficult financial situations, some of the large estates gradually declined in the hierarchy of the landed gentry. In the social and cultural sense many of these small gentry owners belonged to the group of large landowners, if they had at least fifty hectares, although their membership in this group was sometimes rather subjective and not necessarily recognized by the landed gentry possessing hundreds of thousands of hectares. These petty gentry owners prevailed in Wilno, Nowogródek, Warsaw, Białystok, and Tarnopol provinces. The tradition of Polish noble origin was still very strong among about 200,000 small farmers in the northeastern regions of interwar Poland. It was much weaker among about 400,000 petty owners in eastern Galicia, where they mostly belonged to the Greek Catholic Church and had a strong Ukrainian national identity, or in Polesie, where they were usually Orthodox and thought of themselves as "local" people, Poles, or Byelorussians.[60] In relation to the size of their farms, their family and social connections, as well as their national consciousness, these owners were situated closer or further away from the bulk of the Polish landed gentry. Owners of farms below fifty hectares, even if they had gentry roots, fell out of the category of large landowners as defined in the present study.

A clear dividing line ran between Polish and non–Polish owners. Although there were some German and even Russian gentry families among them, their representatives only exceptionally married into Polish gentry families. In interwar Poland such marriage was usually subject to adoption of the Polish culture by the "foreigner." Polish gentry more frequently married French, British, or Jews, rather than Germans or Russians. The latter were very rarely accepted in Polish landed gentry circles. One of the few exceptions was Olga (née Reutern) Strukova, who married Eugeniusz Tyszkiewicz of Landwarów. Her first mother–in–law, Ananya Strukova, possessed a huge estate of Bostyń in Polesie (21,700 hectares). Mixed marriages were sometimes recorded among cosmopolitan aristocrats who broke social conventions. Such was the case of Jarosław Potocki of Rzepichów who divorced his first wife and married a dancer.[61] But this was an exception rather than a rule. On the other hand, religion was not a very strong barrier; although most of the Polish landed gentry were Roman Catholics, there were cases of marriages with other Christians, or Muslims. The Jewish landowners, even with a longer tradition of land ownership, only exceptionally entered Polish landed gentry circles. It was perhaps the easiest in Galicia.[62]

Finally, the large landowners in interwar Poland included several thousand Polish, and foreign, owners without noble roots. Some of them simply purchased land as a good investment, or as a place for recreation. Even in this group, however, family or social connections could make the owner closer, and the lack of such contacts further, from the landed gentry circle. These complicated relations are illustrated by a few examples. Tadeusz Chłapowski was born into a well–known and rich Great Polish gentry family. After a "tempestuous youth" he went abroad and worked as a manual laborer in many

countries. He then came to the Boryslaw oil mining region of Galicia
and rose to the rank of chairman of an oil company. After World
War I he bought an estate at Cieśle near Poznań as an industrialist
of noble origin returned to the countryside.

Stanisław Prince Lubomirski maintained only a small part of
his family's fortune and engaged in banking and industry. He was
a businessman but formally remained a landowner as well. General
Józef Dowbór–Muśnicki, commander of the First Polish Corps in
Russia during World I, managed the small estate of Lusowo in Poznań
Province; he was of the Lithuanian nobility, but sought landowner's
status elsewhere. General Władysław Sikorski also had an estate in
Parchanie near Inowrocław; many other officers, not always of noble
origin, had small estates like this. The Goetz family had made a fortune in the Galician brewing industry in Okocim, had been ennobled
by Emperor Franz Joseph as the Goetz–Okocimskis, and had bought
large estates. After three generations, in interwar Poland, Baron Jan
Goetz–Okocimski was the owner of Okocim in Brzesko County and
Skowieszyn in Tarnobrzeg County (altogether 10,500 hectares), and
belonged to the conservative elite in Cracow, Baron Leopld Kronenberg of the Jewish banker family, traditionally supporting Polish national aspirations, as the owner of Wieniec in Włocławek and Łęińsko
in Łódź Province (6,800 hectares). Despite some "objections," he was
generally accepted among the Polish landed gentry. Stanisław Lilpon,
by contrast, bought his estate of Wilhelmów near Warsaw later and
was treated as a bourgeois who purchased land to enter this circle.[63]

One of the richest Polish industrialists of the interwar period,
Andrzej Wierzbicki, remembered that "all Polish industrialists aimed
at buying a piece of land at the first possible moment. . . . They
bought land not to invest—they had better investment opportuni-
ties . . . they were simply land hungry."[66] Apart from a sort of
social snobbery, some of them followed a strange brand of a Polish
noble atavism. The owners who could hardly be treated as the landed
gentry because they did not engage in agriculture and enjoyed their
estates as a rural residence included, for instance, such industrialists
and bankers as Władysław Żukowski of Łazy near Olkusz, Tadeusz
Popowski of Ruszki near Kutno, and Adam Trepka of Gryków and
Rychłocice in Łódź Province (2,300 hectares). Even Alfred Falter,
the Upper Silesian businessman with connections to German capital,
thought to be one of the richest people in interwar Poland, had an
estate in Great Poland. These examples show that there were divisions between the landed gentry and nongentry landowners, but the
limits were not always clear.

Table 2.4

Average Total Area of Large Private Estates
in Poland in Hectares, 1921–1938

Province	1921	1939	1939:1921 in Percent
Poland	**593**	**522**	**88.0**
Warsaw	358	358	
Łódź	531	436	
Kielce	657	570	
Lublin	917	889	
Białystok	461	457	
Central Poland	521	488	93.6
Wilno	344	318	
Nowogródek	600	493	
Polesie	2,103	2,121	
Volynia	961	893	
Eastern Poland	772	684	88.6
Poznań	438	367	
Pomerania	212	174	
Silesia	1,640	1,391	
Western Poland	325	269	
Cracow	615	723	
Lwow	891	772	
Stanisławów	898	866	
Tarnopol	943	869	
Southern Poland	838	802	95.7

Source: Author's calculations according to: Mieczysław Mieszczan-kowski, *Struktura agrarna Polski Międzywojennej [Agrarian Structure of Interwar Poland]* Warsaw, 1960, p. 338, Table 148; *Statystyka Polski*, t. V,, "Wielka własność rolna" (*Statistics of Poland*, vol. 5. "Large Landed Ownership") Warsaw, 1925, pp. 1–2, Table 1; Jan Stecki, *Zestawienie ogólne ze statystyki większej własnośći ziemskiej na r. 1939 dokonane przeze mnie na podstawie ankiety przeprowadzonej przez RNOZ [General Statement of Large Landed Estates for 1939 Made by Me Based on the RNOZ Inquiry)* Library of the Catholic University of Lublin, File 537.

Chapter 3

SOCIOPOLITICAL AND ECONOMIC CONDITIONS

Rebirth of Poland

For the first two years of World War I Polish attempts to persuade both sides to include the reconstitution of Poland as an objective of war were fruitless. But as their economic and human resources were gradually exhausted, on 5 November 1916 the German and Austrian emperors decided to attract Polish support by announcing the reestablishment of a rump Kingdom of Poland that they had just occupied. In his New Year's Eve order of 1917 Russian Grand Duke Mikhail responded with a similar proclamation of good intentions, but the March 1917 Revolution soon swept the tsarist government away. Apart from the Polish Legions already fighting on the side of the Central Powers and the Polish Military Organization (Polska Organizacja Wojskowa) of Józef Piłsudski conspiring against Russia, there were also Polish Corps allowed by the Provisional Government in Russia, which also made a proclamation in favor of Poland's independence. The Polish cause received a strong boost when tireless efforts by the pianist Ignacy Paderewski won over President Woodrow Wilson, who included the reconstitution of Poland as one of his peace conditions on 22 January 1917. In Paris in the fall of 1917, the Allies recognized the Polish Committee (Komitet Narodowy Polski) headed by Roman Dmowski.

The Bolshevik Revolution of November 1917 facilitated Polish independence efforts to the extent that it removed Russia from the Entente, but the Brest–Litovsk Peace Treaty of 3 March 1918 stablized the status quo of the front, which meant limiting the Polish state to the Kingdom of Poland's territory. Along with this, the Allies were now more interested in setting up Poland as a barrier against Germany in the east. On 11 January 1918 President Wilson made a speech on his Fourteen Points, whose thirteenth point was formulated in the following way:

An independent Polish state should be erected, which should include the territories inhabited by indisputably Polish populations, which should be assured a free and secure access to the sea and whose political and economic independence should be guaranteed by international covenant.[1]

In the summer of 1918 the Central Powers began to collapse. While their armies were holding the front far to the east, they were less able to control the situation in Poland. The German–controlled Regency Council (Rada Regencyjna) in Warsaw proclaimed independence and unification of Poland on 7 October. On 27 October the Polish Liquidation Commission (Polske Komisja Likwidacyjna) in Cracow practically took over power from the Austrians. In 1918 Jędrzej Moraczewski, the first prime minister of reborn Poland, noted:

It is impossible to express all the excitement and fever of enthuasism which gripped Polish society at this moment. After one hundred and twenty years the cordons broke. "They are gone! Freedom! Independence! Our own statehood!"

The national euphoria was accompanied by radicalization of the masses: first, workers' councils ("soviets") were founded in which the revolutionaries began to prevail over members of the Polish Socialist Party (Polska Partia Socjalistyczna). Farm workers' councils and estate committees were beginning to emerge with a clear program for land redistribution by force. On 7 November a local socialist government under Ignacy Daszyński was established in Lublin that, under the influence of its radical peasant members, announced a land reform.[3] Since the landowners, conservatives, nationalist, and middle class strongly opposed radical plans for expropriation, the country was on the edge of a civil war in which independence could be lost; revolutionary forces in Russia and Germany were ignoring the question of national ambitions in their pursuit of a European revolution.

While the various self–governments in Poland were gradually getting rid of the control of their former German and Austrian patrons, the Polish question depended increasingly on the victorious Entente. In the summer of 1918 the whole Entente finally decided to support the idea of an independent Poland with access to the Baltic Sea. In September the Polish army in France, then comprising about 17,000 men under General Józef Haller, was recognized as an "allied beliigerent army." On 13 November the Polish National Committee in Paris was recognized by France as a de facto Polish government.[4] To the Allies Piłsudski's followers were, at least, suspect in their previous connection with the Central Powers. At home the National Democrats faced a growing wave of popular discontent and radical demands.

Then, all of a sudden, Józef Piłsudski was released from Magdeburg and arrived in Warsaw on 10 November; the Regency Council gave him the remains of their power. The Lublin government of Daszyński accepted him as the provisional head of state, as did most of the moderate socialist and peasant groups. The leftist extremists had already drifted toward the idea of dictatorship of the proletariat and agitated against national statehood. The National Democrats feared that a socialist government, such as Daszyński's, would be sucked into the revolutionary maelstorm, but finally decided to trust Piłsudski. Opposing him would mean allowing a further radicalization of the masses. As Roman Dmowski later said, "It is certain that if we formed a government—let us assume with me as its head—we should well and truly cut the throat of Poland."[5]

Thus in mid–November 1918 Piłsudski became a "bridge to independence," a one–man institution invested with some confidence by most of the major political forces in Poland, except for the revolutionaries. The decree of 22 November, concerning the interim political system of Poland and entrusting Piłsudski with the duties of provisional head of state, was signed by Piłsudski himself.[6] The limitations to Piłsudski's position were soon to appear.

The new government under Jędrzej Moraczewski, which he appointed on 18 November, was from the beginning strongly opposed by the National democrats and all conservative forces in Poland. At that time, however, Piłsudski saw the major threat in the spread of revolution. This is why on 20 November the Moraczewski government announced a declaration anticipating the nationalization of key industries, participation by workers in factory administration, and a radical and reform.[7] These radical social reforms were, however, to be introduced by a freely elected parliament. The policies of the Moraczewski government were a reflection of the socialist program, but they were mainly aimed at attracting the revolutionary masses to the idea of an independent Poland and its democratic institutions. The struggle for social and economic reforms was to be moved from the streets to the parliament.

All through December 1918 the Moraczewski cabinet was attacked by the political right and by the internationalist revolutionaries. The latter, however, were losing ground for their agenda. The bulk of their social and economic program was taken over by the Socialists and presented as a democratic proposal. When Piłsudski felt that the wave of revolution was subsiding in January he broadened the coalition government, under Ignacy Paderwski, on 16 January 1919. His cabinet was recognized by the victories Entente as the government of independent Poland. At the same time the rightist pressure on the government decreased.[8]

When independent Poland was reborn amid revolutionary waves in November 1918 it was not obvious what territorial shape it would take and what its sociopolitical system would be. From the very beginning it was involved in struggles for almost all of its frontiers. The western territories—Great Poland, Pomerania, and Upper Silesia—were claimed by Germany; Teschen Silesia became a bone of contention between Poland and Czechoslovakia; the Wilno region was contested by Poland and Lithuania; the Lwow area was already being fought for by the Poles and Ukrainians; while in the northeast, it soon came to a clash between the Bolsheviks and the improvised Polish army. In December 1918 the Warsaw government of Jędrej Moraczewski controlled only the central part of the Polish territories—the former Kingdom of Poland and western Galicia.

Under these circumstances, in January 1919, Head of State Piłsudski succeeded in gaining international recognition for the Paderewski government, which included leaders of the Paris Polish National Committee favored by the Entente. On 26 January 1919 the first round of elections to the Constituent Sejm was held, which gave victory to the right and center of the parliament: the National Democrats gained 34 percent of the seats, the moderate Peasant party "Piast" 13 percent, the leftist Peasant party "Wyzwolenie" 17 percent, the Polish peasant (Left) 4 percent, and the Polish Socialist party 9 percent. The additional election in Great Poland and other territories incorporated by mid–1919 even strengthened the dominance of the rightist and centrist parties.[9]

During the early months of 1919 the position of the government in Warsaw stabilized, thanks to creation of democratic institutions, introduction of progressive labor legislation, and military successes. In mid–1919 Great Poland and Pomerania were practically under Polish control, along with the Wilno region, and Polesia and a great part of eastern Galicia won from the Ukrainians. The Versailles Treaty of June 1919 confirmed Polish acquisitions in the west with the exception of Upper Silesia, which was to be subject to a plebiscite. The internal situation of Poland was improved, but in mid–1919 there was still a lot of tension in the countryside.

Old Order or New

Independent Poland was reborn under extremely difficult economic and political conditions. The collapse of the Russian state and the social upheaval in the tsarist army and among urban workers had a dramatic impact on the situation of Polish landowners. At first this referred to the easternmost borderland (*kresy wschodnie*). The revolutionary wave spilled far and wide, carrying along masses of Byelorussian and Ukrainian peasants. Military detachments in revolt and groups of peasant rebels attacked manors, confiscated food and horses, and plundered and murdered Polish landlords.[10]

The first climax of terror came at the end of 1917 when the flimsy power of the Russian Provisional Government was overthrown by the Bolsheviks. In the power vacuum various rebel groups in Byelorussia and the Ukraine knew no restraint in looting and killing. On 4 November 1917 a gang of about 1,000 raided Sławuta, entirely destroying the estate and palace and butchering the 80–year–old owner, Prince Roman Sanguszko.[11] A similar raid took place in Antoniny, whose owner, Józef Potocki, survived because he was absent. Other manors that suffered from such attacks included Semerynka and Werboynce of Jan Pruszyński, whose collection of books, Gobelins, tapestries, and china was destroyed; Tymoszówks, near Chehyryn, of Karol Rościszewski, a place in which the composer Karol Szymanowski had spent many years; Korytna in Ploskiri County of Wanda and Stanisław Kossecki; Chabno of Stanisław Horwatt; Ohremowce, whose owner, Stanisław Skibniewski, was murdered, burned, and his ashes scattered, and many others.[12] At the beginning of 1918 eleven members of the family of Kazimierz Szemioth of Iloszka near Kobryń were murdered.[13]

After the collapse of the Austrian and German occupation at the end of 1918 another wave of terror came. Their numerous victims included, for example, Władysław Joworski of Bisówka, Aniela Święicka of Rasztówa, Jan Pruszyński of Semerynka, and cruelly violated and butchered Julia Chodkiewcz and her daughter Zofia of Młynów. The third period of attacks on manors and their owners came with the westward offensive of the Red Army in mid–1920. At that time brothers Antoni and Ignacy Broel–Platerwere killed at Dąbrowica. Other well–known victims included Edward Jeleński, Prince Hieronim Drucki–Lubecki, and young Stanisław Szadurska of Pusza.[14] The Russian Revolution had also a significant impact on the social situation in central Poland. Although there were no spectacular murders, in November and December 1918 large estates in the Kingdom of Poland and western Galicia were frequently looted. Also the first farm workers' soviets were created. On 6 November 1918 a revolutionary peasant Tarnobrzeg Republic was established. The atmosphere of these days can be illustrated by a speech of its radical leader, Reverend Eugeniusz Okoń, who said: "You will not have to bow to the 'enlightened' counts and landlords, you will not pave the streets with peasant skulls; it is with noble skulls that you, peasants, will pave our market squares."[15] Soon a similarly revolutionary Pińczow Republic was created under a Polish Bolshevik, Jan Lisowski.

On 2 December 1918 Provisional Head of State Józef Pułsudski received a delegation of landowners headed by Marian Kiniorski, Ludomił Pułaski, and Kazimierz Fudakowski. They declared their support for the idea of a democratic state but demanded that the government put an end to the revolutionary activities of the peasants. Piłsudski promised to undertake such steps. The supreme authorities of reborn Poland did not intend to support revolutionary changes in the social order.[16] Nevertheless the tensions in the countryside did not cease. The peasants of Zamość and Krasnystaw counties went on strike. At the beginning of December 1918 several thousand peasants penetrated the Rozwadów estate of Jan Goetz–Okocimski. During a scuffle between farm hands and the military in Kozłów in Płock County on 29 December 1918, a couple of peasants were killed. In early January 1919 under their village mayor (*wójt* stole estate potatoes and livestock from Mokrzyszew of Zdzisław Tarnowski, while another group ravaged the Grębów manor of Seweryn Dolański in Tarnobrzeg County.[17] Peasant strikes and protests were basically of an economic nature but gradually, under the influence of radical and revolutionary agitation, they developed into a political movement.

In early 1919 trade union activities were started by farm hands and on 16 March 1919 the first congress of farm workers created the Trade Union of Agricultureal Workers (Związek Zawodowy Robotników Rolnych, or ZZRR). The new union was strongly influenced by the revolutionary left and the Polish Socialist party. Attempts by the National Democrats to create a moderate trade union of farmers and foresters were much less successful. In March 1919 farm workers of Lublin Province, headed by communist activities, went on strike. The Paderewski government decided to proclaim a state of emergency in the whole region. In the ensuing clashes eighty–two people were killed and several hundred wounded. Finally, on 5 April 1919, landowners' representatives headed by Jan Stecki and Zazimierz Fudakowski, signed an agreement with the strike committee, providing for an eight–hour work day, paid leaves, increased pay, and some social benefits. The strike was ended.[18]

The agreement eased the tension in the countryside, but only in part. The peasants of the Zamość entail still entered its forests and felled trees. Strikes were repeated in Great Poland.[19] If the government had delayed the land reform preparations, it could have faced a return of the revolutionary wave. Under the pressure of the peasant parties, on 19 July 1919 the Constituent Sejm issued a declaration on the principles of land reform based on a draft prepared by the Peasant party "Piast." The maximum of unexpropriated land was fixed at 60 to 180 hectares in central Poland and up to 400 hectares in the easternmost and westernmost regions. All forests were to be nationalized and the former owners were to receive compensation. The resolution was however not a law; the land reform act itself was to follow.[20]

The Sejm proclamation could only partly satisfy the conflicting interests. Landowners strongly opposed the declaration and its "Bolshevik" nature. The leftist peasant parties were not satisfied and urged more radical measures. The ZZRR protest against the declaration, too moderate in their opinion, was ignored by the parliament, which led to proclamation of a general agricultural strike on 16 October 1919. About 150,000 peasants took part in the strike, which finally collapsed under government pressure and the withdrawal of the Socialists. In the fall of 1919 the ZZRR was dominated by the members of the Polish Socialist party, which moderated the revolutionary vigor of the farmworkers.[21]

Thanks to a certain stabilization of the state's authority at the end of 1919, rural tensions decreased. In early 1920 trade agreements were reached for the five provinces of central Poland, providing for the working conditions of farm laborers receiving allowance in kind (*ordynariusz*), village tenants (*komornik*), and estate handicraftsmen. Peasant strikes became less and less frequent, but in April 1920 there was a farm workers' strike in Great Poland organized without the consent of the ZZRR, and it was stimulated by the Communists and

Germans.[22]

When the Polish offensive in the east broke down and the Red Army started a massive westward drive in June 1920, peasant discontent became a major political factor again. In view of the advance of the Bolshevik troops, some Byelorussian, Ukrainian, but also Polish, peasants started a spontaneous redistribution of estate lands. Farm hands frequently made use of the situation to take over crops or estate land. This was, for example, the case in Hrubieszów County. In the territories occupied by the Red Army special manor committees were founded on large estates. Landowners withdrew: those who stayed were often killed, just like Jan Starzyński of Maliszewo.

On 31 July 1920 the Provisional Revolutionary Committee for Poland (Polrevkom) moved to Białystok. County committees were created over the whole territory between Brodnice and Rypin in the northwest to Garwolin and Radzyń Podlaski in the southeast. On 5 August 1920 the Polrvkom issued an appeal to the Polish peasant proclaiming the expulsion of landlords and the takeover of their estates in the name of the "Polish nation." In practice this meant nationalization of the expropriated estates according to the principles of the Bolshevik "Decree of Land," although Feliks dzierzyński favored redistribution of some of the expropriated land, the opinion of Julian Marlewski, who opposed it prevailed. The landless peasants were disappointed.[23]

In the face of the advance of the Red Army in July 1920, from the Sejm emerged a coalition government under the "Piast" leader Wincenty Witos. The Socialist Ignacy Daszyński became vice–premier. This was to show the socialist world that Poland was ruled by a "worker–peasant" government and that the Polish–Soviet war was not a "class war" but a national one. At the same time the Sejm had to react to the social challenge of the Bolsheviks. On 15 July 1920 a land reform law was passed. Forced expropriation of estates of above 180 hectares (eastern and western territories, 400 hectares) was to follow at half the market value of land. Taking into account other deductions, landowners would not receive more than 3 percent of the value of the land. The expropriation procedure was made very complicated, so that before the end of 1920, when the Polish–Soviet War was over, only six estates were expropriated according to the July 1920 principles. Of course, voluntary redistribution went on undisturbed.[24]

The Battle of Warsaw in August 1920 is called one of the decisive battles in the history of Europe. If it had been lost by the Poles, probably nothing would have prevented the Bolshevization of Germany, and the fate of Europe would have been quite different. Since it was won by the Polish army, independent Poland was saved. When the Polish–Soviet armistice was signed in October 11920 and the Peace Treaty of Riga of 18 March 1921 determined the Polish–Soviet frontier, the constitutional debate in the Sejm reached the final stage. Among the principles of civil rights, suffrage, and state authority one of the most important issues was the treatment of private property. Article 99 of the constitution, finally passed on 17 March 1921, stipulated that private ownership was the principle of a sound sociopolitical system, so that any expropriation had to be fully compensated. Discussion of article 99 was in fact a reconsideration of the July 1920 land reform law. Finally it was agreed that the partial compensation provided for in this law could not be accepted. This was, to a great extent, due to the fact that after the immediate danger to the state was gone, peasants' feelings were no longer so important. But even some of the parties representing the peasantry supported the inviolability of property rights.[25]

The suspension of the land reform and economic difficulties aggravated the atmosphere in the countryside. In October 1921 the ZZRR proclaimed a strike by farm workers in Poznań Province, which was suppressed by the military. In August 1922 the Poznań strike was revived; it included 1,400 Great Polish estates. In 1923 more strikes took place as a result of hyperinflation; later the strikes decreased because of currency stabilization. While in 1923 about 849,000 farm workers went on strike, in 1925 this number had decreased to about 149,000.[26]

In the easternmost territories the social atmosphere was even worse. After the Polish–Soviet armistice of October 1920 the Byelorussian and Ukrainian peasants would not give up the "liberties" of the revolutionary period. In many areas of Wilno, Nowogródek, and Polesie provinces various brigade gangs continued to ravage estates.[27] In September 1923 the gang of "Mucha" Michalski raided the Nacz estate of the Czarnockis, while other gangs burned down four estates in Słonim County, one estate in Nieśwież County, and one in Baranowicze County. In Czurlony, in Wilejka County, brigands murdered a government administrator.[28] The climax of these raids which frequently came from beyond the Soviet border, was in the summer of 1924 when after a series of attempts in Łuniec, Nieśwież, Stołpce, and Baranowicze counties, the Polish government decided to create a special force called the Border Defense Corps (Korpus Ochrony Pogranicza).[29]

Stabilization of rural relations was also due to the progress of the land reform process. The radical peasant parties that opposed the principle of full compensation urged expropriation without compensation. The moderate Piast party accepted compensation but would not wait with the expropriation of large estates. On the other hand the conservatives pressed the National Democrats to prevent any wider expropriation. If it had not been for the desire of the Piast and National Democrats to form a parliamentary majority government in 1923, the land reform question would have remained unsolved for a longer time. However, in an agreement known as the Lanckorona Pact of 17 May 1923, both parties agareed to a compromise solution: voluntary redistribution at full compensation and the government's right to force the redistribution of land unless an annual quota of 200,000 hectares was distributed.[30]

The collapse of the majority government because of hyperinflation in December 1923 slowed down preparations for the reform. In May 1924 Piast and Wyzwolenie moved that these preparations be accelerated. The new coalition government of Władysław Grabski presented a draft law. The National Democrats wanted to raise the maximum of unexpropriated land while Wyzwolenie resolved to adopt only the no–compensation principle. In the course of the fierce parliamentary struggle two ministers of agriculture gave up. The final land reform law was passed on 28 December 1925.[31] It could not satisfy either the landowners or the radical peasant parties, nor could it solve most of the problems of the Polish countryside, but it was a great political compromise.

During the years of prosperity the social atmosphere in the countryside improved. It was not until the Great Depression that the tensions grew again. For several years farm workers and landowners had struggled over pay and collective agreements. Otherwise the depression affected all farmers, large or small, so the economic difficulties did not, as a rule, aggravate the conflict between the peasants and landowners—however, there were a few cases. For instance, in 1933 about 12,000 peasants of Łańcut County, irritated by the arrogance of the Łańcut entail administration and the dissolution of the peasant Wici youth organization, organized a "march on Łańcut." The action was stopped by the police and military.[32] Generally speaking, however, as a result of the depression the traditional conflict between manor and village was largely replaced by the conflict of interests between the countryside and the towns, between the farmers, impoverished by the declining prices, and the urban entrepreneurs, who could more effectively dictate prices for industrial goods. Also, the great peasant strike of 1937 was mostly directed against urban monopolies and the more and more authoritarian governments.

War Damage

World War I damage in the Polish territories was, in relative terms, one of the worst in Europe. This damage was added to by the Polish–Ukrainian and Polish–Soviet military operations of 1918–1920. Out of 388,000 square kilometers (111,197 square miles) of the 1921 territory of Poland, about 90 percent was affected by some kind of military operations in the years 1914–1920, while stationary warfare affected about 85,000 square kilometers (32,819 square miles), that is, about 22 percent of Poland's territory.[33] The Carnegie Foundation estimated the overall damage to Polish agriculture over 1914–1920 at about 4,300,000,000 gold francs. About 20 percent of horses were lost along with about 29 percent of cattle. In 1919 crops in the former Kingdom of Poland were at only 55 percent of the prewar level, while at only about 38 percent of that level in the easternmost borderland.[34]

There are few data illustrating the degree of damage to large estates and small farms. For instance, in 1919/20 the area under winter crops in the southern provinces was generally smaller in large estates than in small holdings. Only in Cracow Province was it different: the overall area under winter crops accounted here for 24.8 percent of the arable land area, while on large estates this share was 25.4 percent. In Lwow Province respective shares were 26.6 and 19.3 percent, in Stanisławów Province 21.8 and 12.6 percent, and in Tarnopol Province 16.7 and 6.3 percent.[35] The rule seemed clear: the farther east, the worse the damage. If proportions between damage to large estates and small farms in the southern provinces can be treated as representative for the whole of Poland, the damage to large estates was large than to small holdings.

The war damage affected various parts of interwar Poland in an uneven way. The former German partition suffered relatively less. Only in the East Prussian borderland, which changed hands during the 1915 and 1920 campaigns, was the damage very serious. For instance, the Pomeranina Cibóż estate (1,170 hectares) near Działdow, belonging to Ignacy Mieczkowski, was successively plundered by the German, Russian, and Soviet troops. The German military vandalized the nearby Jabłonowo estate of Zygmunt Narzyński and despoiled the owner's family tombs.[36] Several other Pomeranian and Poznanian estates were also affected by requisitions and war damage, but after the front moved eastward in 1915 the agriculture of the German partition was in relatively good shape and could even enjoy a kind of a war prosperity.

The former Kingdom of Poland witnessed the fluctuations of the front line in 1915 and the effects of the Polish–Ukrainian and Polish–Soviet military operations after 1918. The most war–damaged areas included Chełm County, where about 42 percent of farm buildings were destroyed, as well as Hrubieszów and Tomaszów counties in the east and Ostrołęka, Kolno, and Prrzasnysz counties in the north.[37] Only the Zamość entail suffered losses of about 8,000,000 rubles, while the value of assets lost by its owner, Maurycy Zamoyski, in Russian banks was estimated at further 500,000 rubles.[38] Huge damage resulted from seven months of heavy fighting in Rawa Mazowiecka County, where several villages and estates were entirely destroyed.. Grójec, Pinńczów, Płock, and Błonie counties in the central part of the former Kingdom of Poland were relatively less damaged.

On the other hand the eastern territories suffered from immense destruction. Between the rivers Niemen (Nemunas) and Jasiełda the losses in buildings were estimated at 60 percent and in the Kosów Poleski County at 69 percent. About 50 to 60 percent of buildings were destroyed in Pinńsk and Brest counties and in Horochów County in Volhynia. These areas were also the most depopulated. Huge forest areas were ruined. In 1926 it was estimated that only 37 percent of the forest area in Polesie was in fair condition.[39] When, after the World War I destruction, the estate owners started reconstruction, the Soviet invasion of 1920 came, bringing further damage and losses.

In the fall of 1920 Oskar Meysztowicz of Rohoźnica in Wołkowysk County noted: "We have not found even a single bushel of grain or potatoes, even a single hectar of land under crops, while most of the buildings [lie] in ruins."[40] Another landowner described the conditions in Polesie:

> The whole countryside between Baranowicze and Brest is a desolate desert. . . . Only here and there grassy pavements or solitary wells mark the place of a former village, while crushed walls or a protruding chimney of a distillery bear

witness to a formerly rich manor house.[41]

Wincenty Witos, who visited the eastern provinces in late 1920, noticed the ruins and the absence of many owners, who were still in the army or had not returned from the evacuation.[42] A similar picture was presented by the writer Maria Rodziewiczówna, who lived in a small estate in Hruszowa in Polisie.[43]

Many examples of estates entirely ruined in the easternmost borderland may be quoted. In Woropajewo Konstanty Przeździecki, in the northern part of Wilno Province, the huge forest damage was due to the fact that the German-Russian front ran across the estate for several months. The same applies to the Czurlony estate of the Krasicki family in the southern part of Wilno Province, where farm buildings were ruined along with the palace, park, and a great part of the forest. In Koziczyn (Święciany County of Wilno Province), which belonged to Zygmunt Bortkiewicz, the German troops felled most of the forest, plundered the manor house, and requisitoned all the cattle in 1916. The destruction was completed when the Polish-Soviet front moved through the estate twice in 1919 and 1920. The Łazduny estate (Oszmiana County of Wilno Province) of Hipolit Korwin-Milewski was 90 percent damaged.[44]

Out of twenty-six farm buildings of the Kołdyczew estate in Nowogródek Province none remained in good shape. When in 1920 the owner, Tadeusz Szalewicz, managed to put together one of the buildings and to gather some horses and cattle, the Soviet offensive came and everything was lost again.[45] According to an inquiry by the Baranowicze Agricultural Society, over the years 1913-1923, the area of wasteland had grown from 5 percent to 46 percent of the total land area, while the number of horses in the fourteen estates examined decreased from 420 to 144 of cattle from 713 to 131, and of pigs from 311 to 160.[46]

The situation in Polesie was very much the same. In 1919 only about 10 percent of arable land was under cultivation in the large estates of Brest, Prużana, and Korbryń counties. Most of the fields became wasteland filled with bushes and trenches. In many cases the ruined estates never recovered. Only few owners, such as Jan Roth of Brest County or Stanisław Puzyna of Kobryń County, managed to restore the prewar economic standing of their estates.[47]

In Volhynia the war damage was also disastrous. In Smordwa an estate of 7,130 hectares in Dubno County, belonging to Aleksander Ledóchowski, the crops were burned by the Russians, the manor by the Austrians, and the palace was plundered and destroyed by the nearby peasants in 1920. Nevertheless, Ledóchowski managed to reconstruct the estate, which later was one of the most efficient in Volhynia. The Poryck estate in Włodzimierz County (4,840 hectares) belonging to Stanisław Czacki, was affected by four waves of destruction: by the Austrians in 1914, Russians in 1915, Ukrainians in 1918, and Soviets in 1920. Entirely destroyed were the estates in Horochów County, such as Zamlicze (1,150 hectares) of Aleksander Sumowski, and Zaturce (710 hectares) of Stanisław Lipiński. The situation in Sarny County was equally bad.[48]

Some Volhynian estates never recovered from World War I damage. In 1933 a landowner recorded his impressions from an excursion:

> Yesterday I visited a Volhynian estate which had once belonged to the family of my mother. . . . The spot where the palace once stood is all covered with wild bushes (the palace burned down by the Muscovites during the war) and only a huge, neglected park, still showing traces of the hands that had cared for it, can bear witness of the former prosperity.[49]

Cracow Province suffered much less. Only in its northeastern parts did some military operations take place. But in Lwow, Stanisławów, Tarnopol provinces the effects of the war were horrible. The Przeworsk entail of Prince Andrzej Lubomirski (8,580 hectares) was devastated by Austrian and Russian requisitions, and by fires. Its losses were estiamted at about 6,500,000 zlotys US$730,000 of that time). About 2,000 hectares of forest were burned down by the Russians in Ruda Różaniecka, an estate of Hugo Wattmann–Maelcamp in Lubasców County (altogether 12,000 hectares). The large estates in Stanisławów Province were even further wasted. In 1919/20 the area under cultivation in Tłumacz, Horodenka, Rohatyn, and Kołomyja counties did not exceed 10 percent of the total arable land area.[50]

The situation in Tarnopol Province was probably the worst in Poland. In Zborów County the area under cultivation in 1919/20 was only about 13 percent of the total arable land area, whole on large estates it was only 3 percent. The Jagielnica latifundium of Antoni Lanckoroński was subsequently destroyed by the Russians, Ukrainians, and the Red Army. The Skała entail of Agenor Gołuchowksi lay fallow as late as in 1922. By th fall of 1920 Zaleszczyki County had changed hands seven times; almost all its thirty–eight large estates lay in ruins. The Torskie estate of Zofia Łoś had four kilometers of trenches and its fifty-six farm buildings were ruined. On the Kniaź estate of Izabela Jaruzelska buildings, livestock, and crops were requisitioned and destroyed four times in the years 1914-1920.[51] Huge losses were also recorded in Podhacjce, Trembowla, and Złoczów counties. Repair of this huge war damage was to require a lot of time and astronomical funds. The alrge private owners could rarely afford the reconstruction themselves. Hence they took extraordinary measures by selling land, felling forests, organizing mutual aid funds, and applying for government credits. Subsequent governments usually favored demands for credits for reconstruction purposes and requests for reduced taxation. But that does not mean that large landowners were only recipients of government aid. Apart from regular taxes, the large landed properties were assessed an extraordinary levy by the law of 11 August 1923, executed especially by the government of Władysław Grabski in 1924 and 1925.[52] The overall sum of the levy in relation to agriculture was 280,000,000 zlotys (US$31,000,000 of that time), and most of this sum was exacted from large private estates. The large private landowners had also to pay about 100,000,000 zlotys ($11,000,000) in a special forest levy for reconstruction of other sectors of the national economy.[53] The question of taxation of large private estates will be discussed further on, but it is worth stressing here that, apart from the costs of reconstruction of their own estates, the landowners also bore a significant part of the costs of reconstruction of the whole Polish economy after World War I.

Reconstruction went on for years. By the end of 1922 only about 47 percent of farm buildings were reconstructed, and at the end of 1923 about 600,000 buildings were still in ruins, most of them in the eastern borderland. In the spring of 1923 about 370,000 hectares of arable land still lay fallow.[54] Generally speaking, the reconstruction process was terminated around 1926, when prosperity began, but some regions, such as Nowogródek Province or Podolia, did not come up to the prewar standards of the economy by 1939.

The Range of Large Private Estates

The decline of large landed properties in the Polish territories had gone on since the partitions. In 1772 the large noble estates covered about 57,000,000 hectares, that is, 78 percent of the area of the Polish-Lithuanian Commonwealth.[55] The land holdings of large private owners later decreased because of confiscation of estates, after the partitions and the 1830 and 1863 national risings, and the appropriation of land with the emancipation of peasants, voluntary redistribution, and the liquidation of easements (*serwituty*). Altogether, in 1913 large private estates in the 1772 territory covered about 26,300,000 hectares, including about 15,300,000 hectares of Polish private estates.[56]

On the eve of World War I the large private estates in the former Kingdom of Poland covered about 4,272,000 hectares, of which about 95 percent was in the hands of Polish owners.[57] In Galicia about 2,168,000 hectares belonged to large private owners, of which about 85 percent was in Polish hands.[58] In Prussian Poland private estates of more than 100 hectares constituted about 2,653,000 hectares. Polish owners possessed about half of this area.[59]

For the eastern territories various estimates can be quoted. Rejecting extreme figures, it may be assumed that in 1913 the large private landed property in Lithuania, Byelorussia, and the Ukraine covered about 17,400,000 hectares, of which about 50 percent had belonged to Poles. In the Wilno *gubernia* the Polish owners had 1,225,000 hectares (60.3 percent of all large estates), in the Kaunas *gubernia* 972,000 hectares (60.1 percent), in the Minsk *gubernia* 1,583,000 hectares (49.5 percent), in the Mohylev *gubernia* 666,000 hectares (27.9 percent), in the Vitebsk *gubernia* 774,000 hectares (38.7 percent), in the Volhynian *gubernia* 1,048,000 hectares, in the Podolian *gubernia* 677,000 hectares, and in the Kiev *gubernia* 676,000 hectares. It was estimated that in the three latter the share of the area in Polish hands was about 47 percent. After World War I and the Bolshevik revolution about 12,700,000 hectares of large landed property were liquidated in Lithuania, Byelorussia, and the Ukraine, including about 5,702,000 hectares of Polish estates.[60]

It may have seemed that when the Polish state was reconstituted after 1918 the area of the large private estates would be precisely estimated, at least in view of the peasant pressure to parcel out large landed property. This was not the case and the delicacy of the land reform was probably the reason. Bowing to popular demands to start land redistribution the first census was organized in 1921, when not all the territorial problems were finally settled. The census did not cover the whole area of Poland, about 500,000 people were still abroad, and demobilization was not complete. Some of the administrators, or even the owners, did not know the exact data concerning their estates. Many smallholders underestimated the area of their plots in hopes of benefiting from the land reform, while the large owners did the same to minimize the extent of the expected redistribution. Additional calculations published in 1925 only partly improved the quality of the census results. The gaps in the existing evidence were to a large extent filled by Mieczysław Mieszczankowski, whose calculations will be presented here as a foundation for further estimates.[61] Furthermore, the second census, of 1931, failed to give precise data on the area of large private estates. The census was carried out during the Great Depression, when the voluntary parcelling out within the land reforms was declining and the government was not interested in stressing the failure of the land redistribution program. Therefore the census data were presented in a way that prevented precise comparisons with the 1921 data. By 1939 there had been no third census. Some fragmentary data gathered by the Supreme Council of Landowners' Organizations, calculated by Jan Stecki, referred to only 5,700,000 hectares of land.[62]

It should be noted that the area of large private estates in Poland presented in Table 3.1 includes only the estates of Polish citizens within the frontiers of the Polish Second Republic. Some of the landowners who held Polish citizenship had estates abroad. This was the case of the German Silesian tycoons and also of some Polish owners. For instance, Ksawery Branicki of Wilannów had 1,500 hectares at Montrésor in France, later inherited by the Rey family; Adam Stadnicki of Nawojowa had an estate at Fraim in Slovakia; Konstanty Skirmutt of Mołodów had a vineyard near Brindisi in Italy. The overall area of foreign landed property in the hands of Polish citizens is not known.

Table 3.1 shows that the overall area of large private estates decreased by 20.1 percent over the years 1921-1938. This decrease was most significant in Lublin, Kielce, and Warsaw provinces in central Poland, and in the eastern provinces of Polesie and Nowogródek. The rate of the large estate decline in western Poland, as well as in Stanisławów and Volhynia provinces̄ was the slowest. Noteworthy is that the rate of decrease of the total land area of large private estates was higher than that of public estates. While the share of the large private estates in the total land area in Poland fell from 30.4 percent in 1921 to 24.3 percent in 1938, the share of public estates decreased from 17.7 percent to 16.2 percent. At the same time the share of small holdings increased from 51.9 percent in 1921 to 59.5 percent in 1938.[63]

Table 3.1

Total Area of Large Private Estates in Poland
in Hectares, 1921–1938

Province	1921	1931	1938	1938:1921
POLAND	11,532,900	9,805,000	9,231,200	79.9%
Warsaw	951,500	749,600	695,100	73.0%
Łódź	502,000	404,000	374,300	74.5%
Kielce	556,000	437,400	405,300	72.8%
Lublin	835,800	634,000	588,000	70.4%
Białystok	444,500	361,000	334,600	75.2%
Central Poland	3,289,800	2,586,400	2,397,300	72.9%
Wilno	872,900	770,200	717,700	82.2%
Nowogródek	746,900	586,600	564,000	73.1%
Polesie	1,800,500	1,370,100	1,277,100	70.9%
Volhynia	818,600	783m700	730,200	89.2%
Eastern Poland	4,238,900	3,510,600	3,271,000	77.1%
Poznań	1,143,200	1,104,200	1,059,900	92.7%
Pomerania	500,200	483,000	460,000	91.9%
Silesia	188,600	184,400	179,400	95.0%
Western Poland	1,832,000	1,771,800	1,699,200	92.8%
Cracow	379,800	307,500	293,400	77.2%
Lwow	844,600	781,900	744,900	88.2%
Stanisław	382,400	380,700	363,000	94.9%
Tarnopol	556,300	466,100	444,200	79.8%
Southern Poland	2,163,100	1,936,200	1,845,600	85.3%

Source: Calculated according to Mieczysław Mieszczankowski, *Struktura agrarna Polski międzywojennej [Agrarian Structure of Interwar Poland]* Warsaw, 1960, p. 338.

The total land area of large private estates in interwar Poland decreased mainly as a result of redistribution liquidation of easements, and parcelling among family members. Redistribution of land as provided for by the land reform act of 1925 was voluntary. The major motives encouraging landowners to sell land included the necessity to find resources for reconstruction and the desire to gain extraordinary profits during the years of prosperity. For instance, the costs of reconstruction of the Jagielnica latifundium of Antonio Lanckoroński were mostly met by distributing 1,700 hectares of agricultural land. More commercial was the sale of lots from the Wilarów estates of Ksawery Branicki in the Warsaw suburbs of Służew, Wawer, and Anin. Many suburban villas were soon built on these lots.[64]

As can be seen from Table 3.2 the quota of 200,000 hectares per annum was fulfilled only during the inflation and in the years of prosperity 1926–28. During the Great Depression voluntary distribution collapsed because of the dramatic fall in prices for foodstuffs and land. Landowners were less ready to offer land at falling prices, while

Table 3.2

Distribution of Land in Poland in Hectares
1919–1938

Year	Total Area Parcelled	Year	Total Area Parcelled
1919	11,800	1929	164,500
1920	54,300	1930	130,800
1921	180,400	1931	105,300
1922	254,200	1932	74,100
1923	201,700	1933	83,500
1924	118,300	1934	56,500
1925	128,300	1935	79,800
1926	209,800	1936	96,500
1927	245,100	1937	113,100
1928	227,600	1938	119,200

Source: *Mały Rocznik Statystyczny 1939 [Concise Statistical Yearbook for 1939]* p. 70.

potential peasant purchasers could not afford to buy extra land as their income radically declined. The government failed to demand compulsory redistribution for fear of a further decline of land prices. Altogether 2,654,800 hectares of land were redistributed in Poland in the years 1919–1939, of which 1,863,400 had belonged to large private estates.

The question of easements (*serwituty*) has already been mentioned. The common use of private property not only complicated a clear separation of property units, but was also a serious burden for the economy of the large private estates. In 1921 about 1,540 such estates were burdened with these *serwituty*. Most of these estates were situated in the former Russian partition. In Warsaw Province about 16 percent of estates had to cope with these easements, in Łódź Province about 22 percent, in Kielce Province 18 percent, in Lublin Province 11 percent, in Białystok Province 21 percent, in Wilno Province 9 percent, in Nowogródek Province 15 percent, in Polesie Province 17 percent, and in Volhynia Province 17 percent of estates had easements to liquidate.

In other parts of the country only few large private estates were still burdened with *serwituty*. Most of the easements encompassed meadows, pastures, and forests. In Polesie and Volhynia the easements were frequently bilateral: not only could the peasants use the landlords' land, but also vice versa—the manors had the right to use the peasant land (so–called *tołoka*). On 7 May 1920 the Sejm passed a law eliminating easements in the former Kingdom of Poland, either by means of voluntary agreements, or legal enforcements. On 10 January 1922 this law was extended to the northeastern borderland.[65]

Altogether, about 595,300 hectares of large private estate lands were given to peasants in exchange for the abolition of the common use of pastures, meadows, and forests. The highest rate of easement liquidation was recorded in the years 1926–1930, when from 50,000 to 100,000 hectares of easements were abolished every year.[66] In the central provinces easements were exchanged for land or money, while those in the eastern borderland provinces were mostly for land. This is an indirect proof of the particular shortage of cash in the hands of large private landowners in the eastern provinces. Abolition of easements required long and laborious negotiations between landowners and local peasants. The process not only took a lot of time and energy, but also generated many conflicts. Clear property relations were established at the cost of the resignation by the landowners of some parts of their estates or by financial compensation. In the latter case, the costs involved were a serious burden for a large estate economy. This was the case of the Wielkie Soleczniki estate (1,930 hectares) of Karol Wagner in Wilno Province. The owner gave up about 525 hectares of land in exchange for abolition of the common use rights to his land. The Zamość entail had great problems with the easements. Local peasants had had customary rights to enter the entail and exploit its pastures and forests. In the 1920s the volume of timber felled by the peasants in this entail was estimated at several thousand cubic meters per annum. By 1929 about 66,000 hectares of the entail, that is about one-third of its total area, was distributed among the peasants in exchange for abolition of the easements. It is noteworthy that these 66,000 hectares accounted for 11 percent of the whole area of large estates given up in return for easements in Poland.[67]

In the 1930s easement liquidation slowed down because only the most difficult cases still remained unsolved. By 1939 the process of abolition was mostly completed. Nevertheless, it must be remembered that all through the interwar years this process caused serious disruptions in the economies of the large private estates.

Some of the large private estates were also liquidated as a result of distribution among family members. If heirs of a large landowner received bequests of more than 50 or 100 hectares, they remained within the statistically accepted group of large estate owners. Otherwise, distribution of an estate could make some of the heirs fall into the category of small farm owners. To prevent this, large estates were sometimes bequethed only to some of the potential heirs; quite frequently siblings who received land bequests were obliged to pay off those who settled elsewhere. Sometimes such payments were a serious burden for the large estate economy, but the lack of a specific statistical evidence makes it impossible to measure this phenomenon.

The declining share of large private estates in the total land area in interwar Poland was accompanied by an even more rapid decrease in agricultural and arable land area. While in the years 1921–1938 the total area of large private estates decreased by 20.1 percent, the arable land area of these estates fell by 33.4 percent and the area of pastaures and meadows decreased by 20.7 percent, the area of forests declined by only 5.6 percent. As a result the land use structure of large estates changed. In 1931 agricultural land in Poland accounted for 67.5 percent of the total area, while on the large private estates only for 47.3 percent. At the same time arable land accounted for

49.0 percent of Poland's total laand area and for 32.9 eprcent on the
Polish large private estates. While forests covered 22.0 percent of
the territory of Poland, on the large private estates they covered 42.6
percent. In 1931 the total area of the large private estates in Poland
accounted for 25.9 percent of the total area of Poland, but in relation
to the agricultural land area this share was only 18.0 percent, and
in relation to the arable land area only 17.3 percent.[69] The land use
structure was also strictly correlated with the size of estates: the
alrger the estate, the higher the proportion of forests and wasteland
and the lower that of arable land.

Evolution of the Market

In the first years of the new Poland the market condition was
mainly subject to the effects of the war. Agricultural output was much
lower than it had been before 1914 and the shortage of basic farm
products made the government introduce a system of controls. For
social reasons the peasant holdings were frequently exempted from
obligatory deliveries, so most of the market supply quota came from
large estates. This is why landowners could hardly benefit from the
rapid increase of food prices. When the Polish–Soviet War was over
and the postwar reconstruction allowed for an increase in the food
supply, in 1921 the controls were abolished. In 1923 a certain market
surplus of farm products was recorded for the first time.

The postwar reconstruction of Polish agriculture was accompanied by constantly accelerating inflation. Food producers could pro-
tect their incomes if they shortened the time gap between selling their
products and spending the money. They could not, however, avoid
the "price squeeze" effect: prices of farm products grew more slowly
than those of manufactured goods. When creeping inflation turned
into hyperinflation in 1923, Polish agriculture faced a collapse of the
amrket. The depression lasted until 1926, outliving the 1924 budgetary and monetary reforms of Władysław Grabski. Bad harvests
in 1924 caused a slight increase of prices, but because of a depressed
market, the farmers could not fully benefit from it. The good harvests of 1925 brought agricultural prices down again, although the
price squeeze was reduced. The general trends of prices in Polish
agriculture can be seen in Table 3.3

Table 3.3

Agricultural Prices in Real Terms and the Price Squeeze in Polish Agriculture, 1914–1938

Year	Prices of Goods Bought by Farmers	Prices of Goods Sold by Farmers	Price Squeeze
1914		78.8	
1922	82.4	60.8	-22.4
1923	102.5	57.3	-45.2
1924	110.4	88.8	-21.6
1925	105.9	102.2	-3.7
1926	90.0	84.1	-5.9
1927	96.1	102.9	+6.8
1928	100.0	100.0	0.0
1930	98.5	67.6	-11.2
1931	98.5	59.5	-30.9
1932	90.4	59.5	-30.9
1933	72.6	42.6	-30.0
1934	70.3	37.0	-33.3
1935	66.3	35.8	-30.5
1936	64.6	38.7	-25.9
1937	66.2	49.2	-17.0
1938	65.0	43.0	-22.0

Source: Władysław Grabski, *Kryzys rolniczy.* Memoriał na I Zjazd Ekonomistów Polskich w Poznaniu w maju 1929 r. (*Agricultural Depression.* Report to the First Congress of Polish Economists in Poznan in May 1929) Warsaw, 1929, p. 33; *Koniunktura gospodarcza Polski w liczbach i wykresach w latach 1928-1938 [Market Situation in Poland in Figures and Graphs in the Years 1928-1938)* Warsaw, 1939, p. 22.

In the summer of 1926 the Polish economy entered a time of prosperity. Agricultural prices grew and the price squeeze diminished. In 1927 farm products were sold at prices relatively higher than industrial prices. While the industrial prices of 1928 were 16.8

percent higher than those of 1913, the agricultural prices were 26.8 percent higher.[70] Since land prices were increasing, many landowners voluntarily sold parts of their estates. The demand for land remained relatively high: many smallholders believed in the future and applied for credits to purchase land.

A slight decrease in agricultural prices was recorded at the end of 1928, but the real disaster started in the summer of 1929. For the six subsequent years prices of all farm products decreased becasue of shrinking markets, both at home and abroad.

The market situation for the farmers was further aggravated by "hunger supply," that is, the desire of the farmers to increase their returns by means of increased supply, usually at the cost of their own personal consumption. The fall of agricultural prices in Poland was one of the worst in the world. In relative terms it was only worse in the United States, Bulgaria, and Lithuania. The bottom was reached in 1935, when prices of wheat fell to 31.8 pecent of the 1928 level, rye to 29.6 percent, potatoes to 34.2 percent, pork to 33.9 percent, milk to 45.2 percent, and eggs to 36.1 percent.[71] The agricultural situation was made even worse by the growing price squeeze. Farmers had to sell more and more to be able to buy the same amount of manufactured procucts. Sales of fertilizers, agricultural machinery, and other industrial goods bought in the countryside were next to zero. The mood among Polish farmers at that time was well described by Wiktor Osten-Sacken, who said, "It is not a depression.It is the atmosphere of the sinking Titanic."[72]

In 1936 the recovery of the world market produced a gradual improvement of the market in Poland. Prices of farm products also increased because of the industrial recovery stimulated by the government investment policy of Eugeniusz Kwiatkowski. But in 1938 agricultural prices decreased again. It could have been only a temporary phenomenon, but the fact is that by 1939 agricultural prices in Poland remained far below the predepression level and the price squeeze was still working against agriculture. Out of the twenty-one years of interwar Poland's existence, only a few could be called years of prosperity; most of the time the economy was weak. The decline of large private estates in interwar Poland should also be seen in the light of this situation.

Chapter 4

THE ECONOMY OF LARGE ESTATE OWNERS

Agriculture

In 1921 the large private estates disposed of about 22.9 percent of the arable land area in Poland, in 1931 about 17.3 percent, and in 1938 about 15.0 percent.[1] The decline of this share was the major reason for the decrease in agricultural output on large private estates and their share in the total output in interwar Poland. This phenomenon is illustrated by Table 4.1. The share of large private estates in the

Table 4.1

Crops on Large Private Estates in Poland
1921–1938

Crop	Output in 1,000,000 Quintals			Share in Total Output in Percent		
	1921–24	1929–32	1921–24	1935–38	1929–32	1935–38
Wheat	44.4	5.0	4.0	38.9	26.3	19.8
Rye	12.7	9.3	8.0	26.2	14.9	12.4
Barley	4.3	3.1	2.6	31.2	21.6	18.6
Oats	7.6	4.4	3.5	20.7	17.8	13.4
Potatoes	72.0	48.7	43.2	25.0	15.6	11.8
Sugar beet	23.6	25.3	18.2	59.6[a]	67.8	64.9
Corn	0.2	0.1	0.1	17.4	7.9	9.0
Clover		4.9	5.8		24.9	19.8
Legumes		0.5	0.4		29.3	27.0
Rape		0.2	0.4		48.1	57.0
Flax		0.1	0.4		48.1	57.0
Hops				42.3	41.8	

[a]Crops in 1923 and 1924

Source: Wojciehch Roszkowski, *Gospodarcza rola większej prywatnej własnośći ziemskiej w Polsc 1918–1939 (Economic role of Large Private Estates in Poland, 1918–1939)* Warsaw, 1986, pp. 177–78.

four major grain crops and potatoes decreased more than was average, while fodder land commercial crops decreased less than the average or in a few cases even increased.

Yields per hectare on large estates were generally higher than on small farms. Since there is no way to precisely sort out the statistical evidence on large private and public estates, it is assumed that the data published by the Chief Census Bureau refer to private estates. The error is probably not too big, as the private estate accounted for more than three–fourths of all large estates. Table 4.2 shows multiple average yeilds of large estates and small farms.

Table 4.2

Average Yields on Estates (over 50 Hectares)
and Small Farms (Below 50 Hectares) in Poland
in Quintals per Hectare, 1918–1923, 1927–1938

Crop	1918–1923		1923–1926		1927–1938	
	Estates	Farms	Estates	Farms	Estates	Farms
Wheat	13.4	10.8	13.8	10.6	14.6	11.3
Rye	12.5	10.5	12.7	10.6	13.5	10.9
Barley	15.8	11.8	16.6	13.2	15.5	11.4
Oats	13.4	11.1	13.3	11.4	13.9	11.1
Potatoes	130.0	112.0	127.0	110.3	136.0	113.0
Sugar beets	199.0	161.0	222.5	156.0[a]	220.0	196.0[b]

[a]Yields for 1925–1926; [b]Yields in 1938

Source: *Udział ziemian w rozwoju kultury rolniczej w Polsce [Participation of Landowners in the Development of Polish Agirculture]* Warsaw, 1929, p. 20; Library of the Cathonic Universi—y of Lublin, Jan Stecki Archive, File 593, p. 49; Maria Czerniewska, "Grunty orne, struktura zasiewów i plony w latach 1927–1938" ["Arable Land, Crop Structure, and Yields in the Years 1927–1938"] *Statystyka Rolnicza,* 1937, p. 121, Table XVI; *Statystyka Rolnilza,* 1938, p. 11, Table IV.

It is apparent that large estates not only had higher yields, but the disparity seemed to grow. While in the years 1918–1938 the average yields of wheat on large estates grew by 8.9 percent, on small farms they increased only 4.6 percent. The same increments in rye yields were 8.0 and 3.8 percent and potatoes 4.6 and 0.9 percent. Only in the case of sugar beets did the difference decrease. Also, in other crops large estates had higher yields. For instance in 1938 the rape yields on large estates were 12.0 quintals per hectare and on small farms only 9.0 quintals, the corn yields, respectively, -15.0 and 14.2 quintals, and legume yields 13.5 and 8.5 quintals. Only buckwheat yields on large estates were lower (7.4 quintals per hectare) than those of small farms (7.5 quintals).[2] The greatest differences between large estate and small farm yields were recorded in Łódź, Warsaw, Cracow, Poznań, and Stanisławów provinces, the lowest in the northeastern borderland (Wilno, Nowogródek, and Polesie).

Of course, not all the agricultural output was sold. In terms of the marketable surplus output large estates were even more efficient than small farms. It was estimated that, with 17.0 percent of the arable land and 21.5 percent of the total ouput large estates supplied about 45 percent of the marketable farm products in Poland. While each hectare of arable land on small farms in Poznań Province supplied about 0.8 quintals of wheat, 3.5 quintals of rye, and 0.7 quintals of potatoes, an average estate supplied about 1.5 quintals of wheat, 2.9 quintals of rye, and 3.2 quintals of potatoes.[3] During the Great Depression large estates supplied to the market about 14,000,000 quintals of grain, while small farms about 13,500,000 quintals. Therefore one hectare of large estate land produced about 440 kilograms of the grain market supply, and one (hectare of small farmland about 90 kilograms.[4] According to another estimate, in the years 1930–1932 large estates sold from 46 to 55 percent of all harvested rye, 75 to 81 percent of wheat, 54 to 57 percent of barley, and 22 to 28 percent of oats. In the same period small farms sold about 12 percent of all harvested rye, 20 percent of wheat, and 8 percent of barley and oats.[5]

The higher marketability of the agricultural production of the large estates resulted in their serious troubles during the Great Depression, since they were more sensitive to price changes. Moreover, large estates could not increase their market surplus at the cost of their own consumption. Smallholders reduced their own consumption to be able to sell the "hunger supply." Estate owners would have had to reduce the consumption of their workers, and this was impossible without aggravating social conflicts.

It is, of course, impossible to cite all the best large estates, but at least some of them should be mentioned. In terms of agricultural output, the highest standards were reached by the Poznań and

Pomeranian estates, as well as by some of the estates situated in Warsaw, Łódź, Lublin, and Kielce provinces. The highest grain yields were recorded in Gola (Gostyń County) of Edward Potworowski, Dobrojew (Szamotuły County) of Franciszek Kwilecki, Gryżna (Kościan County) of Józef Lossow, Szelejewo (Koźmin County) of Stanisław Karłowski, and many others too numerous to mention.

Sugar beets were a speciality of the large estates. In 1925 plantings on large private estates supplied 71.7 percent of the sugar beets processed in sugar mills, and in 1933 as much as 81.4 percent.[6] The highest yields were recorded in Kielce Province. The best sugar beet planters were Alfred Cłapowski of Bonikowo (Kścian County), Jan Brochwicz–Donimirski of Łysomice near Toruń, Józef Sczaniecki of Łaszczyn (Rawicz County), Kazimierz Kwilecki of Gosławice, Mieczysław Chłapowski of Kopaszewo (Kościan County), and many others. Large private planters were associated within the Unions of Sugar Beet Planters (Związek Stowarzyszeń Plantatorów Buraka Cukrowego) in Warsaw, and Poznań. During the Great Depression the unions supported sugar beet prices through a system of supply quotas. Some of the planters also had shares in sugar mills, and since the sugar industry was a monopoly they gained special benefits from the high retail price of sugar.

The role of large private estates in grain crop production decreased overall, while it grew in fodder and industrial crop raising. In 1927 several landowners, such as Adam Czartoryski of Gołuchow, Władysław Kościelski of Miłosław, Stanisław Łącki of Posadowo, and Kazimierz Lubomirski of Horodenka, founded the Semina Company for the cultivation of pastures and grassland. The future Polish ambassador to London, Edward Raczyński, developed a farm for growing the Rogalin variety of lupin. The most outstanding rape planters included Wojciech Wyganowski of Zbiersk (Kalisz County) and Roman Janta–Połczyński of Łabiszyn (Wągrowiec County). In 1933 the Union of Oil Plant Producers (Związek Producentów Roślin Oleistych) was established, and landowners played a leading role in it. The leading hop growers were Aleksander Ledóchowski of Smordwa (Dubno County in Volhynia) and Jan Kleniewski of Kluczkowce (Puławy County).[7]

In discussing the role of large landowners in agricultural production it is necessary to mention the influence of private estates on the development of agricultural technology and cultivation. Before World War I and even in the interwar period, most of the professionals in Polish agriculture were landowners. They also played an important role in organization and operation of "farmers' circles" (kółka rolnicze) in which they shared htheir expertise with smallholders. Of course, not all the landowners engaged in this social activity, but the most outstanding organizers of the farmers' circles included Franciszek Bętkowski, Leon Janta–Połczyński, and Adam Schedlin–Czarliński, and Gustaw Raszewski (Greater Poland), and so on. About 50 percent in the Polish landowners belonged to agricultural associations in interwar Poland.[8]

Some of the large private estates were famous for their seed production. Among several seed–producing companies run by landowners the following should be mentioned: The Sandomierz–Great Polish Seed–Production Company (Sandomiersko–Wielkopolska Hodowla Nasion) headed by Alfred Chłapowski and Stanisław Karłowski, the Poznań Siew Company, the Granum Company, the Seed–Producing Company (S. A. Hodowli Roślin) of the brothers Bogusław, Edward, and Józef Kleszczyński, and others. In Dańków (Groójec County) Aleksander Janasz developed a new variety of wheat ("graniatka Dańkowska").

Horticulture was generally underdeveloped in interwar Poland, but some of the orchards grown by large landowners matched European standards. These included Kluczkowce and Szczekarków of Witold and Przemsław Kleniewski near Lublin, Zassów near Mielec of Tadeusz Łubieński, Broniszów near Cracow of Jan Śląski, and Nowa Wieś near Grójec of Tadeusz Daszewski. Large vineyards were developed by Cyryl Czarkowski–Golejewski of Wysuczka (Borszczów County), and Zofia Łoś of Torskie (Zaleszczyki County) in Tarnopol Province. Podhorce of Julian Brunicki and Pudliszki of Stanisław Fenrych were famous for vegetable crops.

In terms of animal breeding interwar Poland was an average European country. The available statistical evidence is reliable in relation to the overall number of livestock, but the distribution of this livestock between large estates and small farms is only approximate in view of the lack of data for 1921. Furthermore, the Chief Census Bureau included the cattle and pigs of farm workers among those belonging to small farmers, although these animals grazed on estate pastures. Therefore the number of livestock in large private estates given in Table 4.3 is only an approximate estimate. It is, nevertheless, clear that after the reestablishment of livestock breeding in the 1920s the relative share of large private estates in Polish livestock production gradually decreased in the 1930s.

Table 4.3

Number of Livestock on Large Private Estates in Poland in the Years 1921–1938

Year	Cattle 1,000 Head	Percent	Pigs 1,000 Head	Percent	Horses 1,000 Head	Percent	Sheep 1,000 Head	Percent
1921	743	9.1	832	15.3	262	7.9	276	12.0
1930	1,009	10.7	859	14.2	335	8.1	313	12.0
1931	997	10.0	1,029	14.1	335	8.1	313	12.0
1932	945	10.0	850	14.5	323	8.2	303	12.2
1933	911	10.1	834	14.5	314	8.3	291	11.4
1934	909	9.8	940	15.3	309	8.2	288	11.3
1935	901	9.2	754	11.2	303	8.1	300	10.7
1936	913	8.9	762	10.8	300	7.8	317	10.5
1937	922	8.7	812	10.6	301	7.7	330	10.3
1938	886	8.4	719	9.6	297	7.6	336	9.8

Source: Wojciech Roszkowski, *Gospodarcza rola większej prywatnej własncśći w Polsce 1918-1939 [Economic Role of Large Private Estates in Poland, 1918-1939]* Warsaw, 1986, p. 193.

According to the 1921 census data it may be assumed that the intensity of animal breeding was decreasing with the increase of the area of estates. The only exception was with sheep and goats, which were kept mainly on estates between 500 and 1,000 hectares. The highest concentration of animals per one hectare of agricultural land of estates was recorded in the Cracow, Silesian, and Tarnopol provinces (cattle), Poznań, Pomeranian, and Cracow provinces (pigs), Polsie and Kielce provinces (horses), and Pomeranian, Poznań and Łódź provinces (sheep).[9] It must be remembered, however, that large estate animal breeding had a significant role only in provinces where landowners disposed of a considerable part of the agricultural land, that is in Great Poland, Pomerania, and Warsaw provinces.

The intensity of animal husbandry in large private estates was generally lower than on small farms. For instance, during the Great Depression the average number of cattle per 100 hectares of agricultural land of large estates oscillated between 9.8 in central Poland

and 13.7 in the southern provinces, while that on small farms was 35.1 in central Poland and 55.6 in the southern provinces.[10] On the other hand the livestock of the large private estates was usually of a better quality. As a result of careful breeding, the average weight of large estate cattle was 525 kilograms, while the same average in small farms was about 425 kilograms. The average annual milk yield in Poland in the 1930s was 2,600 liters for large estate cattle, while the cattle bred by small farms rarely produced in excess of 2,000 liters.[11]

Unfortunately, the higher quality of large estate animals did not pay, as higher costs could not bring higher returns, especially during the Great Depression. One of the agricultural experts commented that "the landowners showed less intuition than peasants, who, breeding mostly 'tails,' produced almost free fertilizers. The landowners, on the other hand, were more ambitious but bred contested bills of exchange."[12] Therefore it was no wonder that the large estate animal husbandry declined in the 1930s.

Despite that, large estate animal breeding was very important in terms of the zootechnological prospects of the Polish agriculture. Most of the pedigree barns belonged to large landowners. The Union of Stockbreeders [Zweięzek Hodowców Bydła] of the Central Agricultural Association and the Association of Milk Producers [Zrzeszenie Producentów Mleka] were also dominated by landowners, such as Jerzy Ciechomski of Rutkowice (Włocławek County) and Jan Eustachy Kowerski of Miastków (Garwolin County). The record milk yield of single cow—9,827 liters per annum— belonged to the Radzików dairy of Stanisław Janasz near Warsaw. The best large estate dairies included Dłużewo (Mińsk Mazowiecki County) of Stanisław Dłużewski, Kawć eczyn (Kalisz County) of Aleksander Olędzki, Brudzew (Koło County) of Ignacy Kożuchowski, Łęki (Kutno County) of Jan Czarnowski, and others.[13]

The intensity of pig breeding in small farms was also higher than on large estates. In 1931 large estates had 22.2 pigs pen 100 hectares of agricultural and and small farms had 30.0. At the same time the average weight of a large estate pig was about 150 kilograms, while on small farms it was about 135 kilograms.[14] Most of the pedigree pig farms belonged to landowners. During the National Exhibition of 1929 special awards were given to the farms in Snopków of Kazimierz Piaszczyński and Kluczkowce of Przemsław Klieniewski (both in the Lublin Privince), and Kwitcz (Greater Poland) of Dobiesław Kwilecki, Zbiersk (Łódź Province) of Wojciech Wyganowski, Wielkie Soleczniki

(Wilno Province) of Karol Wagner, and Ołyka (Volhynia) of Janusz Radziwiłł.[15]

Horse breeding was the favorite animal husbandry on large estates: it was, in fact, the continuation of a long-time noble tradition. As one of the leading Greater Polish horse breeders, Franciszek Kwilecki of Dobrojewo, said, "Utile cum dulce—horses are our best companions at work in the fields and, when [we are] in need, they are our defenders."[16] Polish horse breeding suffered immense losses during World War I and the Polish–Soviet War. Later, horse breeding developed unexpectedly quickly, which was a result of economic needs, but also of the landowners passion. Horses were the predominant tractor power in Polish interwar agriculture, since motor vehicles were not competitive at all. Also the Polish army purchased a large number of the "remote" horses, which stimulated careful breeding.

The oldest Polish stud farms included Knyszyn of King Zygmunt I August. In the nineteenth century special renown was won by the Sławuta stud farm of the Sanguszkos and the Antoniny stud farms of the Polockis. Both of them were situated in the Ukraine and were destroyed during the Bolshevik revolution. Some of the Arab horses from these farms were transferred to Gumniska of Roman Sanguszko and Beheń of Roman and Józef Potocki. Polish interwar horse breeding was clearly divided between manorial and peasant stud farms. Most of the blood-line and half-bred horses in Poland were on manorial farms. In 1928 large estate owners possessed 15,786 blood-lines including 2,700 thoroughbred horses, while peasant stud farms had only 5,957 half-bred horses and no thoroughbreds.[17]

Manorial horse breeding in interwar Poland could be divided into three groups: thoroughbred, half-bred, and Western draft horses. The highest standards of breeding were reached in Greater Poland, Upper Silesia, and Łódź, Kielce, Warsaw, and Lublin provinces, as well as in southern Volhynia. Altogether, in 1930 there were about 1,000 thoroughbred English horses and about 100 thoroughbred Arabs. The Polish Arab stud farms belonged to the best in Europe, as their owners put the stress on quality and not quantity. This success was largely due to the activities of the Society for Arab Horse Breeding (Towarzystwo Hodowli Konia Arabskiego) founded in 1926.[18] The predominance of manorial farms in terms of quality may be illustrated by the fact that in 1936/37 the Polish army purchased 73 percent of its horses from the large private estates. At the same time the share of manorial stud farms in the total number of horses in Poland was a mere 10 percent.[19] The best stud farms in interwar Poland included, among others, Szelejewo of Stanisław Karłowskim Posadowo of Stanisláw Łącki. Gałowo of Michał Mycielski, Wituchowo of Zofia Mycielska (all in Poznań Province), Poryck of Stanisław Czacki (Volhynia), and Piotrowice of Witold łoś (Lublin Province). Michał Komorowski of Siedliska and Albert Wieloplski of Poraźna were the founders of the Society for Horse Racing (Towarzystwo Wyscigów Konnych) in Służew near Warsaw in 1925.[20] In terms of sheep breeding Poland was rather underdeveloped. The home output of wool covered only about half of the army's demand, while wool imports cost from 40,000,000 to 50,000,000 zloty per annum. Sheep breeding on large estates was less intensive than on peasant farms, but the average yield of wool per one sheep was generally higher on large estates. The leading sheep breeders included Janusz Radziwiłł of Ołyka, who bred Merino sheep, Stanisław Karłowski of Szelejewo (Merino–Precoce sheep), Stanisław Grabiński of Walewice, Franciszek Kuczyński of Gawartowa Wola, and Antoni Birar of Maniewicze.[21]

Other lines of animal production—goat and poultry breeding, as well as agiculture—were developed mainly on small farms. The share of large estates in fish farming is hard to estimate, but it was very high. In Wilno Province, where fish ponds were relatively well developed, the share of large estate ponds in the total area of fish ponds decreased from 98 percent in 1928 to 89 percent in 1938.[22] The best fish–farming estates included Zator near Oświęcim, of Adam Potocki, Osiek (Cracow Province) of Andrzej and Marian Rudziński, Żeromin (Łódź Province) of Aleksander Mazarski, and Ruda (Warsaw Province) of Marian Starzeński. Large ponds were situated in the Komarno latifundium of Antoni Lanckoroński and in the Brzeżany estate of Jakub Potocki in eastern Galicia. Karol Raczyński had a unique trout farm on Złoty Potok near Częstochowa. Extensive fish farming was developed in the Dawidgródek entail of Karol Radziwiłł in Polesie.[23] Some economic importance was also attached to hunting, but it was more a part of the landowners way of life, so it will be discussed in Chapter 6.

There are various estimates of the total agricultural output in interwar Poland and their verification is extremely difficult. Therefore any estimate of the share of large private estates may only be approximate. Such an estimate may be found in private estates in

the agricultural output in Poland was declining. At the same time
it must be remembered that in terms of market supply of food, the
large private estates played a much bigger role.

Table 4.4

**Total Agricultural Output and the Share
of Large Private Estates in Poland
1924–1938 (Current Prices)**

	1934	1929	1938
Plant production in fields and meadows in millions of zloty	1,327.5	1,416.3	735.9
Share of large private estates in percent	29.8	24.0	18.3
Horticultural product in in millions of zloty	29.1	60.0	40.0
Share of large private estates in percent	13.0		
Animal production in millions of zloty	460.8	810.2	347.2
Share of large private estates in percent	12.4	13.2	10.3
Total agricultural output in millions of zloty	1,817.4	2,286.5	1,123.1
Share of large estates in percent	25.1	19.9	15.6

Source: Calculated according to Wacław Ponikowski, "Próba obliczenia wartości wytwórczości roślinnej i zwierzęcej w Polsca" ["An Attempt to Calculate the Value of the Plant and Animal Production
in Poland"] *Rolnik Ekonomista*, 1926, no. 7, pp. 509–518; Wacław
Ponikowski, Próba obliczenia wartości produkcji rolniczej w Polsce w
roku gospondarczym 1927/28" ["An Attempt to Calculate the Value
of Agricultural Output in Poland in 1927/28"] *Rolnik Ekonomista*,
1929, no. 13/14, pp. 19–24.

Forestry

Poland was, excluding the Soviet Union, the fifth largest country
of interwar Europe in absolute forest area. In the early 1920s forests
covered about 23 percent of Polish territory, but about one–fifth of

the Polish forest area was wasteland.[24] There were many, various estimates of the forest area in interwar Poland and the share of the three basic categories of owners: large landowners, smallholders, and the state. Table 4.5 gives an approximate estimate.

Table 4.5
Evolution of the Forest Area in Poland
in Hectares, 1921–1938

Year	8,943,800	4,417,100	2,835,400	1,619,300
1926	8,691,000	4,416,400	2,910,400	1,364,200
1931	8,321,800	4,176,900	3,114,800	1,030,100
1936	8,191,600	4,171,200	3,123,800	996,600
1938	8,179,600	4,169,300	3,136,600	873,600

Source: Wojciech Roszkowski, *Gospodarcza rola większej prywatnej własności Ziemskiej w Polsce 1918–1939 [Economic Role of Large Private Estates in Poland, 1918–1939]* Warsaw, 1986, p. 210.

Data presented in Table 4.5 show a clear trend: the total area of forest in Poland decreased particularly rapidly in the 1920s, the forest area in the hands of large private owners declining at a slightly lower rate. The public forest area generally increased, while the forest area in the hands of small owners dramatically decreased. In the years 1921–1929 the total forest area in Poland fell by about 503,000 hectares (5.6 percent), while the large private forest area decreased by 185,900 hectares (4.2 percent). In the years 1931–1938 the total forest area in Poland fell by only 142,200 hectares (1.7 percent) and the large private forest area by 7,600 hectares (0.2 percent).[25]

The largest private forest estates were situated in the southern and eastern provinces, as well as in Upper Silesia. The Zamość entail of Maurycy Zamoyski had 128,000 hectares of forests, and after the liquidation of easements 70,500 hectares. Its largest forest inspectorates, such as Kocudza (8,950 hectares), Janów (8,725 hectares), and Terespol (7,870 hectares), were of the size of large individual forest latifundia.[26] Thousands of hectares of forests accounted for the Dawidgródek and Nieśwież entails fo the Radziwiłłs, the Rzepichów estates of Jarosław Potocki, Worobin and Dąbrowica of Witold Broel–Plater, and the Bereźne forests of Marek Małyński. In southern Poland the largest forest latifundia included the Skole estate of Hermann Groedel, Żywiec of Archduke Karol Stefan Habsburg, Pieniaki of Tadeusz Cieński, and Nawojowa of Adam Stadnicki.[27]

The economic situation of Polish interwar forestry was largely subject to special legislation. On 16 January 1919 special forest control offices were created, and on 10 July 1919 the Sejm passed a resolution on nationalization of all forests.[28] This resolution was not carried out but it created an atmosphere of uncertainty among large private owners. The budget deficits made the Sejm pass a law of 29 January 1919 concerning a special forest levy, but the levy was not put into practice before 6 July 1923, when another forest levy law was passed.[29] This law made the large owners cut a five–year felling quota within three years. Extensive felling was also made inevitable by the law of 11 August 1923, which concerned an extraordinary property tax to be collected by the Grabski government as part of the budgetary and monetary reform of 1924–1925.[30] Of course, under the existing fiscal and monetary conditions, the collection of both levies was a matter of national emergency, but it must be stressed that Grabski's budgetary reform was made possible by the cost of extensive felling.

Excessive exploitation of forest resources might have decreased after 1926, when the budget was stabilized. Nevertheless, in the years of prosperity extensive felling continued, this time because of the increase in timber prices. According to a presidential decree of 24 June 1927 concerning forest management, the control of large private forests was made more rigorous. Owners of forests of below ten hectares were practically free from any control, but large forest owners were obliged to reforest cut–down areas and to introduce rational management of their forests according to plans approved by the authorities. Special forest inspectors had the right to control large private forest management and to take some actions at the cost of the owners. Sanctions were foreseen for forest owners who tolerated mismanagement.[31]

As a result of these policies the management of large private forests was rationaized. While in 1925 management plans covered 1,776 forest estates covering 2,351,700 hectares, in 1934 this number had grown to 9,870 estates with a combined area of 3,445,000 hectares.[32] Nevertheless, because of the increasing momentum of this management, the large private forest economy was still strongly criticized. In 1929 the Peasant party (Stronnictwo Chłopskie) demanded nationalization of all large private forests, disregarding the fact that small owners were ruining their forests at a much greater rate. Also the supreme director of the state forests (lasy państwowe), Adam Loret, spoke in favor of nationalization of large private forests.[33] However, government policy went in another direction: the presidential decree of 21 October 1932 relaxed the state control of private forest management.[34]

Rational forest exploitation should be based on the balance of annual natural amounts of timber and its felling. In the 1920s the annual felling was much higher than the timber volume. In the public forests the growth of the timber was estimated at about 8,000,000 cubic meters per annum, while the amount felled was 8,500,000 cubic meters in 1923, 8,700,000 in 1924, and 12,100,000 cubic meters in 1925. In large private forests the natural growth was estimated at about 11,500,000 cubic meters per annum and the actual felling was 22,600,000 cubic meters in 1923, 16,000,000 in 1924, and 25,500,000 cubic meters in 1925.[35] Excessive felling diminished at the end of the 1920s and vanished in the 1930s.

As already mentioned, the excessive felling of the 1920s was largely due to the need to finance reconstruction of the estates, the budgetary and monetary reform of 1924–1925, and to the increase in timber prices in the late 1920s. According to some estimates, the property tax and the forest levy collected during the Grabski reform involved felling of about at least 3,500,000 cubic meters of timber per annum. In the years 1926–1928 the excessive felling was also encouraged by the excellent market situation. While in mid-1926 one cubic meter of pine logs cost about twenty zloty, in February 1928 its price grew to about seventy zloty.[36] Therefore many large forest owners made use of the situation to improve their financial standing; and some of them acted against the interests of the Polish state. For instance, in the years 1921–1932 Johann von Pless–Pszczyński felled 310,800 cubic meters of timber above the natural use quota and exported the timber to Germany without paying taxes. He also overburdened his forests with loans.[37] Excessive felling was typical for Alfred Potocki's management of Łańcy. Felling in the Sołotwin estates (Nadwórna County in eastern Galicia), which belonged to Johann Liebig and Company, could be called plundering just like the devastation of the Naliboki Forest in Nowogródek Province by the administration of Vladimir Falz–Fein.[38]

The average natural growth of timber volume in Poland in 1923 was estimated at 2.39 cubic meters per hectare per annum. In public forests this ratio was 2.84 cubic meters, in large private forests 2.44, and in forests belonging to small owners it was 1.62. Data referring to private forests could have been underestimated because they were based on tax statements. The forest economy was most efficient in the southern provinces, where large private forests showed an annual natural growth of timber volume of 3.62 cubic meters per hectare.[39] The overall output of Polish interwar forestry is subject to various estimates. The highest estimate—541,000,000 cubic meters, including about 200,000,000 cubic meters of excessive felling in large private forests—seems exaggerated.[40] It is more likely that in the years 1918–1939 about 482,000,000 cubic meters of timber were felled in Poland, including about 281,000,000 cubic meters in large private forests. The excessive felling in large private forests did not exceed 80–100,000,000 cubic meters.[41] The average share of large private forests of timber production was about 58 percent. In 1924 this share was about 60 percent, in 1929 about 70 percent, and in the late 1930s it did not exceed 45 percent.[42]

In the 1930s large forest owners abolished excessive felling and improved the quality of the produced timber. Exploitation of forests became the least profitable line of production. In 1932 the average price of timber was about 40.0 percent of the 1928 level, the average agricultural price 43.5 percent, and the average industrial price was 65.5 percent of the 1928 level. Under these conditions all incentives to produce timber disappeared. In fact it is hard to understand why large forest owners generally improved the quality of produced timber, since the prices for processed timber decreased even more than those for the firewood.[43]

Karol Kruzenstern of Niemirów (Rawa Ruska County in Lwow Province) once made the appeal: "Forest owners unite."[44] In fact, they reacted by uniting regional unions that had existed in Galicia and in the former Kingdom of Poland into the Association of Unions of Forest Owners (Zrzeszenie Związków Właścicieli Lasów). The association was presided over by Witold Babiński and later by Kazimierz Fudakowski. Leading members of the organization also included Alfred Jankowski, Antoni Jundziłł, Stanisław Komorowski, and Jan Krystyn Ostrowski.[45]

Industry, Banking, and Trade

The nonagricultural activity of large landowners can be divided into two categories. First, there were numerous processing plants on large estates, which may be called manorial industries. Second, many landowners had shares in various urban industrial, banking, trade, and insurance companies. Moreover, while talking about the industrial activities of large landowners, one must remember that some of them belonged to the industrial and financial elite whose basic business activities were outside agriculture.

The basic manorial industries included food processing. The large landowners' share in the interwar Polish food–processing industry was probably quite high, since this industry was, in contrast to other industries, dominated by Polish capital. While the share of foreign capital in the Polish oil industry in 1936 was estimated at about 88 percent, in mining and metallurgy at 74 percent, and in the textile industry at 28 percent, in the food–processing industry this share was a mere 8 percent.[46] As the industry closest to agriculture, food processing was historically the first sphere of industrial activity by Polish landowners.[47]

According to the 1921 census the large landowners in Poland had 1,545 distilleries, 1,619 mills, 697 brickyards, 545 sawmills, 357 creameries, 195 potato–processing plants, 111 butter–making facilities, 102 breweries, 49 sugar refineries and other small factories, some of them being inactive as a result of war.[48] In terms of the value of output the most important part of the manorial food industry was sugar refining, distilling, brewing, and potato processing. Apart from that large estates ran a number of sawmills, brickyards, and turpentine distilleries.

Polish sugar refining was largely affected by World War I damage. The area under sugar beet cultivation had decreased by 53 percent over the years 1913–1919, while the output of 1920/21 was only 26 percent of the 1913/14 level. In the former Kingdom of Poland and in the eastern borderlands about 60 percent of the sugar refineries lay in ruins. In Lesser Poland the two largest plants in Chodorów and Przeworsk were completely destroyed. After the recovery of the 1920s, the Great Depression brought sugar output in Poland down again, so that Polish sugar production of 1938 was lower than that of 1913.[49] The landowners' share in Polish sugar refining was significant. In 1921, forty–nine out of sixty–four active plants belonged to large landowners, twenty–two of them being situated in Greater Poland. Manors supplied from 66 percent of sugar beet production to 75 percent during the early 1930s and 60 percent in 1938.[50]

Sugar output was under the strict control of a cartel whose sales went through the Bank Cukrownictwa (Sugar–Refining Bank) in Poznań. While maintaining high prices for sugar in the home market and supporting the dumping of export sugar, the bank tolerated the decrease in prices of sugar beets. Growers who had no access to the supply quota of the cartel faced losses, but those who belonged to the quota system could derive large profits from the monopoly. Bank Cukrownictwa had as chairman Józef Żychliński of Gorazdowo, and the major members of the board included Stanisław Karłowski of Szelejewo, Stanisław Turno of Objezierze (Oborniki County), Mieczysław Chłapowski of Kopaszewo, Jan Donimirski of Łysomice (Toruń County), and Ernst Fischer von Mollard of Góra (Jarocin County). Shareholders of the largest Polish sugar refinery in Chłmża included Adam Czarliński of Zakrzewko near Toruń and Józef Sczaniecki of Łaszczyn (Rawicz County), Stanisław Łącki of Posadowo, Wilhelm von Hardt of Wzsowo (Nowy Tomyśl County), and Zygmunt Kuratowski–Mielżynski were among the largest shareholders of the Opalenciza refinery. Other landowners who had shares in the sugar–refining industry included Józef Lossow of Gryżyna (Kościan County), Alfred Potocki of Łańcut, Janusz Radziwiłł of Ołyka, Leopold Kronenberg of Wieniec (Włocławek County), Stanisław Mycielski of Borynicz (Bóbrka County), Andrzej Lubomirski of Przeworsk, and Antoni Lanckoroński of Jagielnica.[51]

The Polish distilling industry was also seriously affected by World War I damage. The number of operational plants decreased from 2,459 in 1913 to 1,131 in 1921, and output fell from 2,800,000 hectoliters (740,000 U. S. gallons) of pure alcohol in 1913 to 593,000 hectoliters (156,900 U. S. gallons) in 1921.[52] In 1921 there were 1,545 manorial distilleries, most of them inactive. In 1927 it was estimated that among 1,282 Polish distilleries 1,160 belonged to large estate owners. In Greater Poland, where all farm distilleries were situated on large estates, 62 percent of them belonged to owners of estates of above 500 hectares. It may be estimated that about 95 percent of all farm distilelries in Poland belonged to large landowners and that about 85 to 90 percent of the whole alcohol output in Poland came from such distilleries.[53]

Major manorial distilleries included, among others, those situated in Grzymiszew of Ludomił Pułaski (Konin County), Krucz–Goraj of Wilhelm Hochbert (Czarnków County), Siedliska of Michał Komorowski (Kielce County). Stanisław Czarnecki of Gogolewo (Gostyń County), Józef Lossow, Ignacy Mielżynski of Iwno (Środa County), and others were among the shareholders of the Poznań company, Akwawit.

The brewing industry was also largely destroyed during World

War I. While in 1913 about 500 breweries in Polish territories produced about 7,000,000 hectoliters (1,852,000 U. S. gallons) of beer, in 1924 the number of plants decreased to 221 and their output to 1,632,000 hectoliters (432,000 U. S. gallons). The pre–1913 level of production was not reached again until 1939. In 1921 the number of manorial breweries was estimated at 102, that is, 42 percent; but since they were usually smaller than average, their beer production may be estimated at about 25 to 30 percent of the total output in Poland in 1921.[54]

The two largest breweries in interwar Poland belonged to large landowners. The Princely Brewery of Tychy was the property of Johann von Pless–Pszczyński, and and Okocim Brewery belonged to Antoni and Jan Goetz–Okocimski. The Okocimski fortune in face stemmed from the brewery; the family estates at Okocim and Skowieszyn, covering about 10,500 hectares, were only bought later.[55] Much smaller were the breweries in Medenice of Henryk Kolischer, Busk of Kazimier Badeni (both in Lwow Province), and Artur Potocki in Buczacz (Tarnopol Province).

Manorial potato processing comprised starch and flake production, potato flour, dextrin, and syrup. All these operations were frequently combined in the same plant. The majority of about eighty potato–processing plants were situated on large estates, and their share in the total output of such production was probably around 80 to 90 percent, but because of World War I damage and lack of markets 1938 output was about 70 percent of the 1913 level.[56] Stanisław Janicki owned a big starchworks in Ułęż (Garwolin County), while flake works were, among others, in Ląd (Konin County), belonging to Meyer, Samuel, and Abram Nelken, and Oleśnica (Chodzież County, owned by Rochus Luettwitz).

Manorial flour milling was not so widespread. Of about 6,000 mills in Poland in 1921 only about 1,620 were situated on large estates. Nevertheless, many large landowners had significant shares in industrial flour mills. For instance, Józef Żyehliński, Janusz Machnicki, and Zbigniew Żółtowski were major shareholders of the Cerealia mills in Główna, Kazimierz Esden–Tempski and Janusz Machnicki had shares in the Grudziędz mills company, and Kazimierz Żychliński owned part of the Pleszew mills.[57] It seems that the large landowners's share in Polish flour milling did not exceed about 30 percent.

Of 4,000 creameries in Poland in 1921 about 350 belonged to large estate owners, who also had significant shares in local dairy cooperatives and sometimes were the founders of such cooperatives. This was, for example, the case of Jan Rudowski of Półwiesk (Rypin County), who initiated the Rypin Dairy Cooperative Union. Large estates had also 111 butter and 32 cheese–making plants, most of them in Lwow and Poznań provinces.[58] Other lines of food processing on large private estates included yeast, oil, and chicory production, meat and vegetable processing, as well as wine making. For instance, Stanisław Fenrych managed plots of asparagus, peas, and raspberries, which were processed in his Pudliszki factory in Greater Poland, Cyryl Czarkowski–Golejewski had a winery on his Wysuczka entail in Tarnopol Province, while Józef Lossow and Stefan Sczaniecki had shares in the Goplana chocolate factory in Poznań.

Apart from food processing the most important manorial industries included timber processing. Out of the 1,400 sawmills in Poland in the 1920s, 545 belonged to large estate owners. For instance, large sawmills functioned in Łańcut of Alfred Potocki, the Brzeżany forests of Jakób Potocki, Smogulec of Bogdan Hutten–Czapski, Żołudek of Ludwik Czetwrtyński, Horodec of Kamil Pourbaix, and on many other large estates. In the Zamość entail there were five big sawmills: in Zwierzyniec, Korytkowo, Pańska Dolina, Strzelce, and Długi Kąt.[59] Sawmills on the large estates were, however, usually too small to process the bulk of timber cut in the large private forests, especially in the eastern provinces in the 1920s. In most cases the owners sold their timber standing or semiprocessed to trading companies in which Jewish capital played a large role. For instance, the brothers Nachum, Hermann, Maurycy, and Horacy Heller, who had greatly profited in exploiting the Łuniniec forests of Fyodor Ogarkov, founded the Agahell and the Olza companies to process the timber into veneer and plywood. The Heller brothers gradually took over the huge forest complex between Czuczewicze and Lenin in Łuninec County in Polesia and became the Polish timber–processing tycoons.[60]

Many large estates had their own brickyards. In 1921, of about 1,000 Polish brickyards about 700 belonged to large estate owners. A large brickyard was, for example, situated in the Chorostków entail of Stanisław Siemieński–Lewicki in Tarnopol Province and on Busk of Kazimierz Badeni. Big ceramic works on Białaczów (Opoczno County) belonged to Zygmunt Broel–Plater and his partners, Jan Krystyn Ostrowski and Stanisław Rostworowski. Hieronim Radziwiłł of Balice, Jan Żółtowski of Czacz, Alfred Potocki of Łańcut, and Zygmunt Kurnatowski–Mielżynski of Gościeszyn and considerable shares in other clay- and sand-processing plants.

Given the present state of our knowledge, the overall range of manorial industry can hardly be calculated. In 1938 the various food-processing works on large estates employed about 22,000 workers, that is, about 26 percent of all workers in this sector of Polish industry.[61] At the beginning of interwar Poland this share could have been a little higher. It may be assumed that the share of large landowners in the Polish food-processing production was also close to one-fourth.

The landowners had also a significant share in the food trade. For instance, Leon Pluciński, Juliusz Trzciński, and Leon Żółtowski dominated the Centrala Rolnikow company of Poznań. Kazimierz Dziewanowski, Roman Stroynowksi, Jan Czarnowski, Józef Lossow, and Witold Broel-Plater held many shares in the Spirytus company for the export of alcohol. Włodzimierz Cieński, Jan Gerstman, and Henryk Kolischer owned part of the Lwow distilling trade center, Tytus Wilski was in the Rawa agricultural syndicate, while Stanisław Niegolewski and Gustaw Raszewski were in Gleba agricultural machinery company of Poznań. These trade organizations monopolized the supply of farm products and tried to fix their prices, but the effects were of such policies were usually limited, especially during the Great Depression.

Special mention must be made of the landowners' banks. Short-term credits for land distribution were the main objective of the Bank Ziemiański in Warsaw, founded in 1916, whose capital was raised to 12,500,000 zloty in 1929. Bank Ziemiański's chairman was Jan Czarnowski, and the major participants included Kazimierz Dziewanowski, Eustachy Korwin-Szymanowski, and Adam Luniewski. The Wileński Bank Ziemski S. A. had a similar range of activities, but its capital was only 6,300,000 zloty; the bank suffered greatly during the Great Depression, which was the result of the financial weakness of the landowners of the eastern borderland. Long-term land credits were granted by Towarzystwa Kredytu Ziemskiego (Societies for Land Credits, or TKZ) in Warsaw, Lwow, and Poznań. The Warsaw TKZ was for many years headed by Władysław Glinka of Susk, (Ostrołęka County), and its major participants included Hipolit Wąswicz, Stanisław Godlewski, and Zygmunt Leszczyński. The major figure in the Poznań TKZ was Józef Żychliński. Many large landowners, such as Stanisław Lubomirski, Józef Żychliński, Stanisław Karłowski, Stanisław Turno, Stanisław Mycielski, and Adam Tarnowski, also had a great number of shares in other commercial banks.[62]

Precise estimation of the share of large landowners in Polish interwar banking is very difficult. On the grounds of very complex but only approximate calculations, it may be assumed that in relation to the balance sheet total of all Polish private banks the sums representing the large landowners were about 40 percent and in relation to the balance sheet total of all Polish banks their share probably did not exceed about 15 percent.[63]

It is even more difficult to estimate the overall value of the shares of large landowners in Polish industry, banking, and trade. Many owners of large landed and forest estates belonged to the business oligarchy of interwar Poland, disposing of significant shares in urban industry, banks, trade, and insurance organizations. Studies in the composition of this oligarchy are at their beginning stage: there is a general lack of sources and of estimation of the influence by individuals and business groups. So far, some attempts have been made to list the major shareholders in the Polish economy, but these attempts are still far from perfect.[64]

The ranking of landowners, who had significant shares in Polish industry, banking, and trade, is begun with Józef Żychliński, chairman of the Bank Cukrownictwa in Poznań, and shareholder in many other banks and industries. He was descended from the Polish landed gentry and still possessed the Gorazdowo estate in the Września County (about 2,200 hectares). Stanisław Lubomirski, with connections to Italian business circles, was a large shareholder of the Bank Handlowy S. A. in Warsaw, the Banque Franco–Polonaise, the Vereinigte Laura–und Koenigshuette, and other industrial and insurance companies, Lubomirski retained a part of his family's fortune, the Pławno estate in Radomsko County (1,770 hectares), but was mainly a businessman and not a landowner. The same may be said about number three of the list, Antoni Wieniawski, an industrialist and banker, who had the Chlewnia estate in Błonie County near Warsaw (335 hectares).

The major German tycoons—Johann von Pless-Pszczyński, Kraft Henckel von Donnersmarck, Johann Hohenlohe–Oehringen, and Gottfried Hohenlohe–Schillingfuerst—had an even large investment, not only in Upper Silesian, but also in German industry, so their position is hard to compare with that of Polish businessmen. The other top Polish businessmen and landowners would include Alfred Potocki of Łańcut (participant in Vereinigte Laura—und Koenigschuette, the Galician oil industry, sugar refining, and banking), Janusz Radziwiłł of Ołyka (shareholder in many banks, sugar refineries, and chemical factories), Adam Tarnowski, Stanisław Karłowski (banker and shareholder in the Galician oil industry and Great Polish sugar refineries), Antoni Lanckoroński of Jagielnica, Andrzej Lubomirski of Przeworks, Leopold Kronenberg, Eustachy Korwin–Szymanowski, Józef Lossow, and Stanisław Mycielski.[65]

Generally speaking, the overall landowners' share in Polish interwar industry, banking, and trade can be estimated—only very approximately. A more precise estimate would require an extensive inquiry among varied, scattered, and incomplete sources. At present, let it suffice to say that in food processing this share was about 25 percent, in industry and trade about 10 percent, in transportation and insurance about 10 percent, and in banking about 15 percent, so the overall share of landowners in nonagricultural activities was probably a little more than 10 percent.

The Financial Balance Sheet

The large private estates disposed of a considerable part of the national property. The overall value of the landowners' property in agriculture may be estimated at about 12,573,000 zloty in 1926 and about 10,321,000,000 zloty in 1938. The land accounted for about 60 percent of this value, forests for about 17 percent, buildings for about 12 percent, livestock about 5 percent, and other stock about 6 percent.[66] In relative terms the large private estates were less saturated with capital than small farms. This referred not only, as we have already seen, to the livestock, but also to the farm buildings and the other stock. For instance, in 1928/29 the value of farm buildings per one hectare of agricultural land in Warsaw, Łódź, and Kielce provinces was 1,365 zloty on farms of between two and five hectares, 939 zloty on farms of between five and twelve hectares, and only 713 on estates of above fifty hectares.[67]

On the basis of a careful analysis of some regional and all–Polish inquiries it may be estimated that in 1928 large private estates in Poland employed about 680,000 workers, including 470,000 permanent workmen and 210,000 seasonal workers. In 1938 the number of employees on large private estates decreased to about 523,000, including 373,000 permanent workers and about 150,000 seasonal workers.[68] The large private estate economy was much less labor consuming than that of small farms. The average labor input per one hectare of agricultural land of large estates per annum was 46 days in Greater

Poland, 42 days in Pomerania, and 45 days in the eastern borderland. In small farms this ratio was 74 days in Greater Poland, 65 days in Pomerania, and 60 days in the eastern borderland.[69]

The estate employees were a largely differentiated community. At the top of the hierarchy were the administrators and other non-manual workers, followed by handicraftsmen, permanent workers, and seasonal farm hands. The work conditions of farm workers in interwar Poland were better than those before World War I. Under the partitions estates owners were generally free to hire workers individually. According to the law of 28 March 1919 collective bargaining became the foundation of the labor contracts. The law was, not without some resistance from the landowners, extended over the whole of Poland in 1923.[70] Labor conflicts were frequently quite severe, but less and less violent. Neither side was constantly the winner or loser. The number of such conflicts usually increased after bad harvests and decreased after good harvests.[71]

The financial balance sheet of large private estates in interwar Poland can be estimated only approximately on the basis of very complex calculations.[72] The final results of these calculations are presented in Table 4.6 on the following page.

During the Great Depression the gross agricultural returns of large private estates decreased more or less than those of small farms in relation to what base year is adopted. If 1928 is taken as the base year, the index of gross agricultural returns of small farms in 1932 will be 38.5 percent and that of large estates 39.7 percent, but if 1929 is adopted, the same ratio for small farms in 1932 will be 48.5 percent and that for large estates 37.4 percent.[73] The large estates suffered especially from the decrease of returns from sales of plant and forest products and could only partly make it up by selling processed food. On the whole, for most of the 1930s the gross returns of large estates were relatively lower than those of small farms.

On the other hand, average gross returns per one hectare of agricultural land on large estates were much higher than those of small farms. In 1929 an average small farm earned 116 zloty per one hectare of agricultural land, while one hectare on large estates gave 343 zloty. In 1934 the gross returns per one hectare of agricultural land on small farms was 43 zloty and on large estates 1451 zloty.[74] Apart from sales of farm products, large estates had special sources of income, such as land leases, extraordinary wood cutting, and the sale of land.

The costs of production presented in Table 4.6 were estimated on the basis of regional inquiries into labor costs and proportions of other costs. It may be assumed that the average cost of production on a large estate included from 50 to 80 percent of labor cost, while cost of capital depreciation accounted for about 10 percent, fertilizer less than 10 percent, cost of foodstuffs about 8 percent, light and fuel about 7 percent, and insurance about 4 percent of all costs.[75]

Table 4.6

Balance Sheet of Returns and Expenditures of Large Private Estates in Poland in Millions of Zloty, 1924-1938

Year	Agricul-tural Returns	Redistri-bution	Total Returns	Costs	Debt Service	Taxes	Net Income
1924	1,374	114	1,624	582			196
1925	1,915	114	2,220	826	-74	165	1,171
1926	1,670	267	2,108	901	+28	165	1,070
1927	1,905	350	2,473	1,227	+57	206	1,096
1928	2,208	360	2,843	1,574	+110	274	1,104
1929	1,677	242	2,204	1,435	+55	271	553
1930	1,184	181	1,617	1,268	-33	176	140
1931	1,023	135	1,382	983	-131	128	140
1932	826	90	1,106	688	-195	117	107
1933	757	97	1,014	541	-296	99	78
1934	666	63	888	493	-192	111	93
1935	685	84	919	476	-160	172	
1936	789	97	1,038	444	-189	116	288
1937	1,062	121	1,348	464	-240	137	507
1938	872	136	1,175	466	-191	178	341

Source: Wojcieh Roszkowski, *Gospodarcza rola większej prywatnej własności ziemskiej w Polsce 1918-1939* [*Economic Role of Large Private Estates in Poland, 1918-1939*] Warsaw, 1986, p. 285.

The income and cost–accounting of large estates broke down during the Great Depression, when returns decreased much more than costs. Reduction of costs became the prerequisite of avoiding bankruptcy. The costs of fertilizer and purchased foodstuffs were dramatically reduced, while investments were almost entirely suspended. The labor cost could be decreased only partly, mostly as a result of reduction in employment, because farmhands' unions were determined to keep wages up. Farmworkers' wages were not reduced until 1933. It is a matter of discussion whether landowners substituted permanent workers with lower–paid seasonal farm hands. There were such cases in Greater Poland, but many opposite cases may also be cited in which estate owners preferred to employ more reliable permanent workers. The dramatic reduction of costs during the Great Depression led to extension of the large estate economy and to its growing self–sufficiency.[76]

A considerable part of the financial means of the large estates came from external sources: Long– and short–term credits and arrears in payments. It was estimated that in the 1920s various forms of credit accounted for about 5 percent of funds on small farms and for about 15 percent on large estates. During the Great Depression these ratios grew respectively to 10 and 25 percent.[77]

According to an inquiry by the Union of Polish Agricultural Organizations (Związek Polskich Organizacji Rolniczych), in 1925 the total indebtedness of the large private estates amounted to 1,110,900,000 zloty (214,000,000 contemporary U. S. dollars).[78] During the years of prosperity this indebtedness rapidly increased, since there was general trust in the good economic prospects and many landowners invested in machinery and land drainage. In 1932 the total debt of large estates was estimated at 2,182,000,000 zloty (420,000,000 U. S. dollars). In the 1930s the landowners ceased to take up new credits, but the arrears in debt discharge were hardly balanced by the debt service. As a result, in 1938 the total debt of large estates was still about 2,068,000,000 zolty.[79]

In view of the decreasing area, the average debt on one hectare of agricultural land on large estates grew from about 398 zloty in 1929 to 478 zloty in 1932, and 505 zloty in 1938. Large estates only occasionally benefited from the debt amortization stimulated by the government at the end of the Great Depression. The action was mainly for small farms. In 1931 the average debt per one hectare on all small farms was 143 zloty and that of the large estates 222 zloty. Later this difference further increased.[80] This is why several landowners criticized the government debt cancellation plan as a cover-up for political action against large estates. Several cases may be cited in which large estates even faced bankruptcy because of their relatively increased debt burden in the 1930s. Suffice it to say that while in 1929 the average debt service per one hectare of agricultural land on large estates was equal to 1.3 quintals of rye, in 1935 this ratio grew to 3.6 quintals.[81]

The average tax burden of Polish agriculture had increased considerably over the years 1908/11-1928. In the eastern borderland the increase was 262 percent (large estates 531 percent), in central Poland 228 percent (large estates 401 percent), in the former Prussian partition 180 percent, and in Galicia it was 106 percent (large estates 189 percent).[82] The per hectare tax burden in Poland was not very high, but in relation to agricultural incomes it was among the highest in Europe. It is, by the way, no wonder that the post–World War I reconstruction and unification of Poland could only be financed from the country's own resources.

The large private estates paid every year about 20–25,000,000 zloty of the land value tax, from 17,000,000 zolty (1925) to 76,000,000 (1928) of the income tax, about 40–45,000,000 zloty of the property tax (the 1920s), and from 50,000,000 to 100,000,000 zloty of communal and other taxes. Altogether the tax payments by large estates increased from 196,000,000,000 zloty in 1924 to 275,000,000 in 1928, then decreased during the Great Depression to about 99,000,000 zloty in 1933 and grew again to 177,500,000 in 1938.[83]

The question of whether large estates or small farms were more burdened with taxation has been a political issue, subject to various estimates. One the one hand, interwar landowners frequently alarmed the government about the excessive tax burden. On the other hand, the peasant parties tried to show an opposite picture. Post–World War II Marxist authors in Poland also tried to prove that small farms in interwar Poland had been more burdened by taxes than the estates. This thesis cannot be proven. Even if the calculations by its adherent, Mieczysław Mieszczankowski, are taken as a basis, it is clear that in 1929 small farms paid about 13.20 zloty of all taxes per one hectare of agricultural land, while large estates paid 20.10 zloty. In fact the latter figure should be raised at least to about 56.00 zloty.[84] It should not come as a surprise, since rates of the land value tax for farms above 60 hectares were 24 percent higher than those for smaller farms, while the income and property taxes were paid almost exclusively by landowners.

The higher tax burden on large estates as compared with small farms seems undeniable. At the same time, however, two points must be made. First, the large estate owners delayed tax payments, especially during the Great Depression. The question of whether their arrears were higher than thsoe of the smallholders cannot be settled for lack of precise evidence. Second, from the social and economic point of view, it was also important what the tax burden in relation to income was. In 1929 taxes paid by smallholders accounted for about 11 percent of their average gross return. If we accept the underestimate made by Mieszczankowski for large estate owners this ratio would be 6 percent, but if we properly assess all taxes paid by the landowners, the same ratio would increase to 16 percent.[85] The difference is substantial and the accuracy of calculations not too high, so we should not jump to conclusions. It only seems just to say that, in relation to their gross returns, large estate owners did not pay less taxes than smallholders.

The net incomes of large private estates, presented in Table 4.6, show a shocking decline. My estimates, based on the assessment of all components of the cost and effect calculus, appear to be a little higher for the 1920s and much lower for the 1930s, as compared with the net incomes of large estate owners estimated by the fiscal authorities.[86]

Nevertheless, the following conclusions seem to be justified. First, in the years of prosperity the increase of gross returns, due to rising prices of farm products, excessive wood cutting, and the acceleration of land distribution, was accompanied by a rapid growth of costs, mainly in labor, connected to increasing wages. While the net incomes of the large estates were almsot stable in the years 1925–1928, the social income, including hired workers' wages rapidly increased. This can be seen in Table 4.7. Second, during the Great Depression the net incomes collapsed dramatically. In the years 1932–1934 the net incomes of large estate owners was more or less equal to the income from land sales. In other words, to make both ends meet, landowners as a social group were forced to sell land. Third, the share of estate owners in the social income of their estates was decreasing. While in 1924 about 73 percent of the social income produced in the large estates remained with the owners, in 1935 this share decreased to about 37 percent. Apart from the fact that wages of farm hands and their standard of living were rather low, large estates supported more than

Table 4.7

Social Income of Large Private Estates in Poland, 1924-1938

Year	Social Income in Zloty	1928+100	Social Income in Zloty per Hectare	1928+100
1924	1,125,200,000	60.5	195.3	52.9
1925	1,581,900,000	85.6	281.6	76.3
1926	1,556,000,000	83.7	284.7	77.1
1927	1,722,300,000	92.6	328.1	88.9
1928	1,859,800,000	100.0	369.2	100.0
1929	1,284,700,000	69.1	263.0	71.2
1930	843,800,000	45.4	177.2	48.0
1931	759,300,000	40.8	163.7	44.3
1932	571,600,000	30.7	125.2	33.9
1933	459,500,000	24.7	102.6	27.8
1934	425,500,000	22.9	96.2	26.1
1935	472,300,000	25.4	108.0	29.3
1936	568,000,000	30.5	133.6	36.2
1937	792,300,000	42.6	188.6	51.1
1938	620,700,000	33.4	151.1	40.9

Source: Wojciech Roszkowski, *Gospodarcza rola większej prywatnej własncści ziemskiej w Polsce 1918-1939 [Economic Role of Large Private Estates in Poland, 1918-1939]* Warsaw, 1986, p. 268.

half a million hired workers. Fourth, because of the incomparability between labor costs on large estates and small farms, any comparisons of net incomes of both categories of farms do not seem reasonable. For the same reason the social incomes of both large estates and small farms are not comparable.

Chapter 5

THE POLITICAL ROLE OF THE ARISTOCRACY AND LANDOWNERS

Landowners' Organizations

Even today some authors try to present the image of interwar Poland as a country ruled by the bourgeoisie and the landowners. Without going into details of the theory of political rule, it should be stated that interwar Poland was a country of a mixed socioeconomic structure in which elements of state capitalism were accompanied by private monopolies, free market competition, small–scale production, or even subsistence economy.[1] In these circumstances it would be wrong to speak about domination by any particular social group. Many social groups exert influence on the governments of interwar Poland. Thus the term "groups of interest" may quite well reflect the specific nature of the sociopolitical system of the Polish Second Republic. In the present chapter an attempt will be made to show the political participation and to determine the influence of large estate owners on political decisions that were most important to them. Of course, all conclusions must be very cautious, since there are no methods of precisely measuring this influence, especially in history.

The major form of organization for large estate owners, mostly landed gentry, were landowners' societies (*związki ziemian*). The first such association was created as a company for the promotion of the economic interests of Polish estates in Great Poland in 1901. It was a response by Polish landowners to the challenge of the notorious German Colonization Commission (Ansiedlungskommission). In 1918 the Landowners' Society of the Great Duchy of Poznania numbered 547 members. In interwar Poland it continued its activities as the Great Polish Landowners' Society (Wielkopolski Związek Ziemian) under Jan Żółtowski and Jan Lipski. In 1929 the society had 552 members possessing about 270,000 hectares of land.[2]

On 14 June 1915 a similar organization was established in Warsaw under the German and Austrian occupation. Its temporary goals included mutual aid for estates ruined by military operations. In July 1916 the organization was called the Landowners' Society in Warsaw (Związek Ziemian w Warszawie). At first it was chaired by Ludomił Pułaski and from 1919 by Jan Stecki. During the Polish–Soviet War the society continued the self–relief activities, organized credit aid and land distribution, as well as representing estate owners in negotiations with farm workers. In 1929 the organization numbered 3,993 members who had about 900,000 hectares of land. Its major leaders included Jerzy Ciechomski, Jan Czarnowski, Kazimierz Fudakowski, Stanisław Godewski, Zygmunt Leszczyński, and Józef Targowski.[3]

In independent Poland further landowners' societies were created. On 14 March 1919 the Landowners Union was founded under Adam Stadnicki in Cracow. In March 1921 it was changed into the Landowners' Society in Cracow (Związek Ziemian w Krakowie). Its goals included the promotion of common interests of the members and stimulation of the development of agriculture in Poland. In 1929 this society had 618 members who possessed about 325,000 hectares of land. Also in 1919 a landowners' union was founded in Lwow. In 1921 its name was changed to the Landowners' Society of the Eastern Provinces of Lesser Poland (Związek Ziemian Wschodnich Województw Małopolski). In 1929 it had 821 members with about 520,000 hectares of land.[4]

After the conclusion of the Brest–Litovsk Treaty many Polish landowners from Volhynia joined hands to defend their land. In 1919 a Union of Volhynian Poles was founded in Warsaw. On its initiative, on 12–14 April 1920 a gathering of the Polish Volhynian landowners created the Volhynian Landowners' Society (Związek Ziemian Wołynia) in Luck under Stanisław Czacki. In Poland, as well as self–defense against forced redistribution and excessive taxation. In 1929 it had 340 members with about 240,000 hectares of land. Later the society was headed by Aleksander Ledóchowski and Janusz Radzwiłł.

On 1 March 1921 Polish landowners from the Wilno and Nowogródek regions founded their own Northeastern Landowners' Society (Kresowy Związek Ziemian) in Wilno to promote development of agriculture and defend Polish ownership of land. In 1929 it numbered 1,402 members who had about 800,000 hectares of land. For many years the society was headed by Antoni Judziłł. in 1927 the Pomeranian Landowners' Society (Pomorski Związek Ziemian) was founded under Jan Śląski. In 1929 it had 270 members with about 93,000 hectares of land.[5] Theoretically the landowners' societies could include not only estate owners but also leasers, managers, and all persons interested in the adopted programs. In practice they embraced almost exclusively estate owners, mainly belonging to the landed gentry. Statute tasks were formulated in various ways, but everywhere the major objectives included, as in the Warsaw society, "trade solidarity" and "promotion of the interests of estate owners." Only in the Poznań and Pomeranian associations were wider social goals mentioned. Therefore one of the organizers of the movement, Seweryn Dolański, was right to describe the landowners' societies as "trade unions of landed capital," although in practice, the coats-of-arms of their members also counted.[6]

The idea of the unification of all landowners' societies was conceived in early 1919. At that time the landowners had already developed a program that declared the essential importance of the large estates for Poland and that was an attempt to neutralize radical demands by the peasants. A conference held in Warsaw on 28–29 July decided to create the Supreme Council of Landowners' Organizations (Rada Naczelna Organizacji Ziemiańskich, or RNOZ). The council was founded under pressure created by the Sejm resolution of July 1919 on the principles of a future land reform. From its very beginning, RNOZ strongly criticized "utopian" and "doctrinal" slogans such as "land for everyone," and defended the landowners' property rights. But the general objective of the council was to organize a stand by large estate owners on all important socioeconomic and political issues that might affect their interests.[7]

In 1929 RNOZ included seven landowners' societies and a separate Union of Associations of Forest Owners (Zrzeszenie Związków Właścicieli Lasów). Altogether, RNOZ represented 7,996 members, that is, about 45 percent of the owners of estates of above 50 hectares, which comprised approximately 3,150,000 hectares of land, that is, about 32 percent of the total large estates' area. All German, Russian, and many Polish estate owners remained outside the landowners' societies. The council was headed by Kazimierz Fudakowski (1919), Jan Stecki (1923–1924), Kazimiez Lubomirski (1924–1925), Maurycy Zamoyski (1925–1927), Kazimiez Lubomirski again (1927–1930), Stanisław Dąmbski (1931), Zdzisław Lubomirski (1931–1935), Stanisław Wankowicz (1935–1936), and Adolf Bniński (1936–1939). The official publication of the council was the weekly *Gazeta Rolnicza*, edited by

Jan Lutosławski.[8]

Large estate owners also united in trade associations, which tried
to influence the government economic policies on various agricultural sectors. They also pretty much dominated the Trade Union
of Professional Farmers and Foresters (Związek Zawodowy Rolników
i Leśników z Wyższym Wykształceniem), created in 1920, which organized conferences of agricultural experts. Women landowners had
their own all–Polish organization, the Supreme Council of Women
Landowners (Rada Naczelna Ziemianek), founded in 1923, which stimulated various social and educational activities in the countryside.[9]

The influence of the large estate owners of the general agricultural associations was especially noticeable in their umbrella organizations. In 1921 a loose federation of the Central Agricultural Society
(Centralne Towarzystwo Rolnicze), in Warsaw, the Economic Association (Towarzystwo Gospodaracze) in Lwow, the Lesser Polish, Agricultural Society (Małopolskie Towarzystwo Rolnicze) in Cracow, the
Central Agricultural Association (Centralne Towarzystwo Rolnicze)
in Poznań, and the Poznań Chamber of Agriculture (Poznańska Izba
Rolnicza) were united into the Union of Polish Agricultural Organizations (Związek Polskich Organizacji Rolniczych) under the leadership
of the landowner, Marian Kiniorski. Later, the union was presided
over by Kazimierz Fudakowski.

After the May 1926 coup d'état the union was increasingly dependent on government subsidies. The *sanacja* government exerted
growing pressure on the union's authorities: for instance, in the fall of
1927 the government threatened to withhold subsidies unless person-
nel changes were made in the union. In 1928 tighter unification was
undertaken, and in 1933 the Union of Polish Agricultural Chambers
and Organizations (Zwi azek Izb i Organizacji Rolniczych R.P.) was
created. From 1935 on it was chaired by another landowner, Kajetan
Morawski. Although new forms of agricultural organization still depended largely on the government, its landowner members still played
an important role.[10]

In 1928, 4,771 owners from among 10,180 large estates that were
the subject of study belonged to general agricultural societies. The
highest membership of large estate owners in these societies was
recorded in Polesie (68 percent) and in Lublin Province (61 percent), while the lowest was in Wilno Province (23 percent). Large
landowners presided over several regional agricultural societies. For
instance, Karol Raczyński of Złoty Potok was the chairman of the

Częstochowa society, Antoni Rostworowski that of the Lublin society, Michał Krasiński the Grodno society, Jan Strawiński the Słonim society, and Roman Skirmuntt the Piński society.[11]

Political Life before 1926

Before World War I political groups representing large landowners were important in Prussian Poland, Galicia, and in the Russian partition. In (Austro–Hungarian) Galicia, a group called the *"stańczycy,"* who derived the name from the pragmatic and conservative program of the "Teka Stańczyka" ("Stańczyk's Portfolio"), had formulated the program of "trialism." In its opinion, the idea of independence had to be renounced in favor of gradual improvement of the quality of national life under the three partitioning powers. They also argued that the Polish–Lithuanian Commonwealth had collapsed mainly because of its internal defects, and they openly criticized the shortcomings of the Polish noble tradition. Logically, they also made attempts to come to terms with other nationalities living in Galicia, mainly the Jews and Ukrainians. In 1907 the group founded the Party of the National Right (Stronnictwo Prawicy Narodowej), headed by Zdzisław Tarnowski. This party was the most important component of the parliamentary bloc led by the Galician governor, Michał Bobrzyński, who was also one of the party's leaders.[12] The eastern Galician group of conservatives, called the ("Podalians"), had a different political philosophy: since they opposed the national aspirations of the local Ukrainians, their sympathies were with the National Democracy party.

However, the power of the loyalist conservative *stańczycy* was gradually declining. Universal suffrage gave new political power to the Galician peasants, while the fierce struggle for extending the franchise in eastern Galicia increased the influence of the National democrats, who opposed the liberal policies toward the Ukainians followed by conservatives. Following the lead of the National Democrats, the Podolians also took up the "Russian" solution. During World War I the *stańczycy* were only one of the factions of the Supreme National Committee (Naczelny Komitet Narodowy), which organized Polish cooperation with Austria–Hungary in Galicia and aimed for the "'trialist" solution. This program expected the creation of Galicia as the third part of the Habsburg Monarchy. With the bankruptcy of the "Austrian" solution and the granting of the Chełm region to the Ukrainians under the provisions of the Brest–Litovsk Treaty of March

1918, the Party of the National Right lost most of its former support. The influence of conservative loyalists in the German partition was even smaller. The majority of Polish landowners in this region supported the National Democrats, as any political compromise with the German authorities was deemed very unpopular.[13]

In the Russian partition the situation was complicated. In the former Congress Kingdom of Poland the National Democrats, headed by Roman Dmowski, managed to win over a large part of the landowners, Maurycy Zamoyski, the heir of the huge Zamcść entail, was one of their major supporters. The conservative Party of Political Realism (Stronnictwo Polityki Realnej), founded in 1905 under the leadership of landowner Józef Ostrowski, generally followed the loyalist line of the Cracow conservatives, but with the Russian empire. These Political Realists were compromised in the eyes of the Poles, since they were heavily engaged in supporting the Russian throne and were receiving proportionately less in return.

One group of conservatives in the Russian partition had been closer to the Austrian solution advocated by the Galician National Right. However, attempts to create a separate National Conservative party (Stronnictwo Narodowo–Zachowawcze), made by Zdzisław Lubomirski and Seweryn Czetwertyński had failed and their followers joined the Political Realists. There was a lot of mutual distrust between National Democracy, advocating Polish nationalism, and the Party of Political Realism, especially in easternmost Kresy, where politicians such as Aleksander Meysztowicz, Edward Woyniłłowicz, Czesław Jankowski, and Konstanty Skirmuntt opposed Polish nationalism in order to not antagonize local Byelorussian and Ukrainian peasant. In 1908 this group, connected with the daily *Kurier Litewski* in Wilno, became the Regional Party of Lithuania and Ruthenia (Stronnictwo Krajowe Litwy i Rusi).[14]

At the beginning of the war, neither Russia nor its western allies pursued the cause of Polish independence as a war aim. The Galician conservatives generally supported the Austrians. In 1915 the Central Powers occupied the former Kingdom of Poland. After the Act of November 1916, by which the Austrian and German emperors promised the Kingdom of Poland some autonomy, Russians appeal weakened among the landowners of the former Kingdom of Poland: several prominent conservatives from the Russian partition began to put their faith in the Central Powers. When the Regency Council was founded in 1917, it was composed of Józef Ostrowski, Zdzisław

Lubomirski, and Zdzisław Lubomirski, and Archbishop Aleksander Kakowski—all followers of the Party of Political Realism.

In October 1917 the Petrograd National Conservative Party (Stronnictwo Narodowo–Zachowawcze) of Aleksander Meysztowicz and Stanisław Radziwiłł recognized the Polish Regency Council. The Party of National Labor in Ruthenia (Stronnictwo Pracy Narodowej na Rusi), headed by Franciszek Pułaski and Janusz Radziwiłł, also supported the council. Even some National Democratic landowners, such as Jan Stecki, cooperated with the Regency Council. In December 1916 the Party of National Labor (Stronnictwo Pracy Narodowej) was founded in Poznań, and was headed by Adam Żółtowski of Jarogniewice. At first this party hoped for the Polish autonomy promised by the Austrian and German emperors in November 1916, but by the end of the war, it decided that the Entente program had a better chance.

The pro–Russian orientation was supported by the National Democrats who dominated the Interparty Political Alliance (Międzypartyjne Kolo Polityczne), founded in October 1915. When in February 1917 the first Russian Revolution swept the tsarist regime away, the Russian Provisional Government offered the reunification of Polish territories in close alliance with a new Russia. The pro–Russian program of National Democracy then gained more support among the landowners of the Russian partition. Some of them joined the Polish National Committee (Komitet NarodowyPolski), organized in Paris by the National Democrats and recognized by the Entente as the official Polish representatives. Maurycy Zamoyski became the treasurer of the committee and subsidized its activities. With the Bolshyvik revolution and the Brest–Litovsk Treaty the Russian solution collapsed, but the hope for the final victory of the Entente kept the conservative followers of the Paris Committee afloat. At the same time, more and more landowners from the Russian partition began to support the anti–Russian profram of Józef Piłsudski and his ideas on the restoration of the Jagiełłon federation of Poland–Lithuania–Ruthenia. In 1918, though, some of the Polish landowners in Byelorussia, such as Roman Skirmuntt, were among the leaders of an independent Byelorussian government.[15]

In the reborn Poland the political groups representing landowners had to choose between the National Democrats and the followers of Józef Piłsudski, and could not formulate a position of their own. This was largely due to the decline of their power base: the war had resulted in the social and political emancipation of the peasantry, while the hostile attitude of the conservative groups to land reform had alienated those peasants who might have otherwise supported them. The strongest rightist party that emerged from the war was National Democracy, from which the landowner conservatives basically differed in their strong opposition to land reform. Nevertheless, two conservative groups allied themselves with National Democracy during the 1922 elections: these were the National–Christian Popular Party (Narodowo–Chrześcijańskie Stronnictwo Ludowe), founded in 1920 by Edward Dubanowicz and Christian Democracy (Stronnictwo Chrześcijańsko–Demokratyczne). Together they created Christian National Unity (Chrześcijańska Jedność Narodowa), which won a plurality, but not an absolute majority, of votes. As for conservatives, they received but few. The strongest faction supported by some landowners was National Democracy. Maurycy Zamoyski was National Democracy's candidate for president in 1922. For the landowners, however, the problem was that National Democracy did not fully support their views on land reform and other social issues.

Other estate owners belonged to various monarchist or conservative political factions, such as the Party of National Labor in Poznań and the Party of the National Right in Cracow, reconstructed in 1920, which was close to the conservative Cracow newspaper *Czas (Time)*. The latter party lost a lot of its former importance because of its refusal to accept the need for social reforms. It held that the Constitution of March 1921 was "too democratic" and called for a limited franchise. It also opposed the land reform. Otherwise it remained true to its former opposition to nationalism, emphasizing the danger to the multinational state. Although the Cracow conservatives were listened to and respected and their *Czas* was one of the most popular newspapers in Poland, their political strength in parliamentary representation was next to none.

In February 1919 a Party of Constitutional Labor (Stronnictwo Pracy Konstytucyjnej) was created by Jerzy Baworowski. It was supported by Janusz Radziwiłł, Henryk Potocki, Aleksander Meysztowicz, and Aleksander Skrzyński, the former Political Realists or the followers of Galician conservatives: this party had even gained some votes in the 1919 elections. Another group of landowners, such as Tadeusz Szułdrzyński, Leon Żółtowski, and Mieczysław Chłapowski, founded the Christian–National Agricultural Party (Chrześcijańsko–Narodowe Stronnictwo Roinicze) in Poznań in November 1920. Finally, a group connected with the Wilno daily *Słowo* *(Word)*, including Marian Broel–Plater, Czesław Jankowski, and Stanisław Mackiewicz, also had some political influences.[16]

During the 1922 elections most of the landowners sympathized with National Democracy and its allies. The National–Christian Popular Party and the Christian–National Agricultural Party won elections to the Sejm, while other conservatives did not. The Party of Constitutional Labor disappeared from parliament. An attempt to organize the support of the landowning circles by the Piłsudski bloc was a failure. The national State Union (Unia Narodowo–Pańsudski) bloc was a failure by the Piłsudski's followers, attracted only a small percentage of landowners' votes: it still looked too radical to the landowners. In 1923 the Christian–National Agricultural Party crossed the former partition frontier; its achievements in maintaining relative social peace and order in Greater Poland had attracted many landowners from other regions. On 19 June 1925 this party merged with the National–Christian Popular party to form the Christian–National Party (Stronnictwo Chrześcijańsko–Narodowe), headed by Tadeusz Szułdrzyński.[17]

Nevertheless, the conservative parties had very limited parliamentary representations, so that when the estate owners' interests were threatened by the land reform program, most of the landowners supported National Democracy, the strongest single party in Poland, although it was unable to win a parliamentary majority. About 5 percent of The Constituent Assembly was composed of estate owners, whereas it was only 6 percent in the Sejm of 1922–1927. Fourteen percent of the Senate of 1922–1927 was made up of estate owners.[18] The lost presidential election of 1922, the 1923 Lanckorona agreement of the National Democrats and the moderate peasant party Piast and the failure of the Wincenty Witos government, which was based on that agreement, as well as the National Democrats' attitude of compromise with the land reform in particular, drove many estate owners from National Democracy. The climax of these feelings came during the Congress of United Landowners in Warsaw in September 1925.[19] The land reform law of December 1925 simply aggravated the already existing atmosphere of extreme disappointment among estate owners.

After the May Coup d'État

The May 1926 coup d'état finally split the group. Some of the estate owners drew near National Democracy again. This was particularly apparent in the Warsaw Landowners' Society, which passed a declaration calling the coup "an insult to moral principles." The Cracow *Czas* group and followers of the Galician Party of the National Right saw the coup as a threat to the reign of law,[20] Other estate owners adjusted their loyalties and social solidarity to the principles of Piłsudski's *sanacja* bloc. The most pro–*sanacja* attitude was demonstrated by the Wilno *Słowo* group, led by Eustachy Sapieha and Stanisław Mackiewicz, and supported financially by Jan Tyszliewicz, Albrecht Radziwiłł, Aleksander Meysztowicz, and Artus Potocki. Some Galician conservatives and the Warsaw branch of the Party of the National Right, headed by Janusz Radziwiłł, were also willing to cooperate with Piłsudski, but not without conditions. The third group, the Christian–National party, split. While Jan Stecki would ultimately cooperate with the government, the faction led by Stanisław Stroński and Edward Dubanowicz reached out for an alliance with National Democracy and strongly criticized the coup.[21]

Soon after the coup some conservative politicians and followers of Piłsudski remained in touch, each trying to test the intentions of the other side; the role of mediator in these contacts was played by Władysław Glinka. The most active pro–Piłsudski conservative, such as Stanisław Mackiewicz, thought it necessary to support the coup in order to prevent the new regime from being dominated by leftists, although in fact, there was no danger of this. Józef Piłsudski himself thought in terms of a wider coalition and suggested an eminent conservative, Zdzisław Lubomirski, for the presidency, but Lubomirski refused. On 27 May 1926 a conservative committee was established under Janusz Radziwiłł, but it included representatives of various conservative orientations, to talk with Marshall Piłsudski. During the presidential elections of 1 June the most unyielding opponents of the coup from the Cracow group of the Party of the National Right, headed by Michał Bobrzyński, and the Poznań faction of the Christian–National party, supported Adolf Bniński as the candidate against Ignacy Mościcki who had been designated by Piłsudski.[22]

When Piłsudski reorganized his cabinet in September 1926, he included two important landowners from eastern Poland, Aleksander Meysztowicz and Karol Niezabytowski. The Radziwiłł committee seemed reassured about Piłsudski's social moderation and national solidarity: on 26 June 1926 the Warsaw supporters of the Party of the National Right founded the Union of Conservative State Labor (Związek Zachowawczej Pracy Państwowej) under Kazimierz Lubomirski.

The union generally accepted the coup. Only the Poznań conservatives were still determined to oppose the new regime, but their leader, Tadeusz Szułdrzyński, came to Warsaw and promised to act for stabilization in Greater Poland.[23]

On 25 October 1926 Piłsudski came to Nieśwież, the seat of the entail of Albrecht Radziwiłł in eastern Poland, to posthumously decorate his aide–de–camp Stanisław Radziwiłł, killed by the Bolsheviks in 1920. But the presence of many prominent landowners and conservative politicians made the meeting an expresison of mutual confidence.[24] In December 1926 the Polish Conservative Organization of State Work (Polska Organizacja Zachowawczej Pracy Państwowej) was created under Eustachy Sapieha, while the Warsaw and Łódź branches of the Party of the National Right united with the Cracow conservatives. Both groups declared themselves in favor of the *sanacja* government.

In 1927 the political situation among the landowners was stabilized. One group, generally connected with the Christian–National party and sympathizing with National Democracy, declared neutrality toward the new regime, while an even stronger group more or less actively supported the Piłsudski government. Both groups approached each other in July 1927 but still remained as separate factions. The cooperation by the latter group with the govenment was finally agreed upon at another meeting—Walery Sławek (Piłsudski's right–hand man) with landowners on the Dzików estate of Zdzisław Tarnowski on 14–16 September 1927.[25] In October 1927 Sławek also met with the representatives of the eastern Galician conservatives at the Jabłorów estate of Konstanty Dzieduszycki; the participants in this meeting expressed their support for the Piłsudski government.

On 24 October 1927, the three major conservative parties—the Polish Conservative Organization of State Work, the Party of the National right, and the Christian–National party—passed a joint declaration favoring the strengthening of the executive power, civil rights for the national minorities as long as they remained loyal to Polish statehood, respect for private property, and a social policy of solidarity. The three parties agreed to create a joint committee to coordinate their policies, especially during the upcoming elections. On 10 December 1927 the committee (Komitet Zachowawczy) was created. It was headed by Janusz Radziwiłł , Adam Żółtowski, and Eustachy Sapieha. But as a result of cooperation by some of the leaders of the Christian National party with the government, that party split: 15 January

1928 participants in this cooperation, such as Zygmunt Leszczyński, Marian Rudziński, and Leon Janta–Połczyński, seceded to form the Christian–Agricultural party (Chrześcijeńskie Stronnictwo Rolnicze) while opponents of the Połsudski regime, headed by Tadeusz Szułdrzyń ski, stayed under the old party name.[26]

In the years that followed, politicians favoring the Piłsudski regime dominated the estate owners' group. The *sanacja* government generally respected the political objectives of the landowners, and so the Piłsudski regime managed to attract their support. In 1927 Maurycy Zamoyski gave up the presidency of RNOZ to Kazimierz Lubomirski, a collaborator of Piłsudski's. The RNOZ presidents who followed him also generally favored cooperation with that government. In the 1928 elections conservative landowners gained as many as twenty seats in the Sejm from the *sanacja* bloc list, and the Christian–Agricultural party was defeated. As an illustration, Artus Dobiecki, Konstanty Dzieduszycki, Edward Kleszczyński, Stanisław Mackiewicz, Konstanty Rdułtowski, Janusz Radziwiłł, Eustachy Sapieha, Adam Stadnicki, and Józef Targowski were elected to the Sejm; Stanisław Dąmbski, Agenor Gołuchowski, Jan Goetz–Okocimski, Zdsisław Lubomirski, Zdzisław Tarnowski, and Stanisl aw Wań kowski became senators. By the late 1920s even the Christian–National party leaders were expressing moderate support for the government.[27]

Nevertheless, the conservative groups cooperating with the government were only a part of the Piłsudski bloc of supporters. Even as members of this bloc they could not realize all their ambitions, although they supported the government financially. In many issues they pressed their own viewpoint and strongly disagreed with government policies; for instance, the growing statism of the Piłsudski regime was not at all popular among the conservatives. This was clearly expressed during two meetings with government representatives of Janusz Radziwiłł's palace in Warsaw in 1928 and 1929.[28] The conservative newspapers—*Słowo* of Wilno, *Czas* of Cracow, *Dziweń Polski* of Warsaw, and *Dziennik Poznański* of Poznań—advocated the conservative vision of Poland, but it surely was not the vision held by the whole government.

The crackdown on the opposition, launched by the *sanacja* in September 1930, created discomfort or even disgust among the government's conservative allies. *Czas* openly criticized this action. Nevertheless the leading conservative supporters of the Piłsudski regime, such as Zdzisław Lubomirski, Zygmunt Leszczyński, Józef Targowski,

Leon Janta–Połczyński, Jan Stecki, and Janusz Radziwiłł, ran in the 1930 elections. The conservatives' policy toward the Brest trial of the opposition leaders allowed mild criticism within the government bloc, but no public discussion of the regime's abuse of power. Gradually, however, some of the leading government groups's conservatives became more and more critical of the government; in a speech in parliament Lubomirski warned against dictatorship, and in December 1932 Radziwiłł, who was the vice–president of the nonparty bloc's club in parliament and who usually accepted the government's policies, expressed his concern for the deteriorating political situation in Poland.[29]

On 27 February 1933 the conservative groups participating in the Nonparty Bloc of Cooperation with the Government (Bezpartyjny Blok Współpracy z Rządem) met in Warsaw and established a united body called the Union of Conservative Political Organizations (Zjednoczenie Zachowawczych Organiszcji Politycznych). This union was chaired by Janusz Radziwiłł, and the members of the its board included Stanisław Wań owicz, Leon Janta–Połczyński, Stanisław Mackiewicz, and Józef Wielowieyski.[30] The situation of the landowner conservatives in the government bloc became more and more tenuous. The conservatives might have criticized the government for its authoritarian policies, but the more radical members of the *sanacja* establishment were criticizing the conservatives for their ties to foreign capital in Upper Silesia and, sometimes, in search for peasant support, challenged the very existence of large estates; but as long as the government did not act against the landowners' interests, they were generally willing to support it.[31]

This situation began to change at the end of the 1930s, when the minister of agriculture, Juliusz Poniatowski, openly supported the program of land distribution. Because of the decline of large estate incomes, the government was less and less dependent on financial support from landowners, and, therefore, cooperation from the conservative politicians with the government bloc brought less and less profit to landowners. In May 1935 the Supreme Council of Landowners' Organizations paid special homage to the memory of the by–then deceased Marchal Piłsudski. In that same year as many as thirty–four estate owners were elected to the 208–member Sejm, while eighteen owners became members of the sixty–four–member Senate. In 1938 their share decreased drastically: only eleven owners were elected to the Sejm and seven to the Senate.[32]

Conservative support for the political program of the government's Camp of National Unity (Obóz Zjednoczenia Narodowego) in 1937 was weaker than that for the Nonparty Bloc. Janusz Radziwiłł joined the "camp," but without much enthusiasm. At the founding congress of the Conservative party (Stronnictwo Zachowawcze) in Warsaw in December 1937 he made a speech criticizing the government for having lost support among the people; he was not reelected chairman of the progovernment conservative movement that he had led for almost ten years.[33] Party leadership was taken over by Adolf Bniński, a politician with strong sympathy for National Democracy, and who had also been chairman of RNOZ in 1936. The estate owner followers of National Democracy were to gradually regain influence.

An interesting survey of the social composition of the political elites in the Polish Second Republic has been done by Roman Wapiński. According to him, in the years 1918–1926 of 300 top government officials 56 percent were from the intelligentsia, 13 percent were from estate owners, 10 percent from the military, 7 percent from white collar workers, 2 percent from peasants, and 1 percent from the working class. In the years 1926–1939 these proportions changed significantly. The political elite of Poland was then composed of 42 percent from the military, 32 percent from the intelligentsia, 19 percent white–collar workers, 5 percent estate owners, and 2 percent entrepreneurs.[34] In other words, the political influence of the large landowners showed a decrease, especially at the end of the 1930s. Similar results were obtained in a survey of the interwar Great Polish social elites: among its 887 members, that author found only forty-five landowners.[35] Although many of the intelligentsia, military, and white–collar workers had family links with the estate owners society, these data do not show a clear class dominance by estate owners or any other social group in interwar Poland. The only exception might have been in the diplomatic corps that was staffed—especially in the top positions—by landowners, which was due to their personal contacts abroad and their knowledge of foreign languages.[36]

The Efficiency of the Landowners' Lobby

Of course, it is not only numbers and names that count when we analyze the role of large estate owners as an interest group in interwar Poland, but also government policies that either favored or opposed the objectives of this group. Let us now look at the realization of the most important goals of the estate owners: preservation of the landed property, profitability of agriculture, and some other issues.

As early as November 1918 the president of the Warsaw Landowners' Society, Ludomił Pułaski, stated that the major goal of the estate owners was to preserve their landed property. From the beginning they knew this would not happen without some sacrifice on their part. Anticipating the land reform dispute in the Sejm, in March 1919 the joint commission of landowners' societies resolved to offer the speaker of the Sejm a voluntary redistribution of about 840,000 hectares. Landowners from the eastern borderland offered to join in this action if their region would be incorporated into Poland. In order to carry out this plan, the commission suggested the creation of a compulsory union of large estate owners. However, the voluntary redistribution was opposed by the peasants, who were waiting for compulsory expropriation.[37]

During the parliamentary debate on the draft land reform law in 1919, which included a wide range of expropriations, the landowners' societies raised many protests. The Warsaw society warned that the law would erode property rights and cause starvation in towns as a result of a decline of food supply. On 12 July 1919 the joint commission of landowners' societies published an open letter criticizing the Sejm resolution on the principles of land reform. The commission stated that the redistribution of land was necessary but that it should be a voluntary sacrifice and not an act that would open the way for future expropriation by those who had expropriated in the beginning.[38] For breaking ranks with the landowners in this, the Warsaw society expelled Minister of Agriculture Stanisław Janicki and Member of Parliament Seweryn Czetwertyński.

The estate owners' criticism of the 15 July 1920 land reform act was also very sharp, although the law was necessary to strengthen the morale of Polish peasant soldiers in the wake of the Red Army's offensive. The problem was that the reform provided for only 50 percent compensation for the expropriated land. Expressing an opinion held by many landowners, Jan Lutosławski stated that the law "pushed the old Polish culture back to barbarism."[39] The large estate owners also conducted a campaign against carrying out the law, especially when it became contradictory to article 99 of the March 1921 Constitution concerning private property. But it was not only the estate owners who thought the expropriated property should be fully paid for. The principle of private property rights was advocated by many other segments of society and had a wider application than just the defense of large landed properties.

In trying to continue its policy of voluntary sacrifices, in April 1923 the Supreme Council of Landowners' Organizations offered 1,200,000 hectares for voluntary distribution within the following ten years.[40] This was the price the estate owners were ready to pay for the abondonment of land reform. However, the peasant parties, even the moderate Piast leadership, could not be satisfied with this offer. In May 1923 a compromise agreement was reached by Piast and National Democracy, which aimed at creating a parliamentary majority government. This "Lanckorone agreement" between both parties stipulated that every year 200,000 hectares from large estates would be distributed voluntarily, and if the quota went unfulfilled, the government would have the right to forced expropriation of selected estates.[14] This was too much to swallow for the estate owners. Many of them left the National Democratic party. On the other hand radical peasant parties accused the Piast leadership of having betrayed the peasant cause. For a time the estate owners tried to make the National Democratic leadership change its mind, but in vain. In June 1923 President Stanisław Wojciechowski warned the landowers not to treat the matter only from their point of view but to see it against the background of the future of the whole national economy.[42]

Public opinion in Poland followed the parliamentary majority in recognizing the final land reform act of December 1925, based largely on the Lanckorona agreement, as a necessary compromise. A formal stance against the land reform principles formulated by RNOZ in June 1925 and by the Landowners' Congress in September 1925 could not change this, and it created an impression that estate owners cared only for their own property. But since the prices of land rose in 1926–1928, redistribution was good business for the estate owners, their protests against the land reform gradually faded away.

During the Great Depression of 1929–1935, the prices of land fell almost as rapidly as those of farm products. Therefore the estate owners redistributed less and did not fulfill the land reform quotas. In view of the collapse of peasant incomes, the demand for land was very low and the government did not use its right to forced expropriation in order to avoid further fall in land prices. This policy was followed by the minister of agriculture Leon Janta–Połczyński, a landowner himself. But it is difficult to say whether this policy was in the interests of large estate owners only, since the problem affected the whole agricultural sector and there were fewer and fewer peasant buyers of land. In 1932 distribution of heavily indebted estates was demanded by the government. But the real change came in 1934, when the Ministry of Agriculture was taken over by Juliusz Poniatowski, who represented the *sanacia* left wing. He put forward a program of acceleration of land reform through redistribution, consolidation of holdings, and land drainage for the years 1934–1938.[43] The radical program of Poniatowski, who favored the theory of the superiority of small holdings over large estates, stirred up the estate owners emotions and protests again. In November 1936 RNOZ issued a declaration against a harmful, in their opinion, "proletarization" of the Polish countryside.[44]

In the late 1930s, mainly because of Catholic Action's activities, highly regarded in landowner circles, a more balanced view began to prevail among the landowners. In November 1937, the Social Council of the Primate of Poland issued a declaration on the "improvement of the agrarian system in Poland." This document favored a "rational land reform" to ease land hunger among the peasants.[45] The declaration was met with a fierce polemic by Jan Lutosławski, but the younger generation of the estate owenrs thought that such a moderate program was necessary. In 1939 there were, however, growing objections to the radical distribution programs in view of the fact that, despite distribution of one–third of agricultural land from large estates, land hunger did not diminish at all. This did not promise well for solving the overpopulation problem in Poland even if all large estates were subject to being broken up. Moreover, the negative influence of redistribution on Polish control of the eastern borderland was noticeable.[46]

The influence of large estate owners on the government policies can also be noticed in other fields. In view of the disastrous damage from World War I operations and the Polish–Soviet War, on 24 January 1920 the Supreme Council of Landowners' Organizations submitted to the Ministry of Agriculture a memorandum in which it appealed for government aid to ruined large estates and for counteracting strikes by farm workers.[47] These demands were only partly met by the subsequent governments. Although the inflationary market boom of 1920–1923 mostly affected industry, it also helped the reconstruction of large estates. Farmers could avoid the inflationary erosion of their incomes, since they could hold back sales until they needed to purchase industrial goods. But this situation was a result of a general economic policy and the adopted method of postwar reconstruction and not necessarily of the government's preferential treatment of landowners.

The inflation turned into a hyperinflation in mid-1923 and a new cabinet under Władysław Grabski was created in December 1923 to cope with the budgetary and monetary reforms. Grabski's program of January 1924 included an extraordinary tax to be paid by all property owners in Poland. At first, the estate owners raised protests, claiming that the tax would check the progress of reconstruction. The Ministry of Finance issued a communique criticizing those who declined to bear responsibility for improving the budget. At the same time the government hinted at difficulties that could be faced by those who would avoid property tax payments while obtaining credits from the newly organized Bank Polski, a new central bank for Poland.

There were no other sources to cover the huge budget deficit. The landlords were being strongly criticized by the parliamentary left and the peasant parties, the government of Grabski, himself a landowner, was absolutely determined, and so the estate owners acceded to the tax. On 7 March 1924 the Supreme Council of Landowners' Organizations issued a statement to the effect that the estate owners were ready to bear the burden of the property tax and subscription to Bank Polski shares. The first subscribers included many outstanding landowners such as Kazimierz Fudakowski, Marian Kiniorski, Jan Stecki, Janusz Radziwiłł, Michał Komorowski, Jan Lutosławski, and Seweryn Dolański.[48]

The landowners' societies, RNOZ, and the *Gazeta Rolnicza* finally supported the idea of the property tax as an extraordinary sacrifice by the group for the benefit of the whole country. On 12 May 1924 the RNOZ delegation met with Prime Minister Grabski, who showed that there was no other way out of the awful budgetary situation. Although in 1925 property tax payments slowed, which made the second phase of the reform a failure, the initial success of the reform in 1924 was largely due to the fact that large estate owners generally accepted the idea of the extraordinary tax.

During the Great Depression the landowners' organizations frequently alarmed the government by pointing out the disastrous situation of agriculture. As early as August 1928 RNOZ had appealed to the government to prepare adequate measures to cope with the expected price collapse.[49] In May 1929 they demanded a more active export promotion, tax reduction, and low–interest loans. The government reacted with some support for exports: in 1929 a monopoly called the Union of Polish Grain Exporters (Związek Polskich Eksporterów Zboża) was created and was granted the exclusive right to issue export licences qualifying for receipt of state export subsidies.

Once the agricultural situation started to deteriorate, in October 1929 RNOZ demanded that the Ministry of Finance stop collection of the remaining installments on property taxes, but to no avail. In October 1930 RNOZ confronted the government with the disastrous credit situation of the estate owners, and in February 1931 it submitted a memorandum suggesting a reduction of taxes indexed to the fall in price.[50] In September 1932 the Union of Polish Agricultural Organizations passed a resolution on the needed reduction in industrial cartel prices. On 11 May 1933 RNOZ demanded that the government take energetic action to support agriculture through debt cancellation., low–interest loans, and export promotion.[51]

The carrying out of all these measures by the government was rather slow and limited, mainly because of the bad budgetary situation. Despite the reduction of some taxes, their real burden increased in the context of a disastrous collapse in agricultural prices. Debt cancellation begun in 1932 mostly affected owners of small holdings. Therefore in the 1930s the overall indebtedness of large estates did not decrease: if anything, it even grew somewhat. The large estate owners could not force the government to improve their situation. They even had serious troubles in maintaining their own organizations. For example, in 1932 the Warsaw Landowners' Society faced a deficit that made its officials consider dissolution of the organization.[52] Under these circumstances the pressure of the large estate owners on the government could not have been too effective.

The slow recovery from the Great Depression made the large estate owners continue their pressure. In March 1936, while speaking in the Senate, Adolf Bniński, who soon became the president of RNOZ, attacked the government's agricultural policy. In February 1937 the council adopted a resolution setting forth the lack of cooperation between the government and the agricultural organizations, as well as driving landowners from the economic self–management; and in March 1937, already the president of RNOZ, Adolf Bniński made a Senate speech in which he strongly criticized the policies of Juliusz Poniatowski.[53]

In fact, *sanacja* publications frequently touted the "interests of the whole of agriculture" and government propaganda was mainly directed at the peasants, who were considered more important as the base of government support in the countryside. The agricultural theses of the *sanacja* Camp of National Unity, published on 13 August 1938, stressed the necessity for the coexistence of large and small farms in Poland, but expressed more sympathy for peasant holdings. This was not only a result of the government's national social solidarism, but also of its understanding of the grave overpopulation problem of the Polish countryside.[54] In the then discussion on ways to ease the overpopulation problem, RNOZ pointed out the hopelessness of redistribution and appealed for seeking a solution in industrialization.[55] This stance could be understood by Vice–Premier Eugeniusz Kwiatkowski, the promoter of industrialization plans, but at the same time it could not win the heart of Juliusz Poniatowski, the advocate of redistribution, who remained minister of agriculture.

This brief survey of the major ideas of the large estate owners and of their realization seems to show that all extreme conclusions would be incorrect. The group in question was not a ruling class or stratum in interwar Poland and could not force the subsequent governments, both before and after the May 1926 coup d'état, to give in to their demands. The governments usually had in mind the diverse interests of the various social groups and remembered the delicate social balance in a country so economically backward and burdened with so many problems. Of course, the large estate owners cannot be denied as having had some influence on government decisions, but this influence should not be overestimated.

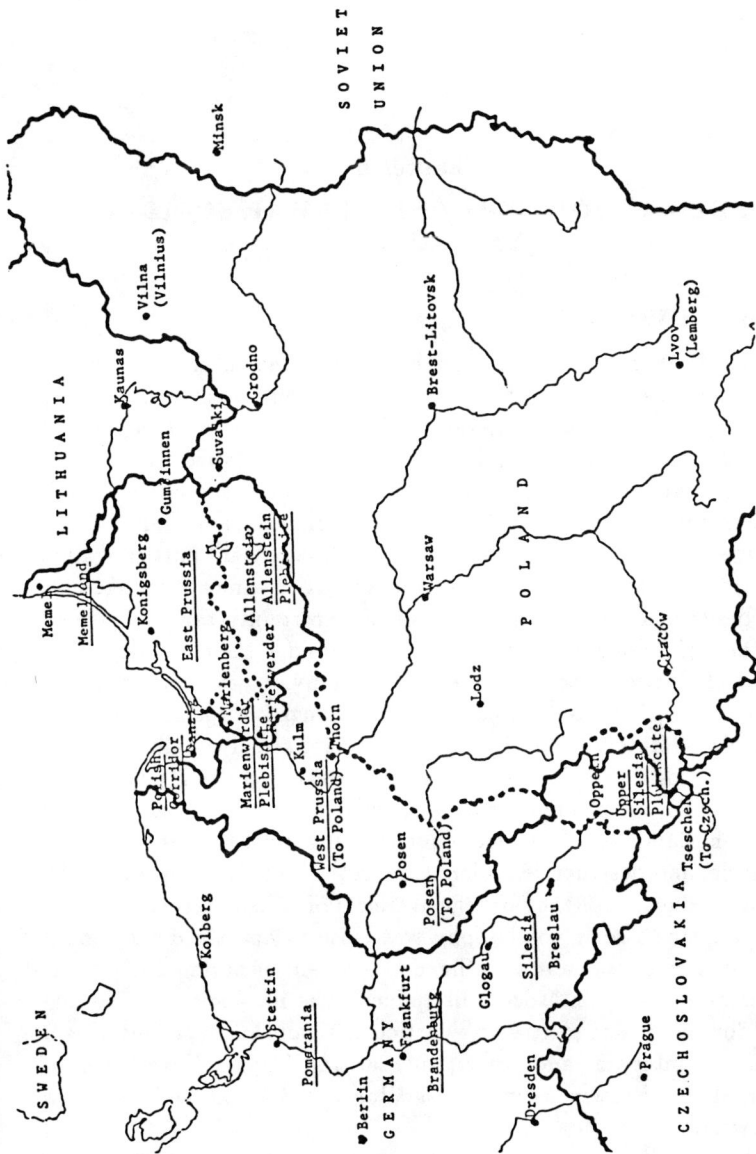

POLAND 1918-1939

Chapter 6

THE LANDOWNERS IN INTERWAR SOCIETY AND CULTURE

Ideas and Values

World War II brought about the political and cultural advance of new social classes, mainly the peasants, who demanded redistribution of large state lands and questioned the historical role of the landed gentry. More or less radical intelligentsia, who followed the socialist credo of Józef Piłsudski's political bloc, supported the popular challenge to the economic and political predominance of the landowners. At the end of World War I, the offensive by the peasant parties against the large estates created among the landlords an atmosphere like that in a besieged fortress. The tension and uncertainty caused by these radical attacks made the landowners reconsider their identity. The effects of this reevaluation were varied. Individual viewpoints could be found ranging from rejection of any thought of social reforms to more a moderate view accepting the need for social equality.

The most radical conservative landowners were ready to oppose any idea of social change. Some of them kept repeating that they still were "an island amidst the sea of ignorance, amidst the depths of controversial and destructive undercurrents."[1] Józef Tyszkiewicz was an outright advocate of the "beneficial effects of [a] counterrevolution."[2] Leon Sapieha's social philosophy was close to apartheid.[3] Zygmunt Broel–Plater of Białaczów outlined a program of nationalist monarchism based on strict social discipline.[4] The ideology of a "special role" for the landed gentry was particularly popular in the older generation of interwar landowners, such as Jan Hupka, Karol Kruzenstern, Michał Korwin–Szymanowski, Jan Lutoaławski, and Stanisław Żórawski.[5]

Not all the conservative landowners were representatives of this kind of extremism. The longtime chairman of the Warsaw Landowners' Society, Jan Stecki, noticed that "an inevitable and by all means desirable social and political advance of the culturally handicapped strata took the shape of a violent attack on the existing legal and social order." But he was of the opinion that it was up to the landowners to prove that "when they are gone, the most zealous workers, the most competent, enlightened, and noble citizens will disappear."[6] Kazimierz Fudakowski, who for many years was chairman of the Supreme Council of Landowners' Organizations, stressed that "the Polish landed gentry has long ago ceased to be a politically privileged stratum, but, settled in the countryside and dealing with farming, has constituted the foundation of culture in our agricultural and rural relations." "Conscious of its own past mistakes," he went on elsewhere, "the Polish landed gentry should present its own ideas and values in our public life."[7]

These opinions echoed the atmosphere of the bastion under attack. Some of the landowners tried to argue that the only way out of this siege was to prove the usefulness of the landed gentry in social activities. For instance, in July 1922 a congress of young landowners adopted a resolution stressing that the masses had gained control of the government but, because of long-term discrimination, they lacked adequate education and political experience. The congress saw the only chance of healing Polish public life in the engagement of all enlighted groups, the landed gentry included, in the social and political work of the reborn state. The young landowners were encouraged to develop various social activities, but first of all to raise the economic standards of their estates, so that they could become true centers of culture in the countryside.[8]

In 1925 the First Congress of Organized Polish Landowners resolved that each member of the landowners' societies was obliged to participate in some social activity, particularly in his own county, and that this participation would be controlled by the societies. The idea of Tadeusz Łubieński of Zassów that the landowners should cooperate with small farmers in defense of the common interest of agriculture was accepted.[9] These resolutions bear the marks of the traditional noble principle "noting about us without us" and of a modern brand of paternalism.

The suggested cooperation with the peasantry developed for better or worse in various parts of the country. In general the post–World War I peasant radicalism gradually became more moderate. In Greater Poland peasants were usually called "farmers" and their relationship with the manors was one of tolerance or even respect.[10]

On the other hand, where Polish landlords faced non-Polish peasants things were more complicated. The tense relationship between Polish landowners and the local peasantry frequently ended in murders of the landed gentry the moment the Soviet Army entered Eastern Poland in September 1939. This was, for instance, the case of Michał Krasinski, the Skirmuntt family, and Hubert Lubomirski of Aleksandria, who were butchered by peasant gangs with the consent of the Soviets.

At the end of the 1930s, the ideology of the landowners was still generally based on the idea of the common interest of agriculture and the special role of large owners as supporters of religious faith and culture in the countryside. This ideology was clearly expressed during the pilgrimage of about 5,000 landowners to the "Black Madonna" sanctuary of Jasna Góra in Częstochowa in March 1938.[11] Eugeniusz Kłoczowski advocated the idea of the landed gentry as "officers of the agricultural army." He also stated that the past role of the landed gentry would not return, but that "an even brighter future is ahead of us . . . if the national culture produced by the landed gentry is absorbed by the whole people."[12]

All this does not mean that the landowners' opinions in interwar Poland were uniform. There were numerous exceptions, not only of rightist extremism, but also of a popular ideology. Emeryk Hutten-Czapski supported the idea that landowners were the supporters of culture in the countryside, but he also accepted the fact that "the foundation of farming in Poland is and will be the peasant farm." The above-mentioned Tadeusz Łubieński of Zassów was a real *enfant terrible* of Polish landowners. He predicted that "the nobility will have to share the land with the peasants" and noticed that the "social work" of the landed gentry was frequently a cover-up for the landowners' desire to control the peasants.[13] The younger generation of landowners more and more frequently accepted the idea that farmers, large or small, would have to become entrepreneurs and that differences in their social backgrounds would gradually diminish as a result of a more equitable distribution of land.[14]

Among the severe critics of the landed gentry was Władysław Grabski, professor of agricultural economy, minister of finance, and the prime minister who carried out the budgetary and monetary reform of 1924. He was descended from a noble family and had an estate at Borowo in Łódź Province, but commented critically on the "idea of estate Poland," which was, in his opinion, still very popular among the landowners in interwar Poland and dangerous to the country's social and economic development. Grabski was of the opinion that it was not important who had land and capital, or which farms were more efficient, but which social group was more dynamic. He thought the peasants offered more potential for expansion than at Borowo in Łódź Province, but commented on the "idea of estate Poland," which was, in his opinion, still very popular among the landowners in interwar Poland and dangerous to the country's social and economic development. Grabski was of the opinion that it was not important who had land and capital, or which farms were more efficient, but which social group was more dynamic. He thought the peasants offered more potential for expansion than landowners and would soon replace them as the dominating social force in Poland.[15] Kajetan Morawski of Jurków in Greater Poland, diplomat and vice-minister of finance, wrote about interwar Poland:

> In this poor country, more agricultural than industrial, in this nation, being a strange mixture of feudalism and revolution, becoming rich was hardly tolerated, and if so, only if connected with public service. Only possession of a piece of land . . . was not objected to among the heirs of many centuries of the noble and peasant tradition.[16]

Although, as we have seen, there were many individual attitudes, the core of the landowners' set of ideas and values was conservatism. Jan Stecki advocated the idea of stagnation of the social world. "The society," he wrote, "never wholly moves forward. It pulls back on the one hand and progresses on the other hand."[17] Kazimierz Fudakowski explained his support for conservatism by the need to stabilize the foundations of social life. Such stabilization of moral principles was, in his opinion, necessary for keeping Poland in Europe. Speaking about the progressives, he expressed the opinion that, with a social utopia in mind, they recognized expropriation, class struggle, and hatred as means, but ultimately accepted them as objectives. He suggested "the sum of benefits acquired by the whole nation" as the final criterion for evaluation of social policies.[18]

"We would not dare," said Jan Bobrzyński, "to repeat after some authors and politicians that parliamentarism is played out. A civilized human being cannot wish it." But at the same time he opposed mob rule and incompetence.[19] Janusz Radziwiłł protested against the identification of conservatism with "reaction." Conservatism, in his opinion, recognized progress and social changes but did not approve of the depreciation of moral values.[20]

Most of the landowners in interwar Poland accepted conservatism in a way similar to Stanisław Estreicher's, who understood it as the defense of the old, historically developed foundations of social life: religious ethics, national consciousness, strong executive power, inviolability of private property, family, and the right of association. "Development should be a continuation of past experience," said Estreicher sententiously.[21] In the eyes of the large owners the connection between conservative values and the role of the landowners seemed obvious: they thought themselves to be the bearers of tradition and the defenders of all values. "The edifice of our national culture," wrote Jan Lutosławski, "pretty scratched up as it is, is maintained in [its] minimum purity and freshness by the country manors first of all."[22]

The landowners' general political attitude was that of loyalty to the government, but their opinion of statism was usually critical. Some of the landowners agreed that in economically backward Poland the government had a significant role to play in the economy. For instance, in 1935 Leon Sapieh stated that "while private initiative declines, it must be replaced by the state."[23] Nevertheless most of the landowners would probably agree with Kazimierz Fudakowski in his criticism of the state–run economy. In his opinion, the "statist spirit of the time" destroyed productivity, income, savings, and capital formation. An entrepreneur was, in his eyes, a target for state bureaucrats, who only wanted to ferret out the source of his income and "shoot it down." Fudakowski observed the "destructive perfection" and the "creative impotence" of socialism. While he supported the idea of a solidarist state, he objected to excessive interference by the government in social life. At the same time he passed a very critical judgment on the individualist tradition in Poland. "Our notorious individualism is mostly nothing else than just the lack of common rules. . . . Most of the enlightened citizens do not hesitate to criticize. . . . They think that speaking up without doing anything is the fulfillment of public duty."[24]

National feelings occupied a prominent place in the landowners' minds. The atmosphere of emotional, or even sugary, patriotism dominated the landladies' organizations. Quite representative of the landowners' nationalism was the resolution of the Congress of Landladies in June 1919:

We demand nothing that is not ours, but Polish souls, Polish households, land, schools, and churches, Polish speech and thought, Polish tombs and crosses and all the legacy of our fathers and grandfathers.[25]

In a country that had regained independence after more than a century of foreign occupation, these feelings were well understood. The national excitement, the slogans of the "Polish National Idea," and the "fluttering of eagles' and angels' wings" were, however, not the only expressions of this nationalism.[26] After all, the patriotic atmosphere of interwar Poland produced a generation capable of resisting the unprecedented onslaught of German and Soviet totalitarianisms after 1939. Landowners played an important role in keeping up this atmosphere.

Of course, this does not mean that the landowners' nationalism was only sweet. Some of the eastern borderland landowners could not help treating their Lithuanian, Byelorussian, and Ukrainian peasants as inferiors and as national enemies. For example, Hipolit Korwin–Milewski was of the opinion that "a Lithuanian is a Pole who feeds geese." Franciszek Qskiera thought all Byelorussian national leaders were paid Bolshevik agents. In his eyes the Polish–Soviet Peace Treaty of Riga in 1921 had not divided Byelorussia but had ceded a "good piece of Polish territory."[27] On the other hand, many local landowners, such as Roman Skirmuntt and Edward Woyniłłowicz would never call their region Poland but Lithuania or Byelorussia and would only favor a federation with Poland. A different example was Janusz Radziwiłł of Ołyka who maintained good relations with the local Unkrainian peasantry; his son Edmund was so popular with them that he was even elected village mayor. Ukrainian peasants also saved the Janusz Radziwiłł family when the Soviet Army entered Volhynia in September 1939.[28]

The intense national feelings of the Polish landowners were sometimes associated with anti–Semitism, which frequently took the shape of an economic struggle. Stefan Górski wrote that "the tendency to be liberated from the Jews and to create our own, strong trade and agriculture is becoming the general objective of all landowners. We cannot afford to lose this struggle."[29] There were cases of landowners advocating hard–core anti–Semitism, for instance in the Legion for the Defense of the Constitution (Legia Obrony Konstytucji). Nevertheless, they were not the rule. Witold Gombrowicz, otherwise a severe critic of the Polish noble tradition, was probably right to describe this phenomenon in the following way:

> The aristocratic anti-Semitism was not dangerous. The "de-
> structive role" of the Jews was condemned, but each noble
> had his own Jew with whom he could talk for hours at the
> porch of his manor house. It was a proof of a long-settled
> coexistence.

According to Gombrowicz, the anti-Semitism of the landowners was
not a reflection of contempt or hatred, but rather the result of un-
skillfullness in overcoming social conventions.[30] In the end it did not
prevent some landowners from marrying rich Jewish girls.

Many German landowners were Protestants, the Russian owners
were Orthodox, and there were also Jewish landowners, while some
of the Polish owners were Protestants, but the majority of the Polish
landowners were Roman Catholics. Catholicism was an important
component of the Polish landowners' world of ideas. Some of the Polish landed gentry, however, treated religion as only a part of tradition.
There were, though, many cases of leading Catholic intellectuals in
landowners' circles. One of them was Władysław Jabłonowski, who
wrote that "Western civilization owes to the Catholic Church not only
the concept of one God . . . but also one law, and one common and
universal morality."[31]

Some of the Catholic authors from among the landowners had
a particularly interesting attitude toward labor. Jadwiga Zamoyska
distinguished three types of work: manual, intellectual, and spiritual.

> The world holds manual work in contempt . . . and does
> not understand spiritual work. . . . Nowadays people seem
> to understand and accept intellectual work only. It does not
> harm their conceit, it even satisfies their pride.

But all the three types of work were, in her opinion, closely intercon-
nected and each type could be performed well only with regard for
the other two.[32]

A specific light may be cast on the spirituality of some landowners
by the *Testament of Władysław Jelski* written for his sons. It included
such instructions as:

> Do not tidy anything up, keep things in order all the time.
> . . . When in conflict with a neighbor put yourself in his
> place to avoid harming him. . . . Beware of pride which
> freezes hearts. . . . You can accomplish all that only given
> the help of Christ the Lord.[33]

Cecylia Plater–Zyberk was a pioneer of Catholic social work in the Polish territories at the end of the nineteenth century. Her work, parallel to that of the most prominent West European Catholic social workers, culminated in the creation of a trade land secondary school in Warsaw. The most outstanding religious writers in interwar Poland included, for instance, Eliżabieta Łubienńska. Father Jacek Woroniecki emphasized the special obligations of the landowners toward their workers and criticized the landowners *vie de chaâteau.*[34]

The Polish landowners' circles produced such outstanding personalities as Archbishop Adam Sapaaieh, a kind of a Polish "inter-rex" during both world wars, Mother Elżbieta Czacka, the founder of the Order of Franciscan Sisters, Servants of the Cross and of the Laski center for the blind near Warsaw, Father Bernard Łubieński, a missionary to the poor, the blessed sisters Urszula and Maria Teresa Ledóchowski, Antoni Marylski, and many others.[35] These spiritual leaders of Polish Catholicism enriched its traditional, national, and popular character not only with deep mysticism but also with practical social values. This kind of apostolate largely affected the formation of the Association of Catholic Academic Youth "Renaissance" (Stowarzyszenie Katolickiej Młodzieży Akademickiej, Odrodzenie), animated to a great extent by the young landowners Jan Czartoryski, Kazimierz Dzieduszycki, Tomasz Rostworowski, Michał Sobański, and others.[36] In fact, the Polish landed gentry played an important role in making Polish Catholicism both more meditative and popular than before.

The Landowners' "Way of Life"

The consumption levels of the landowners are very difficult to estimate because of the lack of reliable statistics, the variety of forms of consumption, as well as the blurring of differences between pure consumption, investments, and social charity. Moreover, the then consumption was, especially during the Great Depression, financed not only from current incomes but also from reserves and extraordinary revenues.

With regard to the net income estimates presented in this work, as well as to the estimates by Czesław Klarner, it may be assumed that the per capita consumption in landowner families was about 12,000 zloty (1,350 contemporary U. S. dollars) per annum in 1929, about 1,000 zloty in 1935.[37] During the years of prosperity some of the funds for consuming were spent on generally accepted cultural investments, which were then, during the Great Depression, changed into money again. Therefore, it may be assumed that the given estimate should be lowered for 1929 and raised for the 1930s. Anyway, the standard of living of the landowners was about twenty times higher than the average for the whole agricultural population in the 1920s and about eight times higher during the Great Depression.

The standard of living of the landowners was changing all through the twenty–one years of interwar Poland. Soon after World War I the everyday life of the group lost many of its former charm because of the immense war damage and the threat of land redistribution. Anna Fudakowska wrote in 1920:

> The beauty and boasts of our life are fading away—the open manor houses, those holiday gatherings of youngsters, crowds of guests . . . gay hunting or cheerful name–day parties going on for three days.[38]

At the end of the 1920s these times seemed to be returning. Guests filled the reconstructed manor houses. Parties, social gatherings, and trips abroad became more frequent, while some of the landowners could afford to buy still very expensive cars.

The Great Depression put an abrupt end to these entertainments. This was even more painful since the landowners had once more become used to better times. Therefore, being economical was not too easy and many owners lived beyond their means. "My brother," recalled Witold Gombrowicz, "always arrived at the Cafe Lourse in an elegant cab, even if he was quite broke; when forced to save his last penny he used to take the cab round the nearest corner only to get out of it at the Lourse with proper chic."[39] At the end of the 1930s the situation began to improve, but not so much as to recall "the good old days."

The foundation of the landowners' way of life was the manor house.

> Surrounded by circles of lime trees, chestnuts, and populars, with a while–pillar porch, the entrance alley lined with old trees and a rosebed underneath the windows, vested in a mantle of memories and enveloped in the mist of history, the manor house . . . connects the past with the present. Moreover, it is a seat of culture, a civilization center of the Polish countryside.

This image, not far from the truth, was recorded by a lady who came

from such a house, Janina Skarbek–Kruszewska.[40]
Among the manor houses there were both rich palaces and small,
wooden buildings. All of them, however, were surrounded by an atmosphere of tradition and care. Hundreds of manor houses were rated
as valuable historical monuments. At least a few of them should be
mentioned: Nieśwież castle of the Radziwiłł sin Nowogródek Province,
Podhorce castle of the Sanguszkos in Tarnopol Province, Krasiczyn
palace of the Sapiehas near Przemśl, Łańcut palace of the Potockis
also in Lwow Province, Kórnik palace of the Zamoyskis in Greater
Poland, as well as many smaller palaces and manor houses, such as
Lewków of Wojciech Lipski, Żelazków of Józef Radoński, Miłosław
of Władysław Kościelski, and Smordwa of Aleksander Ledóchowski.
Numerous small manor houses, some even of wood, were frequently
monuments of high architectural and historical value.[41]

Food consumption by landowners was usually high in quantity
and quality in view of the availability of food produced on the estates
and the generally high incomes. Of course, there were some differences between the richest aristocratic households and small manor
houses. Diversified meals were, however, a natural part of everyday life and the principle of all social gatherings. In most manor
houses random guests from among the landowners could expect to
be invited to a fashionable lunch or dinner. Parties, organized for
holidays, namedays, or family celebrations, were frequently attended
by dozens of neighbors and other guests from the "sphere." Officers,
and especially cavalrymen, were usually welcome, no matter whether
they were landowners or not. Horses were an element of the economic
activity of large estates but also an object of care, love, and pride for
the landowners. Horse races, stepple chases, and other equestrian
events were an important part of landowners' gatherings. The four
Potockis from Łańcut were the best polo team in Poland.[42]

Hunting was also largely a social activity. Most of the landowners were keen hunters and played a leading role in the Polish hunting organizations. Juliusz Bielski of Raszniów (Tłumacz County)
was the chairman of the Union of the Polish Hunting Associations
(Polski Zwięk Stowarzyszeń Łowieckich), Wojciech Gołuchowski of
Janów (Gródek Jagielloński County) chaired the Polish Hunting Association (Polskie Towarzystwo Łowieckie). The exclusive Hunt Club
(Klub Myśliwski) was a meeting place of the landowner elite. Several
aristrocrats and large landowners, such as Maurycy Zamoyski, Ol-
gierd Czartoryski, Eryk Kurnatowski, Zdzisław Lubomirski, Edward

Krasiński, Henryk Potocki, and Władysław Jerzierski, were among the club's leaders. Large estates were frequently exclusive hunting grounds. That was, for instance, the case of Dzilów or Zdzis aw Tarnowski, Ołyka of Janusz Radziwiłł, Woropajewo of Konstanty Przeździecki, famous for wood grouse and black grouse, Poturzyca of Włodzimierz Dzieduszycki, where wild boars were hunted, as they were on Koropiec of Stefan Badeni and Radziechów of Stanisław Badeni. Pheasants were hunted on Lochów of Eryk Kurnatowski. Extensive, days–long hunts, attended by the political elite of the Polish Republic and many foreign diplomas, were organized on the Nieśwież entail of Albrecht Radziwiłł and on Jabłonna of Maurycy Potocki.[43] Some landowners also published interesting hunting reminiscences.[44]

During several days of hunting on the Dawidgródek entail of Karol Radziwiłł, where the largest herd of elk in Poland lived, more than a dozen hunters would kill almost one hundred wild boar and many other game animals. The Mankiewicze palace, the main residence of the Dawidgródek entail, was but a few miles from the Polish–Soviet border, at the confluence of the rivers Olchowa and Horyń. The heir to the entail used a motorboard to show his guests around his exotic domains: the Lubochnia and Straszny Bór (Fearsome Forest) ranges, remote backwoods and islands amid vast marshes, and the lairs of wild animals. The island of Prystyń in the entail was inhabited by a British general, Carton de Wiart. Otherwise, the entail had only few regular villages and some scattered settlements of lumbermen and distillers. The twentieth century and its technical civilization must have seemed far away.[45]

The knightly tradition of honor, still very strong among the Polish landed gentry, was gradually changing its form. Although several instances of duelling were recorded in the interwar period, pressure by the Catholic Church and democratic public opinion reduced the option of solving personal conflicts by bloodshed. The idea of courts of honor prevailed, advocated by, among others, Kazimierz Chłapowski and the League for the Defense of Honor and Dignity (Liga Obrony Czci i Honoru). It was more and more frequently thought, however, that an insult brought dishonor to the insulter rather than to the insulted.[46]

After all, interwar Poland was in the twentieth century. Luxurious consumption by the better-off landowners also included tourism. Jerzy Potocki hunted in India, Canada, Sudan, and Eritrea. Kajetan Czarkowski–Golejewski piloted an airplane from Italy through Turkey, Iran, and India to Thailand, which was a rather astounding trip at that time. Alfred Potocki toured most of the world except for Australia and South America, Janusz Radziwiłł of Ołyka was one of the leaders of the Polish Yacht Club, while Michał Scipio del Campo, a Polish landowner of Italian origin was one of the pioneers of Polish aviation.[47] European trips were undertaken even by many landowners who were not so well off.

Motoring became the favorite entertainment for landowners, Ksawery Drucki–Lubecki was the first chairman of the Polish Motoring Association, while Karol Raczyński chaired the Automobilklub Polski. The leading landowner drivers included Albrecht Radziwiłł , Maurycy Polocki, Kazimierz Dziewanewski, Stanisław Lubomirski, Aleksander Ledóchowski, Antoni Potocki, and Roman Sanguszko. At that time it was not cheap. Jan Krystyn Ostrowski of Ujazd calculated that one mile in his Essex Super Lux 1928 cost him about eight times more than the same trip by train.[48] Therefore, especially during the Great Depression, only the richest landowners could afford to drive a car.

It must be stressed that the standard of consumption by the landowners was as varied as the size of their incomes or their estates. The most extravagant consumption was not typical for more than a dozen or so richest families. Alfred Potocki of Łańcut spent half of the time abroad dropping money in Europe, North America, and Africa. The owner of the Nieśwież entail, Albrecht Radziwiłł , had a palace in Warsaw that cost him about 27,000 zloty (3,300 U. S. dollars) per annum in the 1930s. Janusz Radziwiłł had a palace in Nieborów near Warsaw as well as another in Warsaw and Ołyka palace in Volhynia. Other fashionable Warsaw residences included the Warsaw villas and palaces of Zdzisław Lubomirski, Maurycy Zamoyski, and the Natolin palace of Helena Potocka.[49]

Although this standard of consumption was nothing extraordinary for the American and West European business elites, in a poor and barely rebuilt Poland it raised objections and criticism. Even the National Democratic press, generally sympathetic to the large estates, condemned prodigal hunting in Africa or card losses of thousands of dollars.[50] Of course, each zloty eaten up in this way was a waste for the Polish economy, but ultimately there were not too many cases of this kind.

The average standard of living for a landowner family should not be seen in the context of the luxury of the Łańcut palace. Apart from the richer half of the landowners, living in comfortable manor houses with running water, electricity, many bathrooms, and other facilities, lots of landowners, especially in the eastern borderland, did not have water and and power supplies and frequently had problems with making ends meet. The availability of radio, telephones, and cars in country manor houses was generally no higher than in urban households of comparable income. Visiting a doctor, attending school, and going to cultural events required longer trips or having a second home in a town, and only a small percentage of landowners could afford that. Economizing was especially widespread in the 1930s.[51] Apart from the striking luxury of the richest elite, most of the landowners were better off than an average Pole, but they were not rolling in money.

The Promotion of Arts and Science

Many palaces and manor houses in interwar Poland had rich collections of documents, historical artifacts, and works of art, gathered for many generations. Some of these collections were seriously damaged during World War I but still maintained a high historical and artistic value. For instance, in 1924 the Nieśwież entail collection was reevacuated from Soviet Russia: it included paintings, documents, coins, tapestries, weapons, and even suits of armor estimated at about 212,000 gold rubles. Albrecht Radziwiłł kept the original copy of the Union of Lublin of 1569 in the Kresiński Library in Warsaw, where it was lost during the 1944 Warsaw Rising. The subsequent fate of this precious document is still not exactly clear.[52]

Almost every manor house had family collections and libraries. Some of the richest aristocrats had extensive collections of old books and documents. This was, for instance, the case of the Nieborów Library of Janusz Radziwiłł , the Tarnowski Library in Sucha, the above–mentioned Krasiński Library, the Samoyski Library in Warsaw, and many others. The library and art collection at Rogalin of Roger Raczyński was also open to the public. Jadwiga and Władysław Zamoyski willed their Kórnik palace and library to the Polish nation. Many smaller residences were also seats of valuable collections. For instance, a rather average manor house at Susk Stary near Ostrołęka, rebuilt after damage in World War I, had a rich library carefully selected by Jan Glinka, whose uncle, Franciszek Fiszer, was a popular humorist and philosopher.[53]

Landowners played an outstanding role in supporting various cultural institutions and activities. This role was particularly important at the beginning of reborn Poland, when most of these institutions had to be reconstructed or created anew. For instance, the Central School of Rural Economy (Szkoła Główna Gospodarstwa Wiejskiego), founded in October 1918, was financially supported from the beginning by MichałSobański, Włodzimierz Czartoryski, Antoni Wieniawski, Marian Kiniorski, and Juliusz Tarnowski. In 1927 the school was bequeathed by the Debowice estate of Wacław Highersberger.

Stanisław Hupka of Broniszów endowed a foundation for economic studies with 500,000 Austrian crowns in 1919. Zofia Popiel maintained a school of home economics for country girls in Ruszcza in the years 1916–1921. Thanks to a group of landladies, including Wanda Czartoryska, a trade school for girls was started in Snopków. A similar school in Liskow was financed by the landowners of the Kalisz region, headed by Ludomił Pułaski, in Mieczysławow by Mieczysław Kretkowski, and in Niegłos by Kazimierz Dziewanowski.[54]

The Catholic University of Lublin was founded largely thanks to the support of various landowner families. One of its chief sponsors was Karol Jaroszy ński, a man who had made a fortune in Russia in 1917, lost most of it during the Bolshevik revolution and invested the rest in the university. Other sponsors included Jerzy Moszczyński, Antoni Rostworowski, Stanisław Wessel, he Czertwertyńskis, the Kleniewskis, and the Kowerskis. Aniela Potulicka endowed the university with her whole property, estimated at 6,000,000 zloty (675,000 U. S. dollars).[55]

August Cieszkowski of Wierzenica in Greater Poland, the son of the famous philosopher, bequeathed his estate of Żabików to Poznań University in 1919. The same university received the Laski estate from its founder and first rector, Heliodor Święcicki. Joanna Umiastowska bequeathed her Żemosław estate to Wilno University, Wanda and Zenon Suszycki left their estate at Boguchwała and Latorycz to the Jagiellon University in Cracow. Large book collections were donated to the Ossolineum library and research centers and Lwow University by Adam Czartoryski and Stanisław Badeni, while Albin Rayski left his estates in Michalewice to the Ossolineum. Jakub Potocki of Osieck bequeathed his estates to a foundation for treating tuberculosis and other diseases.[56]

At least a brief mention must be made of the creative role of landowners in Polish interwar culture. Although there were many other attitudes, the Polish cultural life before World War I was strongly influenced by two competing traditions. The radical "progressives" challenged the national and Catholic tradition cherished by the landowners. The climax of this dispute came with Stanisław Brzozowski's criticism of Henryk Sienkiewicz's traditional, patriotic novels. In the interwar years both sides in the conflict evolved. The social and political progressives ceased to be quite so radical, their ambitions being partly institutionalized in the *sanacja* government. They even produced their own self-critics. On the other hand the traditional and conservative circles more and more seriously acknowledged the need for the cultural improvement of the peasants and workers.

Fairly typical of this trend were the novels by Maria Rodziewicz-ówna, who was born to a landowner family in the eastern borderland. Her parents had been deported to Siberia for patriotic activities and had died soon after returning home. Since 1885 she had written at the small estate of Hruszowa in Polesie. In many bestseller novels she presented the hardships, sacrifices, and virtues of the Polish borderland gentry, but also cited their many faults and failures in their relations with the country folk. With naive didacticism she advocated the Positivist "organic work" for the nobles in the countryside.[57] Despite severe criticism of her works by post-World War II writers, the everlasting popularity of her novels is proof of the demand for values in the Polish social life.

The interwar landowners celebrated the forty years of literary work by Józef Weyssenhoff, a descendant of Polonized Livonian German knights. He lived and wrote on the estate called, ironically, Samoklęski (Polish: "Disasters Only") in Lublin Province. His attitude toward noble and aristocratic tradition was more critical than that of Henryk Sienkiewicz, especially in the novel *Syn marnotrawy* (*Prodigal Son*, 1904). Later his criticism of the landed gentry was moderated and he described the charms of their life. Weyssenhoff, who was a master stylist, expressed the opinion that the large landowners defects—not worse than those of other social groups—had been ridiculed by "demagogues and writers of musicals," although the group had also played a constructive role.[58]

There was also Witold Gombrowicz, who was born into a landowners's family. His association with the group was, however, psychologically more complicated. Since his father had come into conflict with the local circle of landowners, this writer tended to parody the landowners' world in the same way that he caricatured other elements of Polish traditionalism. In his opinion, the landowners lived

> a facilitated life. . . . For my father a servant was a natural phenomenon. . . . Simple folk caught this naturalness and were much more eager to bustle about him than about us [the younger generation—author's note], the compulsive master, trying to make the best of bad bargain.

Nevertheless, there was quite a lot of noble self–esteem beneath his witty sarcasm.[59]

There was a big group of popular authors with strong roots in the landed gentry. Melchior Wańkowicz covered the various social and political problems of interwar Poland with a sharply critical eye but with some sympathy for the group. Zofia Kossak started her literary career with Pożoga (*Ravage*), the famous report on the destruction of the eastern borderland gentry during the Russian civil war. Gabariela Zapolska, born as Maria Korwin–Piotrowska into a rich gentry family, had been forced to marry someone she did not love. She left home and started a career as an actress writer. It was no wonder that she was a harsh critic of the landowners.

Orphaned as a young girl, the poetess Kazimiera Iłłakowiczowna was brought up in aristocratic circles in Polish Latgalia. Some of her poems were full of nostalgia for the "good old days" of the borderland gentry. The landowners also produced the Hulewicz brothers: Witold was a writer and journalist, while Jerzy wrote expressionist novels and painted. The philosophers Marian Zdziechowski and Adam Żółtowski, as well as the historian Kazimierz Morawski and many other scholars, were also closely connected with the landed gentry.

Several landowners organized literary and artistic salons on their estates. Probably the best known of these meeting places was the Pławowice manor house of playwright Ludwik Hieronim Morstin, where the most outstanding poets met other writers and artists, including members of the owner's family: Maria Morlstin–Górska and Zofia Starowieyska–Morstinowa. A mere description of the most outstanding names and talents is not enough to demonstrate the cultural role of the landowners. It must be realized that most of the manor houses played the de facto role of local cultural centers. Sometimes these centers were closed meeting places of the artistic or gentry elites, but quite frequently they were open to the wider public.

Social Charity

Some of the landowners' incomes were neither in investments nor spent for personal consumption but used for various social charitable purposes. The range of the group's involvement in financing commonly accepted material needs of the other social classes is very difficult to measure. On the balance sheet of the Turna manor of Kazimierz Popiel the entries under "charity" accounted for about 2 percent of labor cost in the years 1929/30-1934/35.[60] In 1922/23 Ferdynand Radziwiłł used about 5 percent of the expenditures of the Ołykaentail for charity, while his son Janusz spent about 4 percent of the revenues of his estate in Nieborów and about 1 percent in Czumań.[61] The Turna manor was not one of the richest in Poland, but it was otherwise known that not only the richest owners felt obliged to engage in charitable actions. According to a very approximate estimate, these undertakings were supported by about half of the landowners in interwar Poland.[62] All in all, it may be estimated that the funds spent by landowners on social charity, the greatest sums after World War I and in the late 1930s, oscillated between 1 and 2 percent of the cost of labor, that is between 5 and 10,000,000 zloty per annum.

The charity of the landowners was particularly developed in the first years after World War I. As early as October 1918 a group of landowners from the Raciąż region started collecting funds for the Polish army and the National Treasury (Skarb Narodowy).[63] In January 1919 Edward Plater-Zyberk of Osuchów donated 30,000 Polish marks to national goals, while in the summer of 1919 Józefa Potocka made a donation of 5,000 hectares in Pińsk and Nowogródek counties for colonization by Polish and Byelorussian soldiers fighting in the ranks of the Polish army.[64] Adam Stadnicki of Nawojowa and Alfred Potocki of Łańcut also offered land for colonization purposes.

The Polish army in Greater Poland was financed from funds raised by the landowners of Poznań Province, such as Bogday Szembek, who founded a supply base for an infantry regiment in Wysock.[65] Tarnowski of Dzilków financed a detachment of volunteers commanded by his son Arthur.[66] At the same time, Lublin landowners raised 100,000 Austrian crowns for three regiments of the Polish army and the Warsaw Landowners' Society collected considerable sums for the

Polish insurgents in Upper Silesia.[67] In 1919 Stanisław Godlewski of Luszyn founded a committee of Polish farmers to raise funds for field hospitals. The committee included Ludwik Czetwertyński and Maria Rodziewiczówna, while the committee's 150–bed hospital was managed by Maria Tarnowska. Another hospital was founded in Nieśwież in 1920. Izabela Radziwiłł, the wife of the heir to the Dawidgródek entail, was the superior of the Maltese Orders's hospitals in Poland.[68] The list of landowners who donated substantial sums for vairous social and national purposes is very long. Adam Ledóchowski presented land for veterans' colonization on Chorostów and Stanisław Czacki did the same on Wolica in Volynia. Funds for a "social grain action" were raised by Lublin, Puławy, Opatów,and Sieradz landowners in 1922. Large estate owners also offered significant aid to Polish repatriates from Russia, who usually returned without sufficient means for survival, being underfed, sick and broken by the horrors of the Bolshevik revolution.[69]

Aleksander Skarbek donated 8,000 hectares to the Polish state. Aleksander Chomiński of Olszewo in Wilno Province founded a school for country children, which was taken over by the state in 1919. Schools and day nurseries were established by Witold Czartoryski in Pełkinie, Jan Kalenkiewicz in Trokieniki, Stanisław Łoś in Desxna, Stanisław Mańkowski in Kazimierz Biskupi, Jajetan Piechowski in Luboradz, Marian Kiniorski in Suchodębie, Roman Sanguszko in Gumniska, Juliusz Tarnowski in Sucha, and many others.[70] Maurycy Zamoyski, Edward Raczyński, Alfred Chłapowski, Eustachy Sapieha, and Jerzy Potocki covered some of the expendituares of the Polish delegations in Paris, London, and Rome.

The trade school, workshops, and chapel for the blind in Laski near Warsaw, at an amazing religious center founded by Mother Elżbieta Róża Czacka, were supported by her two brothers, Tadeusz Czacki in Pieniaki and Stanisław Czacki of Poryck. The land for the school was donated by Antoni Daszewski, while Katarzyna Branicka gave 300,000 zloty to the Society for the Protection of the Blind (Towarzystwo Opieki nad Ociemniałymi), which managed the school with Mother Czack's nuns.[71]

Many landowners financed the building or reconstruction of local churches. Józafat Budny founded the church in Rejowiec, as did Stefan Swieżawi in Dołhobyczów, Kajetan Piechowski in Dziektarzew, Kamil Pourbaix in Antonówka, Albrecht Radziwiłł in Świrynów, Adam Stecki in Mię dzyrzecz Korzecki, and Antoni Lanckoroński in Muchawka and Rosochacz. Landowners' donations to church activities can be found on many ledgers of the large estates.

Stimulated by the recommendations of their societies, many landowners took part in various other social actions. In 1931/32 they gathered 24,000 tons of grain for the unemployed and in 1932/33 a further 11,000 tons.[72] In July 1936 the Supreme Council of Landowners' Organizations resolved to raise a special fund in the amount of 10 percent of the land-value tax to support creation of the Fund for National Defense (Fundusz Obrony Narodowej, or FON). The target sum was estimated at 1,600,000 zloty. Similar action was soon undertaken by the Union of Agricultural Chambers and Organizations of the Polish Republic. Landowners from Poznań, Nowogródek, Wilno, and Volhynia provinces were the quickest to respond to this appeal. Jewish landowners also joined in.[73] By March 1938 the landowners' organizations had gathered 1,100,000 zloty for FON and about 800,000 liters of liquor for the army. In 1939 landowner circles joined other classes of Polish society in subscribing to the air force loan and in financing supplies for the army.[74]

The generosity of the landowners sprang from several different causes. In some cases bequeathments were due to an absence of heirs, while other endowments were made to avoid other public charges. Sometimes charitable activities were undertaken under pressure by other landowners who cultivated the tradition of a special, paternal role in society. Too, a not insignificant religious motivation msut be recognized: because most of the Polish landowders were Christians, no matter how dearly they cared for their lands and incomes, they frequently remembered the Christian principle that those who had been given more were expected to give more themselves.

Landowners as Seen by Other Social Groups

A characteristic Polish interwar society was the way the polite title *pan* "gentlemen" was used. Originally *pan* meant noble master of an estate. Gradually the term was more and more often widely applied to the intelligentsia and burghers, but was not widespread among the popular masses. The peasants addressed each other with the polite *wy* ("you") or, more familiarly by using the first name. They would, of course, address a landowner or a burgher as *pan*—but the latter would never think of doing the same in return. He would say *wy*, or use the third person singular or the first name. Among high society *pan* would not be enough: here it was also important who was simply a *pan* or a *pan doktor*, *pan professor*, or *pan hrabia* "count"). The importance of the manner address, which could even be called title–mania, tells a lot about the postfeudal nature of Polish society at the beginning of the twentieth century.

The social behavior of the Polish aristocrats and landowners was a combination of "lordiliness" and practical paternalism. A couple of examples may well illustrate such attitudes. When Mrs. Rothschild asked Prince Dominik Radziwiłł of Balice if he knew an impoverished Polish aristocrat about to take the position of doorman at her house, he replied: "Yes, I do know many, but I would not recommend that you engage such a man. Your guests would stop at the door and forget that they came to visit you." [75] A "lordly" attitude was typical of Maurycy Zamoyski, who was not easily pleased by the "international high life," but did respect the values in everybody. [76]

Prince Witold Czartoryski of Pełkinie, who treated hisestates as a "tendency of the historic tradition of the Commonwealth" rather than as his personal property, encouraged his sons to learn crafts, and knew how to communicate with the peasants, even during the peasant strike of 1939, and was death to snobs. The "red prince" Jan Sapieha of Spusza frequently drove his servants to the movies in Grodno. [77] Władysław Zamoyski of Kórnik was well known for ascetic frugality and bequeathed his estates to the Polish nation. On the other hand, the memoirs of Alfred Potocki of Łań cut are a rare example of snobbery. [78] The attitudes of the rank–and–file landowners were a similar mixture of pride and noble "populism."

We have already seen the various ways in which the landowners perceived themselves. Let us now have a quick look at the perception of other social groups. Since they frequently came from the landed gentry and were financially supported by them, the Catholic clergy traditionally supported the landowners. But in the interwar years more and more peasant sons joined the ranks of the priesthood, while priest intellectuals took a more critical attitude toward social inequality. Typical of the latter attitude was Reverend Jan Piwowarczyk, who thought the land reform to be a social necessity and argued with adherents of the thesis that "the cause of the Kingdom of God in Poland" required the retaining of large estates. Piwowarczyk wondered why the landowners should be better fit for heaven than the peasants. [79] The already mentioned declaration by the Social Council of the Primate of Poland in 1937, concerning land reforms, is another confirmation of the changing attitude of the Catholic Church in Poland toward the role of the landowners.

The civil bureaucracy was a varied social group. Some of the state officials came from the petty nobility, while others were burghers' or peasants' sons. The upper strata of the civil service frequently purchased country manors and followed the landowners' way of life out of sheer snobery. But since many of the *sanacja* bureaucracy had gone through socialist, radical "progressive," and democratic organizations, they were quite often very unsympathetic toward the landed gentry tradition. For instance, Tadeusz Ulanowski attacked the landowners as a "legion of the blind and the deaf to any government action to redistribute land."[80] The writer Maria Dąbrowska, a representative of the radical intelligentsia, aimed a lot of bitter words at the landowners; for her, the interests of millions of peasants were always more important and more appealing than those of thousands of large landowners.[81]

Better-off peasants were rather neutral on the idea of land redistribution. A medium-size holder from Witów expressed this attitude in the follow way: "I am not fishing for what is not mine. What I got I made by my own hard work and I don't want to grow rich at someone's expense."[82] Much more radical were smallholders and landless peasants. According to Wincenty Witos, they perceived the manors as "the symbol of a former serfdom." But Witos went on to say:

> Whether they cherished a dream of vengeance or only great pain and bitterness—that I cannot really judge. To be sure, the peasants wanted the manor land but they did not want it for free. . . . The well-known peasant diffidence and the inviolate dogma of private property played a very important role.[83]

The attitude of the most radical peasants and socialists was perhaps well expressed by Czesław Bobrowski who suggested "erasing the noble landowner class from the surface of Polish life." In his opinion, only such an operation against the "vegetative viewpoint" would make possible a "new creativity."[84] This idea was, in fact, very close to the communist point of view: despite the marginal role of the Communists in interwar Poland, their dispute over the existence of large estates is worth quoting. Some of the Polish Communist leaders in Soviet Russia, such as Feliks Dzierżyński, thought it necessary to parcel out large estates among the peasants, at least temporarily, in order to attract them to the idea of the Bolshevik revolution. On the other hand, Julian Marchlewski and others argued that such a redistribution would decrease food supplies and make the goal of "socialization" of land even more difficult.[85]

It seems clear that the attitudes of various classes in Polish interwar society toward the landowners were very diverse. Even among the landless peasants the distaste for the "lords" was accompanied by a special kind of fascination. To sum up thes observations, an inquiry concerning social heirarchy and prestige in interwar Poland may be quoted. Its author, Rajmund Buławski, distributed twenty-five questionnaires among each of the fifteen social groups that he had identified, and asked everybody to present his own ranking of social prestige. The results were strikingly convergent. The top position was taken by "the large landowners" with an average of 1.8, the second place by the industrialists and commercial businessmen with 2.2, the third by the public servants with 3.4, and the fourth by the free professions with an average of 4.0. The clergy took sixth place, the peasants tenth place, and domestic servants took the bottom ranking.[86]

Chapter 7

EPILOGUE

Generally speaking, interwar Poland was a country of relatively high concentration of landed property, but the proportions were not much different from other Eastern and Central European countries. The share of large private estates in the total area of Germany, Austria, Hungary, as well as Spain, Portugal, and Italy, was similar or even higher. With a considerable share of land in the hands of large landowners, the Polish peasant farms were at the same time relatively fragmented. The high concentration of landed property on the one hand, and fragmentation on the other hand, may, but does not necessarily, mean economic backwardness. The case of the Netherlands, where farms were usually very small and agriculture very efficient, could be an illustration of the opposite. Nevertheless, given the historical backwardness of Polish agriculture, this disproportional ownership structure and rural overpopulation were obstacles to economic progress.

From the economic point of view, the existence of the large private estates in Poland seemed, however, quite justified and useful. With lower labor and capital inputs they gave higher yields and returns than small holdings, supplied the army and urban markets with foodstuffs and were an important pillar of the budget and exports. If all large private estates had been liquidated, exports of about 100,000,000 zloty (11,000,000 U. S. dollars) would have been lost and Poland would have become a net grain importer. Since large estates were also characterized by higher gross returns, their liquidation would have limited the home market for industrial goods, while the inevitable increase in agricultural prices would have stimulated an increase in the cost of living, of wages, and production costs in Polish industry. The budget would have lost an important source of tax revenues. All these effects could have been counterbalanced by the acquisition of land by the peasants, but that should not be overestimated. Some of the Central and Eastern European countries that carried out radical land reforms in the interwar period, such as Czechoslovakia and Romania, faced serious problems and a decline in the capacity of their markets. Poland would probably have shared their fate.

The cultural role of the landowners must also be mentioned. Although some of them cared only for their property and incomes, the majority of Polish interwar landowners played an important role in the agricultural societies and farmers's circles, while their estates were frequently centers for advanced agricultural technology. The manor houses were traditional centers of the countryside cultural life, while their owners frequently sponsored social and cultural activities.

Nevertheless, the economic and cultural aspects were not the only parts of the problem. Polish interwar agriculture inherited an overpopulation estimated at 3 to 5,000,000 people, which was the result of a long historical process going back to the spread of the villein and estate economy in the late Middle Ages. No doubt, small holdings could employ more people per hectare of agricultural land than the large estates, while millions of landless peasants were waiting for land. The question was whether even the total liquidation of all the large estates could solve the land hunger. Here serious doubts arise. A thorough study carried out by the Institute of Social Economy in Warsaw at the end of the 1930s concluded that the total area required to make the "redundant" peasants economically self–sufficient amounted to about 7,700,000 hectares. At the same time, the whole reservoir of agricultural land available from an entire redistribution of all private and even public large estates was a mere 4,600,000 hectares.[1]

The significance of these data is pessimistic: even the most radical reform could have only partly solved the rural overpopulation problem while simultaneously diminishing the market supply, causing serious troubles in industry, finance, and the balance of trade. With these conclusions in mind, we should not stick to simplistic stereotypes. The predominance of the efficiency of small farms in animal husbandry must be remembered. Moreover, all the previous conclusions were drawn from average data, but there were not only efficient large estates and backward peasant farms. Sometimes it was the opposite: many large estates were neglected or run from outside, while small farms were better cared for. The Polish interwar situation is not proof of a universal rule of the superiority of large estates over small farms. In different natural, social, and property conditions small farms might prove to be economically viable.

It is also not exactly true what Jan Stecki wrote about the Polish interwar agriculture: "The society and the state are not very particular whether the same ton of grain is produced by twenty people instead of fifteen."[2] Jerzy Ciechomski also noticed only one side of the problem when he said that "efficiency and not the labor factor determine the output growth."[3] These purely economic theses would be right if not for the huge overpopulation problem of interwar Poland. The state simply had to be particular about the growing tension among the landless peasant community and to do something about it. In fact, the economic and social aspects of Polish interwar agriculture were in conflict, so any policy had to be aimed at minimizing any negative effects of the existing situation and the introduced changes.

The destruction of the large private estates in Poland reached the final stage in 1939. Estates situated east of the Ribbentrop–Molotov line were taken over by the Soviet authorities. All their owners who survived the invasion of the Red Army and the purges connected with it, were, according to formal Soviet instructions, subject to arrest and deportation. Only a few landowners avoided this fate. The best known example was Janusz Radziwiłł and his family, reclaimed from the NKVD by the King of Italy. Otherwise, landowners suffered the same horrors of many weeks in terrible jails, eastward journeys in freight cars, and starvation in camps and forced settlement areas. This was, for instance, the fate of Maria Kossakowska of Wielka Brzostowica and her daughters Ludwika Niemcewicz and Anna Mineyko with their children, Jan Strawiński, Władysław Komar, Władysław Serwatowski and families, Juliusz Bielski, Eugeniusz Lubomirski, Zdzisław Tyszkiewicz, and hundreds of others. Most of them died in the Soviet Union; many landowners were killed by the NKVD in the Katyn Forest.[4]

West of the Ribbentrop–Molotov line, the situation of landowners was varied. In the so–called General Gouvernement the Nazis left the large private estates in the hands of their owners but introduced a system of food requisitions and control. The western provinces of interwar Poland, such as Upper Silesia, Poznania, and Pomerania, were incorporated into the Reich. Polish landowners were gradually removed and their estates were expropriated by the German authorities, while the owners, such as Marian Kiniorski and Jan Lipski, were deported to the General Gouvernement. Many prominent landowners, such as Mieczysław Chłapowski, Jan Donimirski, Stanisław Karłowski, Edward Poniński, Edward Potworowski, and Jan Szołdrski, were killed in special public executions that were meant to terrorize the Polish population of the incorporated areas in late 1939. Many other landowners who participated in the Polish resistance perished in Nazi prisons and concentration camps. This was, for example, the case of Adolf Bniński, Stefan Gorski, and Juliusz Trzciński. Edward Krasiński of Opinogóra stood up for a young farmhand beaten by the Gestapo, was sent to Dachau, and killed.

During the Nazi occupation many landowners, especially in the General Gouvernement, supported Polish resistance activities or even joined the Home Army. This was, for example, the case of Edmund Radziwiłł Janusz Radziwiłłof Ołyka. Some landowners, such as Maurycy Potocki of Jabłonna, who had shown no particular interest in social affairs between the wars, made use of their personal contacts with the Nazi officials to help the Polish underground. Adam Ronikier and Janusz Machnicki were the leaders of the Supreme Charity Council (Rada Główna Opiekuńcza), the only Polish mutual aid institution allowed by the Nazis.

When the new Communist authorities were established by the Soviet Army in 1944, the fate of large private property in Poland was doomed. The Communists brought not only a program of nationalization and expropriation, but also a "class hatred" for the landed gentry. According to the land reform decree of 6 September 1944, large private estates above 50 hectares were expropriated and their owners had to leave the county in which they lived. The landowners were also among the first victims of arrests by the "public security" offices. The last heir of the Zamość entail, Jan Zamoyski, was imprisoned in 1945, and again some years later, Witold Maringe, who had directed the Department of Agriculture of the Polish London government–in–exile during the Nazi occupation, was sentenced to life imprisonment in 1951. Kazimierz Fudakowski was also imprisoned for many years. Eryk Kurnatowski and Seweryn Dolański were arrested in 1945 and persecuted even later. In the years 1944–1946 many landowners left Poland for good. As an exception, Alfred Potocki even managed to carry away a trainful of his property, given the assistance of the German authorities. Others stayed, following the motto quoted by the dying Konstanty Skirmuntt in 1946: "Good or bad, this is my homeland; we have to endure and believe in it."[5]

Landowners were for some time allowed to take positions on state farms, but after the end of the 1940s they were removed even from them. After 1956 the persecution of the former landowners generally stopped. Those who survived and stayed in Poland sought various jobs, not always connected with agriculture. Jan Zamoyski worked as a representative for a foreign shipping company. Teresa Lubomirska was employed as a textile worker, Krzysztof Radziwiłł of Sichów, who met some of the Communist leaders at Mauthausen concentration camp joined the puppet Democratic party (Stronnictwo Demokratyczne) and served as the head of protocol in the Foreign Ministry.[6] Many highly educated landowners' sons, such as PawełCzartoryski, Ryszard Manteuffel, Emanuel Rostworowski, and others, became professionals.

In countries that did not have to undergo a social revolution, native large private estates usually evolved from postfeudal institutions into natural elements of a market economy. Liquidation of large private estates by the Communists in Poland after 1944 was only a temporary elimination of a privileged social stratum. Pretty soon a new ruling class emerged, the *nomenklatura* whose economic and political domination in post–World War II Poland was much stronger than that of the landowners in interwar Poland. What is more, the new ruling class lacked the skills and values of the landowner elites. After the land reform of 1944, some of the large estates were not divided and remained in the hands of the government. These State Agricultural Enterprises (Państwowe Gospodarstwa Rolne) were usually mismanaged and proved to be less efficient than small peasant farms. The answer to the mystery of this reversal of efficiences quite clearly lies in changed property relations and not in the very distribution of land. While the performance of Polish agriculture after 1945 is outside the scope of the present work, the overall balance sheet on the destruction of all large private estates by the Communists has shown rather a lot of red ink.

Notes to Chapter 1

[1] For the political activities of landowners in interwar Poland see: Jerzy Jaruzelski, *Mackiewicz i konserwatyści (Mackiewicz and the Conservatives)* Warsaw 1976: Szymon Rudnicki, *Działalność polityczna polskich konserwatystów 1918–1926 (Political Activities of Polish Conservatives, 1918–1926)*, Wroclaw 1981; Wiesław Władyka, *Działalność polityczna polskich stronnictw konserwatynych w latach 1926–1935 (Political Activities of the Polish Conservative Parties in the Years 1926–1935)*, Wroław 1977. For their economic role see: Wojciech Roszkowski, *Gospodarcz rola większej prywatnej własność ziemskiejw Polsce 1918–1939)*, Warsaw 1986.

[2] One of them is Mieczysław Mieszczankowski, *Rolnictwo II Rzeczypospolitej (Agriculture in the Polish Section Republic)*, Warsaw 1983. Otherwise, he was the author of a thorough statistical survey of the interwar agrarian structure of Poland: Mieczysław Mieszczankowski, *Struktura agrarna Polski mi,edzywojennej (Agrarian Structure of Interwar Poland)*, Warsaw 1960.

[3] Mieszczankowski, *Rolnictwo*, pp. 338–358; Bogusław Gałka, "Miejsce i rola ziemiaństwa w strukturze społeczno–ekonomicznej II Rźec- zypopólitej" ("The Role of Landowners in the Socioeconomic Structure of the Polish Second Republic"), *Dzieje Nájnowsze*, 1985.

[4] Karl Marx was not too precise in his understanding of the term "class." He thought that at each stage of social development there are two antagonistic classes. If this scheme was applied to feudalism it would mean a conflict between feudal owners and peasants. Elsewhere Marx noticed a "hierarchic structure of land ownership" in feudalism, practically excluding the bipolar scheme and stated that "classes" were produced by capitalism. Karl Marx, *Das Kapital*, vol. 7, Warsaw 1951, pp. 774–791; Karl Marx, Friedrich Engels, *The German Ideology*, Parts I and III, International Publishers, New York 1947, pp. 44–69.

5 Max Weber, *Wirtschaft und Gesselschaft,* Tübingen 1956, pp. 180, 531–540, 554–585.

6 Irena Rychlikowa, "Problemy pojęciowe i metodyczne w badaniach uwarstwienia ziemiaństwa Królewstwa Polskiego w epoce przekształcania się społeczeństwa stanowego w klasowe" ("Conceptual and Methodological Problems in Research of Stratification of Landowners of the Kingdom of Poland During the Transformation of the Estate Society into a Class Society") *Metody i Wyniki (Methods and Results),* Warsaw 1980, p. 322.

7 Quoted according to M. K. Dziewanowski, *Poland in the 20th Century,* Columbia University, New York 1977, p. 16.

8 On the magnate or aristocratic rule in Poland–Lithuania: Włod zimierz Dworzaczek, *Genealogia* Warsaw 1959. Cf. also two excellent studies in English: Andrzej Kaminski, "The Government" in I. Banac, P. Bushkovitch, eds., *The Nobility in Russia and Eastern Europe,* Yale Colloquium on International and Area Studies, New Haven 1983; Andrzej Kaminski, "Neo–Serfdom in Poland–Lithuania," *Slavic Review,* 1975, vol. 34, no. 2, pp. 253–268.

9 Aleksander Brueckner, *Encyklopedia staropolska (Encyclopedia of Old Poland),* vol. 2, Warsaw 1939, p. 51; A. Mełeń, "Ordynacje w dawnej Polsce" ("Entails in Old Poland"), *Pamiętnik Historyczno–Prawny,* vol. 7, Lwow 1929, pp. 79–89.

10 Norman Davies, *God's Playground. A History of Poland,* vol. 7, Clarendon Press, Oxford 1981, pp. 201–255; J. K. Fedorowicz, ed., *A Republic of Nobles. Studies in Polish History to 1864,* Cambridge University Press 1982, passim.

11 Adam Mickiewicz, *Pan Tadeusz (Lord Tadeusz),* G. R. Noyer's Everyman Library, London 1930, pp. 167–170.

12 A. Bruce–Boswell, "Poland," *The European Nobility in the Eighteenth Century,* London 1953; Teresa Zielińska, *Magnateria polska epoki saskiej (The Polish Magnates of the Saxon Age),* Ossolineum, Wrocław 1977.

13 *Memorandum w sprawie szlachty zagrodowej na wschodzie Polski (Memorandum on the Petty Nobility in Eastern Poland),* Warsaw 1938, pp. 6–8.

14 Antoni Mączak, "Szlachta" ("Novility"), *Encyklopedia historii gospodarczej Polski do 1945 roku (Encyclopedia of Economic History of Poland up to 1945),* Warsaw 1981, vol. 2, p. 366.

15 August Iwanski, *Pamiętnik (Diary)* 1832–1876. August Iwanski,

Jr., *Wspomnienia (Memoirs)* 1881–1939, Warsaw 1968, p. 361.

16 Irena Rychlikowa concluded with a degree of pessimism: "In fact we do not know what the landed gentry was in the transition period between feudalism and capitalism: more of an estate or of a class." Irena Rychlikowa, "Dzieje ziemiaństwa polskiego w latach 1795–1945. Zarys problematyki badawczej" ("History of the Polish Landed Gentry 1795–1945. Outline of the Research Scope"), *Dzieje Najnowsze* 1976, no. 1, p. 116. Cf. also: K. S. Frycz, "Ziemiaństwo" ("Landed Gentry"), *Słowo* 1936, no. 25, p. 6; Witold kula, *Kształtowanie się kapitalizmu w Polsce (Formation of Capitalism in Poland)*, Warsaw 1955, pp. 28–38. Prime Minister Władysław Grabski, himself a landowner, warned against the revival of the "estate ideology" among the Polish interwar landed gentry Wladyslaw Grabski, *Idea Polski (The Idea of Poland)*, Warsaw 1935, p. 87.

17 Leon W. Biegelseisen, *Teoria małej i wielkiej własnośći ziemskiej (Theory of Small and Large Holdings)*, Cracow 1918, p. 7 ff.

18 Rychlikowa, "Problemy," p. 335.

19 *Statystyka Polski*, t. 5, "Wielka własncść rolna *(Statistics of Poland)*, vol. 5, "Large Landed Ownership"), Warsaw 1925, pp. 1–2.

Notes to Chapter 2

1 Ludwik Landau, "Skład zawodowy ludności Polski jako podstawa badania struktury gospodarczej" ("The Occupational Composition of the Polish Population as the Foundation for Research on the Economic Structure"), *Wybór pism (Selection of Works)*, Warsaw 1957, pp. 163, 186.

2 "Stronnictwo Ludowe" ("Popular Party"), *Zaczyn* 1939, no. 5.

3 *Rocznik Statystyki R. P. (Statistical Yearbook of the Polish Republic)* 1930, p. 37, table 1; *Statystyka Polski*, t. V. "Wielka własność rolna" *(Statistics of Poland*, vol. 5, "Large Landed Ownership"), Warsaw 1925, p. 1, table 1; Witold Staniewicz, *Zmiany w strukturze agrarnej Polski (Changes in the Agrarian Structure of Poland)*, Poznań 1926, p. 7.

4 *Organizacje ziemiańskie na ziemiach polskich (Landowners' Organizations in the Polish Territories)*, Warsaw 1929, p. 119.

5 Mieszczankowski, *Rolnictwo*, p. 137, table 26.

6 *Młodzież sięga po pracę (Youngsters Reach for Jobs)*, Warsaw 1938, pp. 20–24.

7 Janusz Żarnowski, *Społeczeństwo Drugiej Rzeczypospolitej 1918–1939 (The Society of the Polish Second Republic, 1918-1939)*, Warsaw 1973, p. 280.

8 Mieszczankowski, *Struktura*, pp. 18, 149–150.

9 *Statystyka Polski*, series C 94 B (*Statistics of Poland*, series C 94 B), pp. vi and 16, table 34.

10 Jan Stecki, *Zestawienie ogólne ze statystyki większej własności ziemskiej na r. 1939 dokonane przeze mnie na podstawie ankiety przeprowadzonej przes RNOZ (General Statement of Large Landed Estates for 1939 Made by Me on the Basis of the RNOZ Inquiry)*, Library of the Catholic University of Lublin, file 537.

11 Stefan Stablewski, *Tezy uzasadniajace konieczność istnienia w Polsce gospodarstw wielkorolnych pozostających w prywatnym władaniu (Theses Justifying the Necessity of Private Large Estates in Poland)*, quoted according to Szymon Rudnicki, *Pojęcie ziemiaństwa w II Rzeczypospolitej (The Concept of the Landed Gentry in the Second Polish Republic)*, manuscript in print made available by the author, p. 4.

12 K Czerniewski, *Struktura społeczna wsi polskiej (Social Structure of the Polish Countryside)*, Warsaw 1937, p. 161; Mieszczankowski, *Struktura*, p. 341, table 151.

13 Mieszczankowski, *Rolnictwo*, p. 137, table 26.

14 Jan Gawroński, *Dyplomatyczne wagary (Playing Diplomatic Truant)*, Warsaw 196⁚, p. 15.

15 The statement of the largest 500 owners may be found in: Wojciech Roszkowski, *Rospodarcza rola*, pp. 356–379. Appendix 1 of the present work includes a statement of the largest 200 landowners.

16 *Ordynacja zamojska (The Zamość Entail)*, manuscript, about 1932, Archive of Modern Records, Warsaw, Ministry of Finance, file 5844; *Gazeta Rolnicza*, 9 June 1939; *Myśl Narodowa*, 1939, no. 21, pp. 318–319; Ewa Komor, *Maurycy Zamoyski*, manuscript in library of the Central School of Planning and Statistics in Warsaw.

17 M. Marczak, *Przewodnik po Polesiu (Polesie Guide)*, Brest 1935, p. 101; Stanisław Dzikowski, *Egzotyczna Polska (Exotic Poland)*, Warsaw 1935, pp. 26–30; *Polesie ilustrowane (Illustrated Polesie)*, Barest 1923, p. 84; Wojciech Roszkowski "Stanisław Radzi-

will (1880–1920)," *Polski Słownik Biograficzny (Polish Biographical Dictionary*, quoted further as *PSB*), vol. 30, pp. 371–372; Wojciech Roszkowski, "Karol Radziwiłł (1886–1968)," ibid.

18 Archive of Old Records, Warsaw, Radziwiłł Archive, part XI, file 317; B. Tuhan–Taurogiński, *Z dziejów Nieświeza (On the History of Nieśwież)*, Warsaw 1937, pp. 125–195; Wojciech Roszkowski (1885–1935), *PSB*, vol. 30, pp. 134–135.

19 Archive of Old Record, Warsaw, Papers of the Potockis of Łańcut, files 453–470; Alfred Potocki, *Master of Lancut*, London, 1959.

20 Teresa Zielińska, "Ordynacje w dawnej Polsce" ("Entails in Old Poland"), *Przegląd Historyczny*, 1977, no. 1; *Ilustrowana Encyklopedia Trszski Everta i Michalskiego (Illustrated Encyclopedia of Trzaska, Evert and Michalski)*, vol. 3, Warsaw 1918, pp. 990–991.

21 F. Serafin, *Wieś śląska w latach międzywojennych (Silesian Countryside in the Interwar Period)*, Katowice 1977, pp. 31–33; S. Wysłouch, *Studia nad koncentracjća w rolnictwie śląskim w latach 1850–1914 (Studies on the Concentration of Agricultural Property in Silesia in the Years 1850–1914)*, Wrocław 1956, pp. 205–218; Stanisław Karwowski, "Jarocin i jego dziedzice," ("Jarocin and Its Heirs"), Poznań 1902; *Dziennik Ustaw R. P.*, 1919, no. 72, item 423.

22 E. A. M., "Na marginesie projektu ustawy o zniesieniu ordynacji ("Note to the Draft Law on Liquidation of Entails"). Warsaw 1936, p. 4; *Monarchia Narodowa*. 16 April 1939. *Dziennik Ustaw R. P.* 1939, no. 63, item 417.

23 Szymon Konarski, ed., *Materiały do biografii, genealogii i heraldyki polskiej (Materials on Polish Biography, Genealogy, and Heraldry)*, vol. 3, Buenos Aires–Paris 1966, p. 223; Marczak, pp. 89 and 93; Tuhan–Taurogiński, p. 189.

24 Dzikowski, pp. 141–143; "Bereńe w Polsce Orrodzonej" ("Berezne in Reborn Poland"), *Ziemia Wołyńska*, 17 March 1929; Edward Maliszewski, *Przewodnik po guberni mińskiej (Guide to the Minsk Region)*, Warsaw 1919, p. 30; N. Rouba, *Przewodnik po Litwie i Białrusi (Guide to Lithuanian and Byelorussia)*, Wilno, no date, p. 190.

25 Rouba, pp. 127–128; Conversation with Stanisław Lipkowski, 18 October 1983.

26 Stanisław Loza, *Czy wiesz kto to jest? (Do You Know Who It Is?)*, Warsaw 1939, p. 243.

27 Roszkowski, *Gospodarcza rola*, pp. 40–42.

28 *Statystyka Polski*, t. 5, "Wielka własność rolna," p. ix.

29 K. Czarniecki, "Ustrój agrarny ziem b. Królestwa Polskiego" ("The Agrarian System of the Former Kingdom of Poland"). *Rolnik Ekonomista*, 1928, no. 20, p. 364; F. Barcióski, *Geografia gospodarcza województwa kieleckiego (Economic Geography of Kielce Province)*, Poznań 1931, pp. 66–67.

30 Witold Ormicki, *Życie gospodarcze Kresów Wschodnich Rzeczypospolitej Polskiej (Economic Life of the Eastern Borderland of the Polish Republic)*, Cracow 1929, map 12; L. Grodzicki, *Struktura posiadania grutów w województwie poleskim (Land Ownership Structure in Polesie Province)*, Warsaw 1936, pp. 33–34; Stanisław Odlanicki–Poczobutt, *Województwo nowogródzkie (Nowodrodek Province)*, Wilno 1936, pp. 412–416; St. Łączyński, T. Żemoytel, *Przebudowa ustroju rolnego w ziemi wileńskiej (Reconstruction of the Agrarian System in the Wilno Region)*, Wilno 1927, pp. 3–4.

31 Stanisław Nowakowski, *Geografia gospodarcza Polski Zachodniej (Economic Geography of Western Poland)*, Poznań 1929, p. 178; *Stan posiadania ziemi na Pomorzu (Land Ownership in Pomerania)*, vol. 2, Toriń 1935, p. 185; Piotr Pampuch, "Reforma rolna w górnośląskiej części województwa śląkiego" ("Land Reform in the Upper Silesian Part of the Silesian Province"), *Pisma Piotra Pampucha (Works of Piotr Pampuch)*, Katowice 1955, pp. 192–193, F. Serafin, pp. 31–35; L. Kohutek, "Struktura reolna Ślć eska" ("Agrarian Structure of Silesia"), Kuźnica, 1935, no. 1, pp. 18–22.

32 *Województwo tarnopolskie (Tarnopol Province)*, Tarnapol 1931, p. 233 ff; S. Pawłowski, *Wielka Własność w gyłej Galicji Wschodniej (Large Estates in Former East Galicia)*, Lwow 1921, pp. 11–12; K. Aufszlag, "Struktura gospodarstw rolnych w wojew stanisławowskim" ("Farm Structure in Stanisławow Province)", *Agronomia Społeczna* 1934, no. 10–11, p. 267.

33 Władysław Grabski, *Społeczne gospodarstwo agrarne (Social Agrarian Economy)*, Warsaw 1923, p. 425; *Stosunki rolnicze Królestwa Polskiego (Agrarian Relations in the Kingdom of Poland)*, Warsaw 1918, pp. 184–185; *Zarys historii gospodarstwa wiejskiego w Polsce (Outline History of Agrarian Economy in Poland)*, vol. 3, Warsaw 1970, pp. 26–62.

34 Melchior Wańkowicz, *Szczenięce lata (Puppet Years)*, Warsaw

1970, p. 110.

35 *Stosunki rolnicze R. P. (Agricultural Relations in the Polish Republic)*, Warsaw 1925, vol. 1, pp.

161–171; Dezydery Chłapowski, "Glos w dyskusji wokół filmu 'Najdłuższa wojna w historii nowoczesnej Europy' " ("Contribution to Discussion on the Movie 'The Longest War in Modern European History' "), *Więź*, 1982, no. 8, p. 16; *Księga pamiątkowa na 75-lecie Gazety Rolniczej (Memorial Book on the 75th Anniversary of Gazeta Rolnicza)*, vol. 2, Warsaw 1938, pp. 690–691.

36 Charles H. Haskins, Robert H. Lord, *Some Problems of the Peace Conference*, Harvard University, Cambridge 1920, pp. 160–176.

37 Edward Woyniłł owicz, *Wspomnienia 1847–1928 (Memoirs, 1847–1928)*, vol. 1, Wilno 1931, pp. 210–211.

38 For instance, "Milołaj Polocki, son of Mieczysław Potocki of Tulczyn, an "international big fish," lived in Rambouillet near Paris. Hipolit Korwin–Milewski, *Siedemdziesiąt lat wspomnień (1855–1925) (Seventy Years of Memoirs, 1855–1925)*, Poznań 1930, pp. 433–434; Jan Drohojowski, *Wspomnienia dyplomatyczne (Diplomatic Memoirs)*, Cracow 1969, p. 26; Bodgan Hutten–Czapski of Smogulec could be treated as another example: cf. Bogdan Hutten–Czapski, *60 lat życia publicznego i towarzyskiego (Sixty Years of Public and Social Life)*, vol. 2, Warsaw 1936, p. 458; Bohdan Hulewicz, *Wielkie wczoraj w małym kręgu (Great Yesterday in a Small Circle)*, Warsaw 1973, p. 12.

39 Roszkowski, *Gospodarcza rola*, pp. 357–376.

40 Stecki, *Zestawienie*.

41 "Zagrożenie polskości na Wołyniu" ("Threat to Polish Ownership in Volhynia"), *Ziemia Wołyńska*, 1936, no. 32.

42 Cf. for instance: Teodor Żychliński, *Złota księęga szlachty polskiej (The Golden Book of Polish Nobility)*, vols. 1–30, Poznań 1880–1915; Gustaw Manteuffel, *O starodawnej szlachcie krzyżacko-rycerskiej na kresach inflanckich (On the Old Teutonic Knights and Nobility in the Livonian Boerderland)*, Lwow 1912; Józef Wolff, *Kniaziowie litewsko-ruscy (Lithuanian and Ruthenian Princes)*, Warsaw 1895; Walerian Meysztowicz, *Gawędy o czasach i ludziach (Tales About Times and People)*, London 1983, p. 10.

43 Stanisław Loza, *Rodziny polskie pochodzenia cutzoziemskiego osiadłe w Warszawie i okolicach (Polish Families of Foreign Descent Settled in Warsaw and Its Neighborhood)*, vols. 1–2, War-

saw 1932–1936; L. Korwin, *Ormiańskie rodziny szlacheckie (Armenian Noble Families)*, Cracow 1934; Szymon Dziadulewicz, *Herbarz rodzin tatarskich w Polsce (Heraldry Book of Polish Tartars)*, Wilno 1929; Czesław Jankowski, *Powiat oszmiański (Oszmiana County)*, vols. 1–3, St. Petersburg 1898; Edward Maliszewski, *Polacy na Litwie (Poles in Lithuania)*, Warsaw 1918.

44 Quotation from Jan Bułnak, "O krajobrazie nowogródzkim" ("On the Nowogródek Landscape"), *Ziemia*, 1925, p. 197.

45 Witold Ormicki, *Spraw reformy rolnej na Śląsku (The Question of Land Reform in Silesia)*, Poznań 1937, p. 4 ff; S. Potocki, *Położenie mniejszości niemieckiej w Polsce 1918–1939 (Situation of the German Minority in Poland, 1918–1939)*, Gdańsk 1969, pp. 94–98; Stanisław Przedborski, *Monografia rolnicza powiatu pszczyńskiego (Agricultural Monograph of Pszczyna County)*, manucript in the Library of the Central School of Rural Economy in Warsaw, pp. 36–37.

46 Serafin, pp. 278–279; Wilhelm Szewczyk, *Skarb Donnersmarcków (The Donnersmarck Treasure)*, Katowice 1973, p. 302.

47 Dzikowski, p. 76; W. Schmidt, "Geneza rosyjskiej własności ziemskiej w b. guberniach wileńskiej, grodzieńskiej i mińskiej (1793–1875) (The Origin of Russian Land Ownership in the Former Wilno, Grodno, and Minsk Gubernias, 1793–1875"), *Miesięcznik Statystyczny*, 1922, no. 5; Stanisław Wołłosowicz, *Ziemia wileńska (The Wilno Land)*, Cracow 1925, p. 74.

48 "Żydowskie gospodarstwa rolne w Polsce" ("Jewish Farms in Poland"), *Rolnik Żydowski*, 1937, no. 9, p. 32; *Statystyka Polski*, series C 62, p. 16, table 34.

49 Stanisław Koszutski, *Geografia gospodarcza Polski (Economic Geography of Poland)*, Warsaw 1918, p. 194; "Zjazd przedstawicieli pracy narodowej na wsi" ("Congress of Representatives the of National Labor in the Countryside"), Warsaw 1937, p. 30, *Hajnt*, 25 January 1932.

50 H. Hescheles, *Żydzi a rola*, *Rolnik Żydowski*, 1934, no. 4, p. 2; Jan Dobraczyński, "Obowiązek antysemityzmu" ("The Duty of Anti–Semitism"), *Myśl Narodowa*, 1937, no. 6, pp. 81–83; Jan Lutosławski, "Kolonizaja żydowska Polski" ("Jewish Colonization of Poland"), *Gazeta Rolnicza*, 7 December 1934, pp. 1304–1305; L. Korwin, *Szlachta mojżeszowa (Mosaic Nobility)*, Cracow 1938; L. Korwin, *Szlachta neoficka (Convert Nobility)*, Cracow 1939.

51 Roszkowski, *Gospodaracza rola*, p. 366; "Czesi na Wołyniu" ("Czechs in Volhynia"), *Ziemia Wołyńska*, 29 July 1928.

52 Roszkowski, *Gospodarcza rola*, p. 66.

53 Karol S. Frycz, "Ziemiaństwo" ("Landed Gentry"), *Myśl Narodowa*, 1935, no. 17, pp. 258–259.

54 Letter of Dezydery Chłapowski to the author, 8 February 1984.

55 Roszkowski, *Gospodarcza rola*, pp. 357–376. Cf. also Małgorzata Szejnert, "Mitra pod kapeluszem" ("Coronet Under a Hat"), *Polityka*, 21 April 1973.

56 Gawroński, p. 140; M. Hugicka, "Ktokolwiek będziesz w nowogródzkiej stronie" ("Whoever Comes to the Nowogrodek Land"), *Ziemia*, 1925, pp. 232–234; conversation with Jerzy Kostrowicki, 10 December 1980.

57 "Ziemiaństwo, rolnictwo, samorzędy województwa łódzkiego" ("Landed Gentry, Agriculture, and Self–Government of Lodz Pro- vince"), Łódź 1928, p. 55.

58 Mieczysław Orłowicz, "Dwory polskie w województwie pomorskim" ("Polish Manors in Pomeranian Province"), *Ziemia*, 1925, p. 12.

59 *Memorandum w sprawie szlachty zagrodowej na wschodzie Polski (Memorandum on the Petty Nobility in Eastern Poland)*, Warsaw 1938, an official Polish publication that lightly exaggerated the number of petty nobles in eastern Galicia and Polesie, trying to stimulate their mass movement in favor of Polish culture. Cf. also: M. Pulnarowicz, *U źródeł Sanu, Stryia i Dniestru (At the Springs of the San, Stryj, and Dniester)*, Turka 1929; *Szlachta zagrodowa Polski (Petty Nobility in Poland)*, Library of the Catholic University of Lublin, file 892; "Szlachta zagrodowa" ("Petty Nobility"), *Monarchia Narodowa*, 23 April 1939; R. Horoszkiewicz, "W poleskich zaściankach szlacheckich" ("In the Noble Villages of Polesie"), *Ziemia*, 1935, pp. 126–129; R. Horoszkiewicz, *Tradycje ziemi pińskiej (Traditions of the Pinsk Land)*, Warsaw 1935; Stanisław Dworakowski, *Szlachta zagrodowa we wschodnich powiatach Tołynia i Polesia (Petty Nobility in the Eastern Counties of Volhynia and Polesie)*, Warsaw 1939. The highest concentration of petty noble farms was recorded in Wysokie Mazowieckie County of Białystok Province (64.3 percent of all land). Cf. M. Skarżyński, *Stosunki rolnicze powiatu wysoko–mazowieckiego (Agrarian Relations in Wysokie Mazowieckie County)*, manuscript in the Library of the Central

School of Agrarian Economy in Warsaw, pp. 17–18.

[60] Conversation with Zofia, née Potocka, Tyszkiewicz, 29 May 1982.

[61] Szymon Konarski, *Szlachta kalwińska w Polsce (Calvinist Nobility in Poland)*, Warsaw 1936; Dziadulewicz, passim; L. Korwin, *Ormiańskie . . .*, passim.

[62] Conversation with Dezydery Chłapowski, 8 February 1984; Andrzej Wierzbicki, *Wspomnienia i dokumenty (1877–1920) (Memoirs and Records, 1877–1920)*, Warsaw 1957, p. 188; Józef Dowbór-Muśnicki, *Moje wspomnienia (My Memoirs)*, Warsaw 1935, pp. 355–356; Marian Kukiel *Władysław Sikorski*, London 1970 1970, p. 87; *Gazeta Rolnicza*, 10 July 1931; Janusz Regulski, *Blaski i cienie długiego życia (Ups and Downs of a Long Life)*, Warsaw 1980, p. 287.

[63] Wierzbicki, p. 188.

[64] Regulski, p. 366; Zygmunt Karpiński, *O Wielkopolsce, złocie i dalekich podróżach (On Great Poland, Gold, and Far Away Journeys)*, Warsaw 1971, p. 166.

Notes to Chapter 3

[1] Quoted in *The Cambridge History of Poland*, vol. 2, p. 488.

[2] *Historia Polski (History of Poland)*, vol. 4, 1918–1939, Part 1, PWN, Warsaw 1969, p. 111.

[3] E. K. (Jędrzej Moraczewski), *Przewrót w Polsce. Rządy ludowe (The Polish Coup. People's Governments)*, Kraków–Warszawa 1919, p. 109.

[4] Marian Leczyk, *Komitet Narodowy Polski a Ententa i Stany Zjednoczone 1917–1919 (The Polish National Committee and the Entente and the United States, 1917–1919)*, Warsaw 1966, pp. 200–202.

[5] Quoted according to R. F. Leslie, Antony Polonsky, Jan M. Ciechanowski, Z. A. Pelczynski, *The History of Poland Since 1863*, Cambridge University, 1980, p. 131.

[6] *Dzinnik Prawa Państwa Polskiego (Legal Gazette of the Polish State*, quoted further as DPPP, 1918, no. 17, item 40.

[7] Text, E. K. (Jędrzej Moraczewski), p. 112 ff.

[8] Władysław Pobóg-Malinowski, *Najnowsza historia polityczna Polski (Modern Political History of Poland)*, vol. 2, B. Swiderski, London 1967, p. 175; Adam Próchnik, *Pierwsze pięnastolecie*

Polski niepodległej (The First Fifteen Years of Independent Po-
land), Warsaw 1957, p. 46 ff; Francesco Tommasini, *Odrodzenie*
Polski (Rebirth of Poland), Warsaw 1928, pp. 15–20.

[9] Adam Próchnik, pp. 54–57.

[10] There is extensive Polish literature on this subject. Cf., e.g.,
Maria Dunin–Kozicka, *Burza od wschodu (Tempest from the East)*,
Cracow 1923; Bohdan Koreywo, *Uśmiechy rewolucji (Smiles of*
the Revolution), Poznań 1920; Elżbieta Dorożyńska, *Na ostat-*
niej placówce (At the Last Outpost), Warsaw 1925; Melchior
Wańkowicz, *Strzępy epopei (Scraps of the Epos)*, Warsaw 1936;
Zofia Kossak, *Pożoga (Ravage)*, Warsaw 1935; Eugeniusz de Hen-
nig Michaelis, *W zamęcie (In the Muddle)*, Warsaw 1929; Józef
Dowbór–Muśnicki, *Moje wspomnienia (My Memoirs)*, Warsaw
1935.

[11] Kossak, pp. 50–51; A. Urbański, *Z czarnego szlaku i tamtych*
rubieży (From the Black Trail and Those Borderlands), Warsaw
1927, pp. 94–97; E. Rzyszczewska, *Mord sławucki w oświetleniu*
naocznego świadka (The Sławuta Murder in the Light of a Wit-
ness's Tale), Lwow 1919.

[12] Kossak, pp. 41–60; A. Urbański, *Memento kresowe (Eastern*
Borderland Memento), Warsaw 1929, pp. 43–45; A. Urbański,
Pro memoria, Warsaw, no date, pp. 46–50; A. Urbański, *Podz-*
wonne na zgliszczach Litwy i Rusi (The Death Knell of the Ruins
of Lithuania and Ruthenia), Warsaw, no date, pp. 102–106.

[13] *Polesie ilustrowane (Illustrated Polesia)*, Brest–Litovsk 1923, p.
107.

[14] Edward Maliszewski, *Polacy na Łotwie (Poles in Latvia)*, Warsaw 1922, p. 20; M. Jałowiecki, *Po dworach i wsi litewskie*
(Through Lithuanian Manors and Villages), Kamień 1928, passim; Edward Woyniłłowicz, *Wspomnienia 1847–1928 (Memoirs,*
1847–1928), part one, Wilno 1931; Walerian Meysztowicz, *Gawędy*
o czasach i ludziach (Tales About Times and People), London
1983, pp. 100, 133.

[15] Tadeusz Spiss, *Ze wspomnień c.k. urzędnika politycznego (Mem-*
oirs of an Imperial–Royal Political Official), Rzeszów 1936, pp.
175–176.

[16] Witold Stankiewicz, *Konfliky społeczne wsi polskiej 1918–1920*
(Social Conflicts in the Polish Countryside, 1918–20), Warsaw
1963, pp. 178–180.

[17] Ibid., p. 45; Spiss, p. 155; Jan Słomka, *From Serfdom to Self-*

Government: Memoirs of a Polish Village Mayor, 1832-1927;
London 1941, p. 210 ff.

[18] Stankiewicz, p. 55; J. Gójski, *40 lat Związku Zawodowego Robotników Rolnych (Forty Years of the Trade Union of Agricultural
Workers)*, Warsaw 1960, pp. 24-30.

[19] A. Czubiński, M. Skrzek, *Strajki rolne w Wielkopolsce 1919-
1922. Materiały archiwalne (Agricultural Strikes in Greater Poland, 1918-1922. Archive Documentation)*, Warsaw 1959, pp.
73-78, 91-92.

[20] Sejm Ustawodawczy, Druk No 839 (The Constituent Assembly.
The Lower House Document No 839); Władysław L. Jaworski,
Prawa państwa polskiego, No. 4, Prawo agrarne od 1 lutego 1918
r. do 1 kwietnia 1920 r. (The Polish State Laws, No. 4, The
Agricultural Law of 1 February 1918 to 1 April 1920), Cracow
1920, pp. 94-102.

[21] *Na cudzym i swoim. Wspomnienia (On Someone Else's and on
One's Own Land. Memoirs)*, no place, 1970, pp. 158-159.

[22] Czubiński, Skrzek, pp. 137—141.

[23] *Tymczasowy Komitet Rewolucyjny Polski (The Provisional Revolutionary Committee for Poland)*, Warsaw 1955, pp. 80-89;
Stankiewicz, pp. 321-326; Walentyna Najdus, *Lewica polska w
Kraju Rad 1918-1920 (The Polish Left in Soviet Russia)*, Warsaw 1971, p. 304.

[24] *Dziennik Ustaw R. P. (Polish Legislation Gazette)* 1920, no. 70,
item 462.

[25] *Documents relatifs á l'application de la réforme agraire en Po-
logne*, no date, no place (Library of Congress 4 HD 1920), pp.
11, 70. *Dziennik Ustaw R. P.* 1926, no. 1, item 1. German text;
"Archiv für Innere Kolonisation" 1921/22, pp. 72-85. French
text: *Documents relatifs . . . .*, pp. 12-39; Olga A. Narkiewicz,
The Green Flag. Polish Populist Politics, 1867-1970, Croom
Helm, London 1976, pp. 169-192.

[26] *Na cudzym i swoim*, pp. 22, 108; Czubiński, Skrzek, pp. 78-135;
Andrzej Ajnenkiel, Czesław Madajczyk, eds., Okólniki Związku
Ziemian z lat 1926-1928 ("Circulars of the Landowners Society
for the Years, 1926-1928"), *Dzieje Najnowsze*, 1970, no. 3, p.
177.

[27] *Przegląd Ziemiański*, 1922, nos. 28-29, pp. 6-7; Jadwiga Skir-
munttówana, *25 lat wspomnień o Marii Rodziewiczównie (Twenty-
Five Years of Memoirs About Maria Rodziewiczówna)*, typescript

in the Library of the Lublin Catholic University, File no. 275, p. 33 ff.

[28] Wojciech Wydżga, *Z wycieczki na Kresy (From an Excursion into the Eastern Borderland)* Warsaw 1923, p. 16; Dzikowski, *Egzotyczna Polska*, p. 186.

[29] M. Romer, *Pamiętniki (Memoirs)*, Lwow 1938, p. 311.

[30] *Zasady współpracy stronnictw polskiej większośći parlamentarnej w Sejmie w 1923 r. (Principles of Parliamentary Cooperation by Polish Majority Parties)*, Warsaw 1923; Wincenty Witos, *Moje wspomnienia (My Memoirs)*, vol. 3, Paris 1965, pp. 36–38; Witold Stankiewicz, "Pakt Lanckoroński" ("The Lanckorona Agreement"), *Roczniki Dziejów Ruchu Ludowego*, 1959, no. 1.

[31] *Dziennik Ustaw R. P.*, 1926, no. 1, item 1; Maciej Rataj, *Pamiętniki 1918-1927 (Memoirs, 1918-1927)*, Warsaw 1965, pp. 331–333.

[32] Irena Rychlikowa, *Szkice o gospodarce panów na łańcucie (Essays on the Economy of the Masters of Lancut)*, Łańcut 1971, pp. 292–295.

[33] B. Domosławski, J. Bankiewicz, *Zniszczenia i szkody wojenne (War Destruction and Damage)*, Warsaw 1936, p. 2.

[34] Ibid., p. 29; Stanisław Rostworowski, Stefan Stablewski, *Rolnictwo i wojna (Agriculture and War)*, Warsaw 1937, p. 57.

[35] Calculated according to data available in the Archive of Modern Records, Warsaw, CTR (Central Agricultural Association), File 953, no pagination.

[36] Księga pamiątkowa na 75–lecie *Gazety Rolniczej (Album in Commemoration of the 75th Anniversary of the Gazeta Rolnicza)*, vol. 2, Warsaw 1938, p. 734; Mieczysław Orłowicz, "Dwory polskie w województwie pomorskim" ("Polish Manor Houses in Pomeranian Provinces"), *Ziemia*, 1924, p. 11.

[37] Zygmunt Limanowski, *Zniszczenia wojenne w budowlach b Królestwa Polskiego (War Damage to Buildings in the Former Kingdom of Poland)*, Warsaw 1918, p. 33; J. S. Wydżga, "Powiat hrubieszowski" ("Hrubieszow County"), *Przeflęd Ziemianski*, 1922, no. 17, pp. 4–5.

[38] *Ordynacia zamojska (The Zamość Entail)*, manuscript in the Archive of Modern Records, Warsaw, Ministry of Finance, File no. 5844.

[39] Witold Ormicki, *Życie gospodaracze Kresów Wschodnich R. P. (The Economic Life of the Eastern Borderland of the Polish Re-*

public), Cracow 1929, pp. 76–77; S. Sw(ianiewicz), "Lasy województwa poleskiego" ("Forests in Polesie Province"), *Las Polski*, 1927, p. 378.

40 *Księga pamiątkowa na 75–lecie . . . .*, vol. 2, p. 879.
41 Tedor Tołłoczko in *Polesie ilustrowane*, p. 95.
42 Witos, vol. 2, p. 378.
43 Cf, e.g., Maria Rodziewiczówna, *Róże dla panny Róży (Roses for Miss Rose)*, Poznań, no date, p. 125.
44 Dzikowski, pp. 122–135; Hipolit Korwin–Milewski, *70 lat wspomnień 1855–1925 (Seventy Years of Memoirs, 1855–1925)*, Poznań 1930, pp. 554–559.
45 Ksiéga pamić atkowa na 75–lecie . . . . vol. 2, pp. 870–875.
46 Danuta Rdułtowska, *Monografia powiatu baranowickiego (Description of the Central School of Rural Economy in Warsaw)*, Warsaw 1929, pp. 65–66.
47 B. Międzybłocki, "Potrzeby gospodarcze Kresów Wschodnich" ("The Economic Needs of the Eastern Borderland"), *Gazeta Rolnicza*, 16 May 1919, p. 379; *Polesie ilustrowane*, p. 103.
48 Rolnik 1867–1937, Lwow 1937, pp. 116–118; *Księga pamiątkowa na 75–lecie*, vol. 2, pp. 851–869; J. Krzyczkowski, *Rolnictwo wielkiej własności prywatnej w powiecie Sarny województwa poleskiego (Agriculture of Large Private Estates in Sarny County of Polesie Province)*, manuscript in the Library of the Central School of Planning and Statistics in Warsaw, Warsaw 1927, pp. 38–46.
49 Letter by Stanisław Bielski to Jerzy Łubieński of 2 July 1933, Archive of Old Records in Warsaw, Łubieński Archive, File no. 10, p. 8.
50 Księga pamiątkowa na 75–lecie, vol. 2, pp. 837–848; RoFile no. 953, no pagination.
51 Rolnik *1867–1937*, p. 141; Archive of Modern Records in Warsaw, CTR, File no. 953, no pagination; *Sytucja w pasie nadgranicznym nad Zbruczem w roku 1922, Archive of Modern Re- cords in Warsaw, TSK (Borderland Guard Society)*, File no. 109, pp. 6–7; J. Pąkowski, "Stan zasiewów i upraw w pow. zaleszczyckim" ("The State of Crops in Zaleszczyki County"), *Głos Ziemiański*, 1920, no. 9, p. 191.
52 *Dziennik Ustaw R. P.*, 1923, no. 94, item 746.
53 *Rocznik Ministerstwa Skarbu za 1924 rok (Yearbook of the Ministry of Treasury for 1924)*, Warsaw 1925, pp. 218–219; *Obciążenia pánstwowymi podatkami bezpośrednimi w roku 1928 (Di-*

rect State Tax Burden in 1928), Warsaw 1930, p. 23; *Dziennik Ustaw R. P.* 1923, no. 87, item 676.

54 *Dziesięciolecia Intendentury Polskiej Siły Zbrojnej 1918–1928 (Ten Years of the Commissariat of the Polish Armed Forces, 1918–1928)*, Warsaw 1929, pp. 143–149; Jerzy Gościcki, "Dziesięciolecie rolnictwa" ("Ten Years of Agriculture"), *Dziesięciolecie Polski Odrodzonej (Ten Years of Reborn Poland)*, Cracow 1928, p. 943; Zbigniew Landau, Jerzy Tomaszewski, *Gospodarka Polski Międzwojennej (The Economy of Interwar Poland)*, vol. 1, Warsaw 1967, pp. 174–175.

55 Stefan Humnicki, *Stan posiadania. Reforma rolna (Land Possessions, Land Reform)*, Warsaw 1929, p. 7.

56 Wojciech Roszkowski, "Stan posiadania ziemaństwa polskiego do 1939 r." ("The Landed Property of Polish Landowners Before 1939"), *Najnowsza historia gospodarcza Polski (Modern Economic History of Poland)*, part 4, Warsaw 1985, p. 62.

57 Zdzisław Ludkiewicz, "Ziemia ludość rolnicza" ("Land and Agricultural Population"), *Dzieje gospodarcze Polski porozbiorowej (Economic History of Post–Partition Poland)*, vol. 2, Warsaw 1922, p. 69.

58 Tadeusz Brzeski, *Materiały statystyczne do sprawy rolnej (Statistical Evidence Concerning the Agrarian Question)*, Warsaw 1919, p. 10; Stefan Schmidt, *Własność folwarczna Małopolski Zachodniej w chwili wskrzeszenia państwa polskiego (Estate Property in Western Galicia at the Resurrection of the Polish State)*, Cracow 1924, pp. 1–88.

59 Emil Caspari, "Polska wielka własność ziemska w Księstwie Poznańskim" ("Polish Large Estates in the Duchy of Poznan"), *Ekonomista*, 1909, no. 1, pp. 376–400; Emil Caspari, "Wielka własnóć ziemska w polskich powiatach Górnego Śląska" ("Large Landed Property in the Polish Counties of Upper Silesia"), *Ekonomista*, 1911, no. 3, pp. 97–116; Stanisław Koszutski, *Geografia*, p. 172; Zdzisław Ludkiewicz, *Rozmieszczenie własność ziemskiej i gospodarstw wiejskich w Polsce (Distribution of Landed Estates and Peasant Holdings in Poland)*, Warsaw 1923, pp. 62–65.

60 Joachim Bartoszewicz, *Na Rusi. Polski stan posiadania (Polish Land Possession in Ruthenia)*, Kiev 1912, pp. 51–53; Zenon Pietkiewicz, "Ukraina (Ruś)" in *Dzieje gospodarcze Polski porozbiorowej*, vol. 1, pp. 420–421; Koszutski, pp. 214–216.

61 Mieszczankowski himself did not avoid inaccuracies of about

37,000 hectares. Mieszczankowski, *Struktura*, pp. 18, 67, 148.
[62] Jan Stecki, *Zestawienie*.
[63] Mieszczankowski, *Struktura*, pp. 147–148.
[64] Księga pamiątkowa na 75–lecie, vol 2, pp. 80–818; *Monarchia Narodowa*, 8 February 1939.
[65] *Statystyka Polski*, vol. 5, p. XIV; *Dziennik Ustwa R. P.*, 1920, no. 42, item 249; 1922, no. 10, item 65.
[66] *Mały Rocznik Statystyczna* 1939, p. 70, Table 3.
[67] L. Kohutek, *Dobra Wielkie Soleczniki (The Wielkie Soleczniki Estate)*, Wilno 1934, pp. 69–79; Albin Koprukowniak, "Likwidacia serwitutów w ordynacji zamojskiej 1920–1932" ("Liquidation of Easements in the Zamość Entail 1920–1932"), *Rocznik Lubelski*, 1960, vol. 3, p. 230 ff.
[68] Archive of Modern Records in Warsaw, Ministry of Finance, File 5877, pp. 98–100.
[69] *Statystyka Rolnicza* 1931/32, p. 17, Table 2; *Mały Rocznik Statystyczny 1939*, p. 72, Table 4; Mieszczankowski, *Rolnictwo*, p. 151.
[70] Władysław Grabski, *Kryzys rolniczy. Memoriał na I Zjazd Ekonomistów Polskich w Poznaniu w maju 1929 r. (Agricultural Depression. Report to the First Congress of Polish Economists in Poznań in May 1929)*, Warsaw 1929, p. 33.
[71] *Mały Rocznik Statystyczny 1939*, p. 249.
[72] Wiktor Osten–Sacken, "Przyczynk i wnioski" ("Reasons and Conclusions"), *Gazeta Rolnicza*, 11 November 1930, p. 683.

Notes to Chapter 4

[1] Calculated according to Mieszczankowski *Struktura*, p. 338; *Statystyka Polski*, vol. 5, pp. 1–2.
[2] *Statystyka Rolnicza*, 1938, p. 11, Table IV.
[3] Władysław Tilgner, *Analiza liczbowa wyników rachunkowych wielkiej i małej własnośći wojewódzwa poznańskiego (Numerical Analysis of Accounting on Large and Small Farms of Poznan Province)*, Poznań 1937, p. 10.
[4] Jerzy Ciechomski, *Produkcja mniejszej i większej własnośći ziemskiej w Polsce (Output of Small and Large Farms in Poland)*, Warsaw 1937, p. 19.
[5] *Prace z zakresu polityki zbożowej w Polsce (Studies in Grain Policies in Poland)*, Poznań 1934, pp. 271–273; K. Powłowski,

"Niektóre dane statystyczne dotyczące wielkorolnych gospodarstw województwo poznańskiego" ("Some Statistical Evidence Referring to Large Estates of Poznań Province"), *Roczniki Nauk Rolniczych i Leśnych*, 1933, vol. 25, p. 319.

6 *Rocznik Statystyki R. P.* 1927, p. 123; *Udział ziemian w rozwoju kultury rolnieczej w Polsce (Participation of Landowners in the Development of Agriculture in Poland)*, Warsaw 1929, p. 50.

7 *Gazeta Rolnicza*, 24 August 1928, p. 1093, 24 November 1933; Z Dziewicka, *Chmielarstwo i jego rozwój na terenie województwo wołyńskiego (Hop Growing and Its Development in Volhynia Province)*, manuscript in the Library of the Central School of Rural Economy in Warsaw, Warsaw 1935.

8 *Ziemiaństwo w pracy społecznej (The Landed Gentry in Social Work)*, Warsaw 1929.

9 *Statystyka Polski*, vol. 5, p. XVI.

10 *Mały Rocznik Statystyczny 1939*, p. 92; Stanisław Antoniewski, *Z ekonomiki gospodarstwo dużych i małych (Economics of Large and Small Farms)*, Warsaw 1938, p. 115.

11 Ciechomski, pp. 26–27; Z. Chojecki, *Produkcja rolnicza i przemył rolniczy w Polsce współczesnej (Agricultural Output and Farming Industry in Contemporary Poland)*, Warsaw 197, p. 201; Antoniewski, p. 114.

12 Władysław Gutowski, "Ratujmy Kresy" ("Save the Eastern Borderland"), *Gazeta Rolnicza*, 5 June 1931, p. 1048.

13 *Udział ziemian*, p. 37, *Gazeta Rolnicza*, 6 January 1925, p. 48, 9 November 1928, pp. 1517–1521, 28 March 1930, pp. 520–529, 3 April 1931, p. 672, 19 January 1934, pp. 61–62, 8 January 1937, p. 28; *Rolnik 1867–1937*.

14 *Mały Rocznik Statystyczny 1939*, p. 91; Roszkowski, *Gospodarcza rola*, pp. 193, 380–381; Pawłowski, p. 212.

15 *Gazeta Rolnicza*, 7 February 1930, pp. 188–196; *Złota księga ziemiaństwa polskiego. Wielkopolska (Golden Book of Polish Landowners, Greater Poland)*, Warsaw 1929, no pagination.

16 Franciszek Kwilecki, " W obronie konia dia armii" ("In Defense of Horses for the Army"), *Gazeta Rolnicza*, 10 February 1928, p. 234.

17 *Udział ziemian,*, p. 34.

18 J. Grabowski, *Warunki, rozmieszczenie typów, posiom okręgi hod- owli koni w Polsce (Conditions, Distribution, Standards,*

and Regions of Horse Breeding in Poland), no place, 1933, pp. 54, 97–101.

19 Ciechomski, p. 25; *Gazeta Rolnicza*, 6 August 1937, p. 854; *Statystyka Rolnicza*, 1938, p. 46.

20 *Złota ksiega . . . .* passim; *Księga pamiątkowa na 75-lecie Gazety Rolniczej (Memorial Book for the 75th Anniversary of Gazeta Rolnicza)*, vol. I, Warsaw 1938, pp. 443–450; "Wystawa wołyń- ska" ("The Volhynian Exhibition"), *Gazeta Rolnicza*, 19 October 1928, pp. 1371–1381.

21 *Gazeta Rolnicza*, 7 June 1929, p. 760–773, 12 October 194, pp. 1117–1118; *Złota księga . . . .* passim; *Ziemia Wołńska*, 14–21 October 1928.

22 *Zarys historii gospodarstwa wiejskiego w Polsce (Outline History of the Rural Economy in Poland)*, vol. 3, Warsaw 1970, p. 598; S. Sakowicz, A. Kozłowski, "Materiały do charakterystyki stosunków rybackich w Polsce" ("Materials Characterizing Fishing in Poland"), *Kwartalnik Statystyczny*, 1930, p. 1005.

23 *Przegląd Rybacki*, 1930, no. 9, pp. 651–562, 1932, no. 7/8, pp. 109–112, 1934, no. 12, p. 474, 1939, no. 8, pp. 310–311; *Rolnik 1867-1937*, pp. 71, 91, 97–98, 108; K. Zaleski, *Gospodarstwo rybne śródlądowe w Polsce (Inland Fishing Economy in Poland)*, manuscript in the Library of the Central School of Planning and Statistics in Warsaw, Warsaw 1937, p. 33.

24 "Lasy polskie w świetle cyfr" ("Polish Forests in the Light of Figures"), *Las Polski*, 1922, p. 347; *Zarys historii gospodarstwa wiejskiego*, vol. 3, pp. 643–645.

25 For details of estimates cf.: Roszkowski, *Gospodarcza rola*, pp. 206–212.

26 Z. Zobczyński, *Przemysł drzewny ordynacji zamojskiej (Timber Industry of the Zamość Entail)*, manuscript in the Library of the Central School of Rural Economy in Warsaw, Warsaw 1936, p. 10.

27 A map showing the largest public and private forest areas can be found in *Kwartalnik Statystyczny*, 1932, vol. 9, after p. 300. Cf. also J. J. Tochermann, *Lasy i gospodarka drzewna Ziem Północno-Wschodnicn (Forests and Timber Industry in the Northeastern Regions)*, Wilno 1938, pp. 9–11; S. Ruśkiewicz, "Rola prywatnej własności leśnej w Polsce współczesnej" ("The Rle of Large Private Forests in Contemporary Poland"), *Las Polski*, 1931, p. 93 ff.

Notes 155

28 *Dziennik Ustwa R. P. 1919*, no. 8, item 117, no. 12, item 1.

29 *Dziennik Ustaw 1919*, no. 11, item 128; 1923, no. 87, item 676, no. 105, item 823.

30 *Dziennik Ustwaw R. P. 1923*, no. 94, item 746.

31 *Dziennik Ustaw R. P. 1927*, no. 57, item 504; B. Nowacki, *Ochrona lasów prywatnych w Polscé (Control of Private Forests in Poland),* Warsaw 1935, p. 8.

32 Henryk Prenier, *Stan i rola wielkiej własnośći prywatnej w gospodarstwie leśnym Polski (The State and Role of Larage Private Property in the Polish Forest Economy),* manuscript in the Library of the Central School of Rural Economy in Warsaw, Warsaw 1936, p. 10.

33 Ruśkiewicz, pp. 247–250; Witold Babiński, "W sprawie upaństwowienia lasów" ("On the Nationalization of Forests"), *Rolnik Ekonomista,* 1929, no. 24, pp. 358–360.

34 *Dziennik Ustaw R. P. 1932*, no. 111, item 932; Witold Babiński, "Nowelizacja prawa leśnego" ("Amendment to the Forest Law"), *Rolnik Ekonomista,* 1933, no. 1, pp. 18–19; Walerian Zaklika, "Polskie ustawy lasowe w świetl polityki leśej" ("Polish Forest Laws in the Light of Forest Policies"), *Przegląd Ekonomiczny,* 1934, no. 53, pp. 104–125.

35 Władysław Barański, *Kwestia drzewna w Polsce (The Question of Timber in Poland),* Warsaw 1928, pp. 26–29.

36 *Wykresy stanu i rozwoju gospodarki leśnej w Polsce w latach 1919-1935 (Graphs Illustrating the State and Development of the Polish Forest Economy),* Warsaw no date, p. 10.

37 R. Fok–Dobrowolski, "Co się działo i dzieje w lasach pszyczyńskich? ("What Happened and What Is Going On in the Pszeczyna Forests?"), *Las Polski,* 1935, p. 212.

38 Archive of Old Records in Warsaw, "The Potockis of Lańcut," File 544, p. 9; K. Warcholak, *Lasy w powiecie nadwórnianskim (Forests in Nadworna County),* manuscript in the Library of the Central School of Rural Economy in Warsaw, Warsaw 1939, passim; Archive of Modern Records, Ministerstwo Rolnictwa i Reform Rolnych, File 271, no pagination.

39 *Rocznik Statystyki R. P. 1924*, p. 129, Table 16; *Udział ziemian,* p. 58.

40 *Zarys historii gospodarstwa wiejskiego,* vol. 3, p. 651.

41 Calcualted according to Barański, *Kwestia,* pp. 26–27; *Mały Rocznik Statystyczny 1936-39.*

[42] Roszkowski, *Gospodarcza rola*, p. 218.

[43] Witold Babiński, *Zagadnienia leśne i drzewne w Polsce (Forest and Timber Problems in Poland)*, Warsaw 937, p. 156; *Mały Rocznik Statystyczny 1937*, p. 229, Table 4.

[44] Karol Kruzensten, "O potrzebie zrzeszenia właścicieli lasów" ("On the Need for Organization of Forest Owners"), *Rolnik*, 25 February 1923, pp. 101–102.

[45] *Gazeta Rolnicza*, 3 December 1926, p. 1175; *Przegląd Ziemiański*, 1923, no. 14, p. 5.

[46] *Przegląd Gospodarczy*, 1937, no. 17, p. 511.

[47] For instance, the first sugar–refining plant in Polish territory was established by Józef Mycielski in Gałowo in 1820. The only blast furnace in Lithuania in the nineteenth century was that in Wiszniewo of the Chreptowiczes. Textile mills were established by the Potockis in Tulczyn and Niemirów, and by the Skirmuntts in Mołodów. Cf. Z. Przyrembel, *Udział ziemieństwa w budowie przemyłu polskiego (The Share of the Landed Gentry in the Development of Polish Industry)*, Warsaw 1937, pp. 10–26.

[48] *Rocznik Statystyki R. P. 1924*, p. 15; *Statystyka Polski*, vol. 5, pp. XVIII–XIX.

[49] *Udział ziemian . . . .*, pp. 50–52; Chojecki, p. 279; Z. Szymaczak, *Działalność Banku Cukrownictwa w Poznaniu na rzecz skartelizowanego przemysłu cukrowniczego w Polsce (The Activities of the Bank Cukrownictwa in Poznan in Favor of the Sugar Cartel in Poland)*, Poznan 1964.

[50] Pawłowski, pp. 316–318; *Dzieje wsi wielkopolskiej (History of the Great Polish Countryside)*, Poznań 1960, pp. 253–254, *Wiadomości Statystyczne*, 1931, no. 22, p. 481, 1939, no. 15, p. 259.

[51] *Rocznik informacyjny a spółkach akcyjnych w Polsce (Information Yearbook on Stock Companies in Poland)*, Warsaw 1930, nos. 537–599.

[52] Marian Eckert, *Przemysł rolno–spożywczy w Polsce 1918–1939 (The Food–Processing Industry in Poland, 1918–1939)*, Poznań 1974, p. 243.

[53] Stanisław Rostworowski, Stefan Stablewski, *Rolnictwo i wojna (Agriculture and War)*, Warsaw 1937, p. 201; *Wiadomcści Statystyczne*, 1928, no. 23, pp. 855–856, 1930, no. 15, p. 637, 1932, no. 2, p. 15.

[54] Eckert, p. 249; *Rocznik Statystyki R. P. 1924*, p. 45, Table 9.

55 *Rocznik informacyiny*, nos. 677, 705; " Śp. bar. Jan Goetz–Okocimski" ("The Late Baron Goetz–Okocimski"), *Gazeta Rolnicza*, 10 July 1931, pp. 1209–1210.

56 *Mały Rocznik Statystyczny 1939*, p. 137, Table 14; Eckert, p. 240; Chojecki, pp. 313–322.

57 *Rocznik informacyjny*, nos. 601, 602, 605, 610, 611; A. Dzik, *Młynarstwo w Polsce (Flour Milling in Poland)*, Warsaw 1928, pp. 27–28.

58 *Rocznik Statystyki R. P. 1924*, p. 45, Table 9.

59 Grażyna Jassem, *Majątek smoguelecki w latach 1918–1937 (The Smogulec Estate, 1918–1937)*, Poznań 1976, pp. 162–167; Zobczyński, pp. 79–81; Rolnik it 1867–1937, p. 124.

60 *Rocznik informacyjny*, nos. 962, 980–982, 1000, 1003, 1059.

61 Eckert, pp. 231–249; *Mały Rocznik Statystyczny 1939*, pp. 134–138; *Wiadomości Statystyczne*, 1928, no. 23, pp. 855–856, 1930, no. 15, p. 637, 1932, no. 2, p. 15.

62 *Rocznik informacyjn*, nos. 2, 6, 16, 31, 35, 37, 46, 47, 64, 69–71; Aleksander Meysztowicz, *O Wileńskim Banku Ziemskim (On the Wilno Land Bank)*, Wilno 1936.

63 For details of this estimate: Roszkowski, *Gospodarcza rola*, pp. 232–234.

64 Zbigniew Landau, "Oligarchia finansowa II Rzeczypospolitej" ("The Financial Oligarcny of the Polish Second Republic"), *Przegląd Historyczny*, 1971, no. 1, pp. 82–86, based his calculations on the information published in *Rocznik informacyjny* (op. cit.) and on the participation of inviduals in the organizations of stock companies. He added up the capital represented by the members of these organizations. This method results in some error since several significant shareholders were represented by proxies. Inclusion of the Bank Polski's capital also deforms the picture, since its authorities included representatives of business groups who did not have to have significant personal shares in Bank Polski's capital. Therefore in my list of the business–landowner oligarchy I do not include Bank Polski capital. Cf. Roszkowski, ıGospodarcza rola, Appendix 11. Despite some inaccuracies, the method suggested by Landau seems the only one possible, given the present knowledge of sources.

65 Roszkowski, *Gospodarcza rola*, Appendix 11.

66 Ibid., pp. 135–148.

67 Wacław Ponikowskie, *Gospodarstwa włościańskie i folwarczne (Peasant Farms and Large Estates)*, Warsaw 1935, p. 224.

68 "Referat statystyczny Związku Izb i Organizacji Rolniczych" ("Statistical Report of the Union of Agricultural Chambers and Organizations"), Ŕolnik Ekonomista, 1934, no. 18; Stanisław Warkoc- zewski, *Położenie robotników rolnych w Wielkoplsce w latach 1929–1939 (The Situation of Farm Workers in Greater Poland in the Years 1929–1939*, Warsaw 1965, p. 50.

69 Antoniewski, p. 113.

70 *Dziennik Ustaw R. P. 1919*, no. 28, item 251.

71 Warkoczewski, passim; H. Cywiński, *Umowy zbiorowe w rolnictwie ziemi płockiej (Collective Bargaining int he Agriculture of Płock Province)*, manuscript in the Library of the Central School of Planning and Statistics in Warsaw, Warsaw 1931, pp. 10, 68 ff.; R. Gerlicz, *Praca najemna na roli w większej własności ziemskiej (Hired Labor on Large Estates)*, Warsaw 1929, passim.

72 For details cf.: Roszkowski, *Gospodaracza rola*, pp. 247–292.

73 Ibid., p. 253; Józef Orczyk, *Studia nad opłacalnością gospodarstw rolnych w Polsce w latach 1929–1938 (Studies on the Profitability of Farms in Poland in the Years 1929–1938)*, Warsaw 1981, p. 39.

74 Mieszczankowski, *Rolnictwo*, p. 290; Roszkowski, *Gospodarcza rola*, pp. 131, 253, 254.

75 Ponikowski, p. 223; W. Tilgner, M. Zeyland, O Biliński, C. Gertner, *Statystyka porównawcza dochodów i rozchodów gospodarstw wielkorolnych i mak orolnych województwa poznańskiego za sześciolecie 1930/31 do 1935/36 (Comparative Statistics of Returns and Expenditures of Large and Small Farms of Poznan Province for the Six Years Between 1930/31 and 1935/36)*, Poznań 1938, no pagination.

76 Wiktor Schramm, "Problem poznawania organizacji gospodarstwa ziemskiego" ("The Knowledge of Farm Organizations"), *Roczniki Nauk Rolniczych i Leśnych*, 1939, vol. 67, pp. 258–259; F. Bogusławski, "Ekstensyfikacja rolnictwa polskiego" ("Extensibility of Polish Agriculture"), *Życie Rolnicze*, 1939, no. 17.

77 Orczyk, p. 96.

78 W. Borowski, *Kredyt rolniczy w Polsce (Agricultural Credits in Poland)*, Warsaw 1927, p. 60.

79 Miedzysław Mieszczankowski, "Zadłużenie rolnictwa Polski międzywojennej" ("Indebtedness in Interwar Polish Agriculture"), *Na-*

jnowsze *Dzieje Polski*, 1963, vol. 6, p. 125; Roszkowski, *Gospo-darcza rola*, p. 271.

[80] Mieszczankowski, *Rolnictwo*, p. 320.

[81] Roszkowski, *Gospodarcza rola*, p. 271; *Mały Rocznik Statystyczny 1939*, p. 249, Table 7.

[82] J. Cieszewski,, W. Englicht, *Obciążenia podatkowe rolnictwa w świetle cyfr (The Tax Burden in Agriculture in the Light of Fig-ures)*, Warsaw 1929, pp. 10–12.

[83] Roszkowski, *Gospodarcza rola*, p. 278, Table 5.5

[84] Mieczysław Mieszczankowski tried to prove his thesis by compar-ing the tax burden of a five-hectare farm with that of latifundia above 2,000 hectares, not noticing that the highest tax burden was faced by estates between 60 and 500 hectares. He also as-sumed that small farms did not delay payments, while large es-tates did. He largely underestimated all tax payments by large estates and ignored the property tax, paid only by large estates, at all. In spite of this, the evidence he published denies his princi-pal thesis. Mieczysław Mieszczankowski, "Podatki rolne w Plsce międzywojennej" ("Agricultural Taxation in Interwar Plland"), *Rocznik Dziejów Ruchu Ludowege*, 19651, vol. 3, pp. 114–158; Mieszczankowski, *Rolnictwo*, pp. 354–355.

[85] Mieszczankowski, *Rolnictwo*, p. 290; Roszkowski, *Gospodarcza rola*, Tables 3.4, 5.1, 5.5

[86] Wojciech Roszkowski, "Próba szacunku dochodów ziemiańskich w Polsce niepodległej" ("Attempts to Estimate the Landowners' Incomes in Independent Poland"), *Roczniki Dziejów Społecznych i Gospodarczych*, 1984, vol. 45, pp. 115–126.

Notes to Chapter 5

[1] Even the Marxian theory of class rule, based on nineteenth cen-tury capitalist relations, included several simplistic assumptions. Cf. Leszek Nowak, "Marksowski model struktury klasowej społec-zeństwa kapitalistycznego" ("Marxian Model of the Class Struc-ture of a Capitalist Society"), *Studia Socjologiczne*, 1972, no. 2, pp. 12–13.

[2] Aleksander Szembek, *Związek Ziemian w Wlelkim Księstwie Poz-nańskim (Landowners' Society in the Grand Duchy of Poznania)*, manuscript, Archive of Modern Records, Warsaw 1929, pp. 66–67.

[3] *Organizacie*, pp. 17–44; Eugeniusz Dłoczowski, "Organizacje ziemiańskie" ("Landowners' Organizations") in *Księga pamiąt-ko- wa na 75-lecie Gazety Rolnieczej (Memorial Book of the 75th Annive˜sary of Gazeta Rolnicza)*, vol. 1, Warsaw 1938, pp. 166–176.

[4] *Organizacje*, pp. 85–90.

[5] Ibid., pp. 73–74, 92–115.

[6] Seweryn Dolański, "Uwagi o chwili obecnej" ("Up-to-Date Remarks"), *Głos Ziemiański*, 1920, no. 7, pp. 137–138.

[7] *Sprawa Rolna*, 1919, vol. 1, pp. IV–XVI; *Organizacj*, pp. 117–122.

[8] Kłoczowski, pp. 166–176.

[9] Z. Ihnatowicz, "Związek Rolników z Wyższym Wykształceniem i jego rola w kształtowaniu polskiej myśli rolniczej" ("Union of Farmers and Foresters with Higher Education and Its Role in Formation of Polish Agricultural Thought") in *Księga pamiątkowa* . . . ., vol. 1, pp. 151–157; Z. Jankowska, *Organizacja ziemianek i jej działalność (Organization of Landladies and Its Activities)*, Ibid., pp. 177–182.

[10] B. Rykowski, *Związek Izb i Organizacji Rolniczych R. P. (Union of Polish Agricultural Chambers and Organizations)*, Ibid., 110–111.

[11] *Ziemiaństwo w pracy społecznej (Landed Gentry in Social Work)*, Warsaw 1929, pp. 15–17; *Kalendarz Rolniczy CTR 1920 (Agricultural Almanac of the Central Agricultural Society for 1920)*, pp. 99–121.

[12] For details cf. J. Buszko, *Zejmowa reforma wyborcza w Galicji 1905-1914 (The Sejm Suffrage Reform in Galicia, 1905-1914)*, Warsaw 1956; Michał Bobrzyóski, *Wskrzeszenie państwa pelskiego (Resurrection of the Polish State)*, Cracow 1920, vol. 1, Stanisław Estreicher "Geneza partii konserwatywnej w Polsce" ("The Origin of the Conservative Party in Poland"), *Czas*, 25 December 1926.

[13] Szymon Rudnicki, *Działalność*, pp. 21–23.

[14] Ibid., p. 27.

[15] Antony Polonsky, *Politics in Independent Poland, 1921-1939*, Clarendon Press, Oxford 1972, p. 67; Rudnicki, pp. 31–35.

[16] Jaruzelski, Mackiewicz, pp. 88–89; Alicja Bełcikowska, *Stronnictwa i związki polityczne w Polsce (Political Parties and Groups in Poland)*, Warsaw 1925, p. 105 ff; "Rada Naczelna Organizacji Ziemiańskich" ("Supreme Council of Landowners' Organizations"), *Dziennik Poznański*, 7 June 1922.

[17] Rudnicki, pp. 116–150, 210; K. J., "Przegrupowania," *Dziennik Poznański*, 12 July 1925.

[18] *Organizacje*, p. 119.

[19] Cf. *Pamiętnik I Walnego Zjazdu Zrzeszonego Ziemiaństwa Polskiego (Diary of the First Congress of Organized Polish Landowners)*, Warsaw 1925, vols. 1–2.

[20] "Okónik Związku Ziemian" ("Landowners' Society Circular"), no. 602 of 19 May 1926, *Dzieje Najnowsze*, 1970, no. 3, pp. 161–162.

[21] Władyka, *Działalność*, pp. 17–19.

[22] Ibid., pp. 23–26.

[23] Ibid., pp. 28–30.

[24] *Stenogramy przemówien podczas zjazdu ziemiańskiego w Nieświeżu (Shorthand Record of Speeches Made During the Nieświez Meeting)*, Archive of Old Records, Warsaw, Radziwiłł Archive, Part XI, File 313, pp. 2–9.

[25] Krystyna Kersten, "Protokół konferencji grup konserwatywnych z udziałem przedstawicieli Marszałka Piłsudskiego w Dzikowie w dniach 14–16 września 1927 r." ("Minutes of the Conference of Conservative Groups with Representatives of Marshal Pilsudski in Dzikow on 14–16 September 1927"), *Najnowsze Dzieje Polski*, 1959, vol. 2, pp. 209–210.

[26] Władyka, pp. 78–97; Jerzy Jaruzelski, "Janusz Radziwiłł (1880–1967)," *PSB*, vol. 30, pp. 215–225; Stanisław Ossowski, "Chrześijańskie, Stronnictwo Rolnicze" ("The Christian Agricultural Party"), *Dziennik Poznański*, 31 January 1928.

[27] Władyka, p. 109 ff.

[28] *Zagadnienie etatyzmu w Polsce. Stenogramy przemówień wygłoszonych na zebrania u J. Radziwiłł w dniu 12 grudnia 1928 roku i 10 stycznia 1929 roku (The Question of Statism in Poland. Minutes of Proceedings at J. Radziwill's on 12 December 1928 and 10 January 1929)*, Warsaw 1929.

[29] *Czas*, 3 December 1932.

[30] Władyka, pp. 204–205.

[31] *Czas*, 28 February 1933.

[32] *Gazeta Rolnicza*, 4 October 1935, p. 1089, 9 December 1938, p. 1412.

[33] Jaruzelski, *Janusz Radziwiłł*, p. 222.

[34] Roman Wapiński, "Problemy kształtowania sięelit politycznych II. Rzeczypospolitej" ("Formation of Political Elites in the Polish Second Republic") in *Społeczeństwo polskie XVIII i XIX wieku (Polish Society in the 18th and 19th Centuries)*, vol. 7, Warsaw 1982, p. 246.

35 Barbara Wysocka, "Elity społeczne Wielkopolski w II Rzeczy-pospolitej" ("Social Elites in the Polish Second Republic"), *Studia i Materiały do Dziejów Wielkopolski i Pomorza*, vol. 11, no. 2, p. 115.

36 The Polish abbreviation of the Foreign Ministry, "MSZ" for Ministerstwo Spraw Zagranicznych, was explained by a diplomat as standing for "Morawski-Skrzyński-Zaleski," the three leading Polish diplomats from the landed gentry. Cf. Kajetan Morawski, *Tamtenbrzeg (The Other Shore)*, Paris, no date, p. 25.

37 Ludomił Pułaski, "Zadania większej własności w dobie obecnej" ("Present Tasks of the Large Estate Owners"), *Ziemianin*, 1918, no. 12, 1–2; "Deklaracja ziemian w sprawie rolnej" ("Landowenrs' Declaration on the Agrarian Question"), *Ziemianin*, 1919, no. 4, pp. 1–2.

38 *Sprawa Rolna*, 1919, vol. 1, pp. 359–367.

39 Jan Lutosławski, "Ustawa o wykonaniu reformy rolnej z dnia 15-tego lipca 1920 roku" ("The Land Reform Law of 15 July 1920"), *Sprawa Rolna*, 1920, vol. 2, p. 149.

40 *Kurier Warszawski*, 15 April 1923.

41 Witold Stankiewicz, "Rakt lanckoroński" ("The Lanckorona Agreement"), *Roczniki Dziejów Ruchu Ludowego*, 1959, no. 1.

42 "Prezydent Rzeczypospolitej o ziemiaństwie" ("The President of the Polish Republic on Landowners"), *Przeglć ad Ziemiański*, 1923, no. 24, p. 6.

43 Jerzy Ciepielewski, *Wieś polska w latach wielkiego kryzysu 1929–1935. Materiały i dokumenty (The Polish Countryside During the Great Depresssion, 1929–1935. Materials and Documents)*, Warsaw 1968, pp. 46–47, 89–92; Archive of Modern Records, Warsaw, KEM, File 1216, pp. 49–69.

44 *Gazeta Rolnicza*, 27 November 1936, p. 1231.

45 *Przegląd Ekonomiczny*, 1938, vol. 21, pp. 167–169.

46 *Gazeta Rolnicza*, 10 March 1939, pp. 232–233; 17 March 1939, pp. 260–261.

47 *Głos Ziemiański*, 1920, no. 3, pp. 42–43.

48 *Gazeta Rolnicza*, 29 February 1924, pp. 233–234; 7 March 1924, p. 258.

49 *Gazeta Rolnicza*, 24 August 1928, pp. 1091–1092.

50 *Gazeta Rolnicza*, 2 November 1929, p. 1451, 14 November 1930, pp. 1748–1750; 17 April 1931, pp. 771–774.

51 *Rolnik Ekonomista*, 1932, no. 20, p. 479; *Gazeta Rolnicza*, 19 May 1933, pp. 472–473.

52 *Okólnik Związku Ziemian (Landowners' Society Circular)*, no. 22 of 1 March 1932, Archive of Old Records, Warsaw, Archive of the Radziwiłł Family from Nieborów, File 484.

53 Adolf Bniński, "O zmianępolityki rolnej" ("To Change Agrarian Policy"), *Gazeta Rolnicza*, 20 March 1936, pp. 297–299. Cf also *Gazeta Rolnicza*, 19 February 1937, pp. 182–183; 19 March 1937, pp. 280–281.

54 Cf., e.g., "Zjednoczona wieć" ("United Countryside"), *Głos Ziemi*, 1937, no. 19; "Wieś w państwie" ("The Countryside Within the State"), *Zaczyn*, 9 June 1938, p. 2; "Tezy rolnicze OZN" ("Agricultural Theses of the Camp of National Unity"), *Zaczny*, 15 September 1938, p. 2.

55 *Gazeta Rolnicza*, 17 February 1939, p. 148.

Notes to Chapter 6

1 According to Mieczysław Jełowicki. Cf. *Pamiętnik I Walnego Zjazdu Zrzeszonego Ziemiaństwa Polskiego*, vol. 1, p. 50.

2 Józef Tyszkiewicz, *Kontrrewolucja (Counterrevolution)*, Warsaw 1931, pp. 11, 24.

3 Leon Sapieh, *Konieczność solidarności europejskiej (The Necessity of European Solidarity)*, Przemyśl 1938, pp. 9–19.

4 Zygmunt Plater, *Wobec sytaucji list otwarty do społeczeństwa polskiego (Open Letter to the Polish Society in View of the Situation)*, Warsaw 1926, pp. 29–37.

5 Jan Hupka, *W sprawie reformy agrarnej (On the Agrarian Reform)*, Cracow 1919, pp. 13–15; Karol Kruzenstern, "Uwagi o naszych stosunkach rolnych na tle ustaw z lipca 1919 i 1920 r." ("Remarks on Our Agrarian Relations Against the Background of the July 1919 and 1920 Laws"), *Gazeta Rolnicza*, 11 June 1923, pp. 522–523; MichałKorwin–Szymanowski, "O nasz program" ("For Our Program"), *Gazeta Rolnicza*, 26 January 1924, pp. 66–67; Jan Lutosławski, *Sprawa rolna jako problemat Polski (The Agrarian Question as the Polish Problem)*, Warsaw 1919; Stanisław Żórawski, "Na posterunku" ("On Guard"), *Gazeta Rolnicza*, 12 May 1930, p. 451.

⁶ Jan Stecki, *W obronie prawdy (Defending the Truth)*, Warsaw 1928, p. 43; *Zadania i obowiązki ziemiaństwa (The Tasks and Duties of the Landed Gentry)*, Warsaw 1921, p. 64.

⁷ Kazimierz Fudakowski, "Nasz stosunek do państwa i do zadań pracy publicznej" ("Our Attitude to the State and the Public Activities") in *Zadania*, pp. 55, 62.

⁸ *Przegląd Ziemiański*, 1922, no. 28/29, p. 2.

⁹ *Pamiętnik I Walnego Zjazdu*, vol. 1, p. 157.

¹⁰ It was only here that a landlady could ask her peasant neighbor if he, "the respected husbandman" (*gospodarz*), would attend a meeting of the farmers' circle. Letter of Wanda Niegolewska of Niegolewo of 14 February 1924 in private collection.

¹¹ Jan Lutosławski, *Ogólnopolska pielgrzymka ziemiaństwa na Jasną Górę (All-Polish Pilgrimage of the Landed Gentry to Jasna Gora)*, Warsaw 1938, pp. 9–23.

¹² Eugeniusz Kłoczowski, "Ziemiania jako oficerowie armii rolniczej" ("The Landed Gentry as Officers of the Agricultural Army"), *Gazeta Rolnicza*, 10 January 1936, pp. 2–5.

¹³ Emeryk Hutten-Czapski, "O niepodzielności i gospodarstw wiejskich i spłatach rolniczych" ("On the Indivisibility of Farms and Amortization in Agriculture"), *Tygodnik Rolniczy*, 1937, no. 45/46, p. 515; Tadeusz Łubieński, *List otwarty do polskiego chłopa (Open Letter to the Polish Peasant)*, Cracow 1919, p. 13.

¹⁴ *Gazeta Rolnicza*, 14 September 1934, p. 1007.

¹⁵ Władysław Grabski, *Idea Polski (The Idea of Poland)*, Warsaw 1935, pp. 87–104; Władysław Grabski, "Wieś jako siła społeczna" ("The Village as Social Force"), *Rolnictwo*, 1936, no. 2, pp. 7–8.

¹⁶ Kajetan Morawski, *Wspólna droga (Common Road)*, Paris, no date, pp. 111–112.

¹⁷ Stecki, *W obronie*, p. 29.

¹⁸ Fudakowski, *Nasz stosunek*, pp. 46, 57.

¹⁹ Jan Bobrzyński, *Na drodze walki (On the Path of Struggle)*, Warsaw 1928, pp. 10–17, 53–55.

²⁰ Janusz Radziwiłł, "Kilka uwag o konserwatyzmie" ("Some Remarks on Conservatism") in *Księga pamiątkowa na 90-lecie dziennika Czas*, p. 63.

²¹ Stanisław Estreicher, *Konserwatyzm (Conservatism)*, Cracow 1928, p. 5.

²² Jan Lutosławski, *Niedomówienia. Zagadnienia większej własności rolnej (Hints. The Problems of Large Estates)*, Warsaw 1915, p.

21.

23 Speech by Leon Sapieh at an election meeting on 5 August 1935, Archive of Old Records, The Potockis of Łańcut, File 1474, p. 5.

24 "Przemówienie prezesa Gudakowskiego z okazji dziesięciolecia istnienia Związku O.R.R.P." ("Speech by the Chairman Fudakowski on the Tenth Anniversary of the Union of Polish Agricultural Organizations"), *Rolnik Ekonomista*, 1931, no. 24, pp. 676–678; Fudakow- ski, *Nasz stosunek*, pp. 51–53.

25 *Ziemianka*, 1919, no. 7, p. 124.

26 Expression used by the sentimentalist writer Helena Mniszek–Radomyska "Loreto a Polska" ("Lorato and Poland"), *Ziemianka Polska*, 1930, no. 20, pp. 5–7.

27 Korwin–Milewski, p. 467; M. Murdeljo (Franciszek Oskierka), *Sęp nam wyjada nie serca lęgc mózgi (Vultures Are Eating Away Our Brains, Not Hearts)*, Wilno 1927, pp. 24, 30.

28 Interview with Izabela Radziwiłł , 10 October 1983.

29 Stefan Gorski, "Unarodowienie handlu rolniczego" ("Polonization of Agricultural Trade"), *Gazeta Rolnicza*, 10 June 1923, p. 533.

30 Witold Gombrowicz, *Wspomnienia polskie (Polish Memoirs)*, Paris 1977, pp. 155–157.

31 Władysław Jabłonowski, "W obronie zachodu" ("Defending the West"), *Myśl Narodowa*, 1927, no. 21, p. 387.

32 Jadwiga Zamoyska, *O pracy (On Labor)*, Poznań 1938, p. 9.

33 *Testament Władysława Jelskiego (The Testament of Władysław Jelski)*, Warsaw 1939, pp. 5–7.

34 Maria Estreicherówna, "Cecylia Plater–Zyberkówna," *Przegląd Powszechny*, 1920, no. 436, pp. 271–281; *Szkoła Cecylii Plater–Zyberkówhy 1883–1944 (The School of Cecylia Plater–Zyberk)*, Warsaw 1987; Elżbieta Lubieńska, *Sam na sam z Bogiem (Soul to Soul with God)*, Warsaw 1935; Jacek Woroniecki, "Rola czynników moralnych w społecznym życiu ziemian" ("The Role of Morality in the Social Life of Landowners") in *Zadania i obowiązki ziemiaństwa.*, pp. 6–12.

35 *Księga sapieżyńska (The Sapieha Book)*, vol. 1, Cracow 1982; Jadwiga Stabińska OSB AP, *Matka Elżbieta Czacka (Mother Elżoieta Czacka)*, Poznań 1981; *O Bernard Lubieński (1866–1933)*, Wrocław 1947; *Matka Urszula Ledóchowska i jej dzieło (Mother Urszula Ledóchowska and Her work)*, Cracow 1948.

36 Konstanty Turowski, *"Odrodzie," Historia Stowarzyszenia Katolickiej Młodzieży Akademickiej ("Renaissance," The History of the Association of the Catholic Academic Youth)*, Warsaw 1987.

37 Czesław Klarner, *Dochód społeczny swi i miast w okresie przesilenia gospodarczego 1929–1936 (Social Income of the Countryside and Towns During the Depression, 1929–1936)*, Lwow 1937.

38 Anna Fudakowska, "Zadanie ziemianek w chwili obecnej" ("The Present Tasks of Landladies"), *Głos Ziemiański*, 1920, no. 6, pp. 116–117.

39 Gombrowicz, *Wspomnienia polskie*, p. 86.

40 Janina Skarbek–Kruszewska, "Dwór wiejski" ("The Country Manor House"), *Ziemianka Polska*, 1930, no. 11, pp. 3, 5. Cf. also J. Obst, *Nasze dwory wiejskie (Our Country Manor Houses)*, Wilno 1919, pp. 95–124.

41 Włodzimierz R. Aftanazy, *Materiały do dziejów rezydencji Materials on the History of Manor Houses)*, Part One, vols. 1–4, Part Two, vol. 5, Warsaw 1986–1988.

42 Maria Ginter, *Galopem na przełaj (Cross-Country Galloping)*, Warsaw 1983, pp. 23–49; Z. Janota–Bzowski, *Notatnik konnego strzelca (Diary of a Mounted Rifleman)*, Warsaw 1981, pp. 24, 41.

43 Stefan Badeni, *Wczoraj i przedwczoraj (Yesterday and the Day Before Yesterday)*, London 1963, passim; Dzikowski, pp. 141–143; Jules Laroche, *Polska lat 1926–1935 (Poland of the Years 1926–1935)*, Warsaw 1966, p. 90; Gawroński, p. 161.

44 Cyryl Czarkowski–Golejewski, *Wspomnienia z rykowisk (Memoirs from the Rutting Grounds)*, Lwow 1927; Jerzy Potocki, *Na wojnie i na łowach (At War and At the Hunt)*, Warsaw 1932.

45 Roman Rogowski, *Do widzenia, stary domu (Good Bye, Old Home)*, Warsaw 1980, pp. 125–129; Henryk Uziembło, *Radziwiłł owska puszcza (The Radziwill Forest)*, Cracow 1934, pp. 9–45.

46 Kazimierz Chłapowski, *Pojedynki a Liga ku Ochronie Czci Honoru (Duels and the League for the Defense of Honor and Dignity)*, Poznań 1911, pp. 5–12.

47 Jerzy Potocki, pp. 41–124; Alfred Potocki, *Master of Łańcut*, p. 145 ff; Kajetan Czarkowski–Golejewski, *SP-AEU. 13 dni lotu nad Azia (SP-AEU. Thirteen Days of Flight Over Asia)*, Warsaw 1932.

48 *Auto*, 1928, no. 11, pp. 541–543; 1929, no. 3, pp. 1–5; 1929, no. 12, pp. 2–3; Witold Rychter, *Dzieje samochodu (History*

of Motorcars), Warsaw 1979, p. 297; *Gazeta Rolnicza*, 22 April 1932, p. 436.

49 Laroche, p. 97; Archive of Old Records in Warsaw, The Radziwiłł Archive, Section XI, File 314, p. 40; Potocki, *Master of Łańcut*, pp. 187–189.

50 Adolf Nowaczyński, "Małopolscy Potoccy" ("The Lesser Polish Potockis"), *Myśl Narodowa*, 3 May 1924.

51 Antoni Kobylański, *Oświetlenia do programu gospodarczego i zmiany ustroju rolnego w Polsce (Explanation of the Economic Program and Change in the Agrarian System in Poland)*, Cracow 1937, pp. 98–106.

52 Archive of Old Records in Warsaw, The Radziwiłł Archive, Section XI, File 315, pp. 1–40, 45; Interview with Izabela Radziwiłł, 7 October 1983.

53 Rogowski, pp. 105–125; *Na rogu świata i nieskończoności (At the Corner of the World and Infinity)*, Warsaw 1985.

54 Jerzy Ryx, "25-lecie 1911–35 z perspektywy pokolenia przedwojennego" ("The Twenty–five Years, 1911–1935, from the Point of View of the Prewar Generation") in *Księga pamiątkowa na 75-lecie* Gazety Rolniczej, vol. 1, p. 59; A. Kiełbicka, "Hupka Stanisław (1880–1919)," *PSB*, vol. 10, pp. 119–111; M. Gostkowska, "Szkoły gospodyń wiejskich w Małopolsce" ("Country Home Economics Schools in Lesser Poland"), *Rolnik*, 16 September 1923, p. 557.

55 G. Łańcucka, *Aniela hr. Potulicka (Aniela Countess Potulicka)*, Potulice 1939, pp. 49–70; J. Iwaszkiewicz, "Ofiarność ziemian na cele oświatowo–kulturalne" ("Landowners' Generosity in education and Culture"), in *Ziemiaństwo i większa własność rolna (Landed Gentry and Large Estates)*, Poznań 1929, p. 36.

56 Ibid., pp. 35–37; *Gazeta Rolnicza*, 15 February 1924, p. 181, 21 November 1924, p. 1162; *Roczniki Nauk Rolniczych i Leśnych*, 1932, vol. 27, pp. 476–478; Archive of Modern Records in Warsaw, Ministry of Finance, File 6251, no pagination.

57 K. Czachowski, *Maria Rodziewiczówna na tle swoich powieści (Maria Rodziewiczówna Against the Background of Her Novels)*, Poznań 1935.

58 Józef Weysenhoff, *Mój pamiętnik literacki (My Literary Diary)*, Poznań 1925, p. 7; *Gazeta Rolnicza*, 4 March 1932, p. 256.

59 Gombrowicz, *Wspomnienia plskie*, pp. 24, 42; cf. also D. de Roux, *Rozmowy z Gombrowiczem (Conversations with Gombrow-*

icz), Paris 1969, passim.

[60] Archive of Old Records in Warsaw, Archive of the Popiels of Turna, File 252, no pagination.

[61] Archive of Old records in Warsaw, Archive of the Radziwiłł s of Nieborow, File 1229, no pagination.

[62] Interview with Jan Zamoyski, 7 March 1981.

[63] *Gazeta Rolnicza*, 8 November 1918, p. 601.

[64] *Gazeta Rolnicza*, 10 January 1919, p. 36, 8 August 1919, p. 715.

[65] Bohdan Hulewicz, *Wielkie wczoraj w małym kręgu (Great Yesterday in a Small Circle)*, Warsaw 1973, p. 128; *Gazeta Rolnicza*, 17 January 1919, p. 51; *Rolnik 1867-1937*, p. 60.

[66] Jan Słomka, *Pamiętnik włościanina od pańszczyzny do dnia dzisiejszego (Diary of a Peasant Since the Corvée to the Present Day)*, Cracow 1929, p. 452.

[67] *Głos Ziemiański*, 1920, no. 1, pp. 5-7; *Gazeta Rolnicza*, 19 September 1919, p. 805; 26 September 1919, pp. 895-896.

[68] *Organizacje ziemiańskie.* . . . , pp. 37-38; *Głos Ziemiański*, 1920, no. 3, pp. 38-39; Czesław Jankowski, "Nieśwież w odrodzonej Polsce," *Słowo*, 2 May 1926, pp. 1-2; Interview with Izabela Radziwiłł , 10 October 1983.

[69] *Przegląd Ziemiański*, 1922, nos. 8, 11, 13, 26-27, 41; 1923, no. 4.

[70] J. Zamorski, *Żywot zasłużonego obywatela (The Life of a Citizen of Merit)*, Warsaw, no date, p. 2; *Gazeta Rolniza*, 9 November 1928, pp. 1513-1514, 16 November 1928, p. 1643, 11 June 1937, pp. 700-701; 28 July 1939, pp. 719-720.

[71] Stabińska, pp. 47, 83, 119.

[72] *Gazeta Rolnicza*, 6 October 1933, p. 987.

[73] *Gazeta Rolnicza*, 24 July 1936, p. 723; *Rolnik Ekonomista*, 1936, no. 15, p. 450, no. 19, pp. 575-576; *Tygodnik Rolniczy*, 1936, no. 33/34, p. 381; *Rolnik Żydowski*, 1939, no. 4, p. 11.

[74] *Gazeta Rolnicza*, 15 April 1938, p. 576, 7 April 1939, p. 338, 21 July 1939, p. 688.

[75] Drohojowski, p. 96.

[76] Konrad Olchowicz, *Pół wieku z Kurierem Warszawskim (Half a Century with Kurier Warszawski)*, Cracow 1974, pp. 304-306.

[77] Interview with Teresa Czartoryska-Rostworowska, 14 March 1981.

[78] Alfred Potocki, *Master of Łańcut*, passim.

[79] Jan Piwowarczyk, *Katolicyzm a reforma rolna (Catholicism and the Land Reform)*, Warsaw 1938, pp. 31-36.

[80] Tadeusz Ulanowski, *Nespa? 15 lat rozjemstwa w kwaterze Marsa i w poczekalni Marksa (N'est-ce pas? Fifteen Years of Mediation in the Headquarters of Mars and in the Waiting Room for Marx)*, Warsaw 1935, pp. 38–39.

[81] Maria Dąbrowska, *Rozdroża (Crossroads)*, Warsaw 1937, pp. 2 ff, 179–198.

[82] *Gazeta Rolnicza*, 28 August 1925, p. 997.

[83] Witos, *Moje wspomnienia*, vol 1, p. 45.

[84] Czesław Bobrowski, "Cyniczna prawda" ("The Cynical Truth"), *Gospodaraka Narodowa*, 15 October 1936.

[85] Julian Marchlewski, "O nowy ład na wsi" ("For a New Deal in the Countryside"), *Goniec Czerwony*, 14 August 1920; Leszek Guzicki, Seweryn Żurawicki, *Historia polskiej myśli społeczno-ekonomicznej (History of Polish Socioeconomic Thought)*, Warsaw 1974, p. 217; Walentyna Najdus, *Lewica polska w Kraju Rad 1918-1920 (The Polish Left in the Land of the Soviets, 1918-1920*, Warsaw 1971, pp. 304, 320.

[86] Rajmund Buławski, "Warstwy społeczne" ("Social Strata"), *Kwartalnik Statystyczny*, 1932, no. 3, p. 201.

Notes to Chapter 7

[1] W. Kaszuba, "Zagadnienie rolnictwa na tle akcji parcelacyjnej" ("The Agrarian Question and Parcelling"), *Drogi Polski*, 1939, no. 3.

[2] Stecki, *W obronie prawdy*, p. 218.

[3] *Gazeta Rolnicza*, 6 August 1937, p. 853.

[4] Walerian Meysztowicz, *Gawędy*, pp. 65–68; Iwański, pp. 312–313; Alfred Potocki, *Master of Łańcut*, pp. 258-261.

[5] Konstanty Skirmuntt, *Moje wspomnienia (My Memoirs)*, manuscript in the Library of the Catholic University of Lublin, File 274, p. 182.

[6] Cf. Szejnert, *Mitra pod kapeluszem*, p. 13.

APPENDIX

List of the Largest Landowners in Poland in 1922

No.	Name Major Estates/County	Hectares
1.	Maurycy Zamoysk—Zamość entail/Zamość	
	Kołbiel/Mińsk Mazowiecki	190,900
2.	Karol Radziwiłł—Dawidgródek entail/Stolin	155,340
3	Jaroław Potocki—Rzepichów Łuniniec	134,830
4.	Fyodor Ogarkov—Czuczewicze–Lenin/Łuniniec	89,270
5.	Albrecht Radziwiłł—Nieśwież	80,000
6.	Witold Broel–Plater—Worobin, Dąbrowica/Sarny	60,010
7.	Karol Stefan Habsburg—Żywiec/Żywiec	53,260
8.	Emanuel Małyński—Bereźne/Kostopol,	
	Niemirków/Równe	48,350
9.	Hermann Groedel—Skole/Skole, Wetlina/Lisko, etc.	44,810
10.	Ferdynand Radziwiłł—Ółyka and Przygodzice	
	entails	42,840
11.	Johann von Pless–Pszczyński—Rszczyna/Pszczyna	42,030
12.	Władysław Pusłowski—Piesek/Kosów Poleski, Albertyn/	
	Słonim, Łohowa/Baranowicze, etc.	38,130
13.	Karol Wojciech Pusłowski—Zawiszcze/Pińsk Telechany	
	and Budy/Kosów Poleski	36,180
14.	Alfred Potocki—Łańcut entail/Łańcut, Stare Sioł Bó-	
	orka, Hanaczówka/Przemyślany	35,400
15.	Jakób Potocki—Osieck/Garwolin, Brzeża/	
	Brzeżany	33,680
16.	Vladimir Falz–Fein—Naliboki/Wołożyn	31,530
17.	Konstanty Przeździecki—Woropajew/Postawy	31,060
18.	Zofia Czechowicz-Lachowicka—Bohdarnówka and	
	Parochońsk/Pińsk	30,470
19.	Jakób Cyryński—Buda-Naliboki/Wołożyn	30,000

20. Antoni Lanckoroński—Komarno/Rudka, Jagielnica/
    Czortków, Rozdół/Stryj   27,800
21. Albert Thurn und Taxis—Krotoszyn, Gliśnica and
    Łąkocin/Odolanów   27,800
22. Franciszek Drucki–Lubecki—Lunin/Łuniniec   26,860
23. Juliusz Tarnowski—Końskie/Końskie   26,780
24. Nadezhda Khrulova—Jelno/Sarny, Jeziory/Stolin   25,040
25. Zdzisław Tarnowski—Dzików/Tarnobrzeg, etc.   24,800
26. Konstanty Chreptowicz–Buteniew—Szczorse/Nowo-
    gródek, Wiszniew/Wołożyn   24,470
27. Ananya Strukova—Bostyń/Łuniniec   21,760
28. Adam Potocki—Krrsszowice/Chrzanów, Zator/
    Oswięim   21,680
29. Roman Sanguszko—Gumniska/Tarnów, Podhorce/
    Złoczów   21,060
30. Vladimir Okhotnikov—Rokitno/Sarny   19,730
31. Zygmunt Sk/'orzewski—Labiszyn/Szublin,
    Czerniejewo/Witkowo   18,870
32. Hubert Lubomirski—Aleksandria and Lubomirka
    Stara/Równe   18,540
33. Witold Czartoryski—Pełkinie/Jarosław,
    Konarzewo/Poznań   18,140
34. Karl Gottfried Hohenlohe–Ingelfingen—Koszęcin/
    Lubliniec   17,720
35. Stanil aw Strawiński—Sieliszze Małe/Sarny   16,590
36. Nadezhda Bobrinskaya—Perechreście/
    Zakoziel/Drohiczyn, etc.   16,490
37. Adam Stadnicki—Nawojowa and Rytro/Nowy Sącz   16,370
38. Guido Henckel von Donnersmarck—Świerklaniec/
    Tarnowskie Góry   16,330
39. Ludwik Czetwertyński—Żołudek/Lida   16,140
40. Janusz Radziwiłł—Szpanów/Równe, Nieborów/
    Łowicz   16,140
41. Konstanty Zamoyski—Wyryki/Włodawa, Dyss/
    Lubartoów   16,120
42. Jerzy Lubomirski—Charzewice/Tarnobrzeg,
    Dojlidy/Białystok   15,720
43. Bolesław Perkowski—Orzechowo/Brześć, Swaryce-
    wicze/Pińsk   15,530
44. Nikolay Kharchenko—Franopol/Brasław   15,480

45. Michał Tyszkiewicz—Ormiany/Święciany, a part
    of the Wołożyn forests/Wołożn   15,420
46. Dzimidowicz–Dzimidecki—rościana/Dzisna   14,490
47. Elzbieta Kurnatowska, née Zamoyska—Łochów/
    Węgrów, Jadów/Radzymin   14,870
48. Józef Przeździecki—Smycz and Posapowo/
    Postawy   14,800
49. Tadeusz Cieński—Pieniaki/Zborów, etc.   14,770
50. Władysław Tyszkiewicz—Tarnawatka/Tomaszów
    Lubelski, a part of the Wołożyn
    forests   14,590
51. Adam Czartoryski—Gołuchów/Pleszew, Sieniewa
    entail   14,470
52. Wojciech Gołuchowski—Janów/Gródek, Kołtów/
    Złoczów   14,320
53. Zygmunt Raczyński—Obrzycko/Szamotuły, Skoraczewo/
    Chodzież, Braczewo/Oborniki   14,130
54. Witold Święcicki—Kabaki/Prużana, Kluki/
    Piotrków   13,790
55. Kazimierz Lubomirski—Myślenice and Bogdarówka/
    Maków Podhalański. Horodenka/
    Stryj, etc.   13,020
56. Michał Baworowski—Żabie/Kosów, Podolian estates
    in the Skałat, Złoczów, and
    Tarnopol counties   12,910
57. Stanisław Szyczewski—Lomsk and Tomaszygród
    Sarny   12,860
58. Hermann Stolberg–Wernigerode—Borzęciczki/Koźim,
    Potarzyce/Jarocin   12,730
59. Karol Raczyński—Złoty Potok/Częstochowa,
    Krasizyn/Krasnystaw, etc.   12,620
60. Anna Tarnowska née Branicka—Sucha–Ślemień/
    Żywiec   12,499
61. Gyodor Kozlaninov—Obrowo/Kosów Poleski   12,499
62. Włodziemierz Dzieduszycki—Poturzyca/Sokal,
    Zarzecze/Jarosław   12,220
63. Chaim Gottesmann—Bielskowodzka Rudka/Sarny   12,000
64. Hugo Wattmann–Beaulieu—Ruda Różaniecka/
    Cieszarów   12,000
65. Krzysztof Mielżynski—Pawłowice/Leszno,

Mchy Śrem, Grodzisko/Gostyń 11,750
66. Stefania Miączyńska, née Orda—Chojno/Pińsk 11,700
67. Krzysztof Radziwiłł —Sichów/Stopnica, Tursko
    Wielkie/Sandomierz, Przyłubie/
    Pułtusk 11,690
68. Benedykt Ryszkiewicz—Pierszaje/Wołożyn, Czarne
    Błoto/Wilno-Troki 11,620
69. Karl Biron von Curland—Perzów, Rybin 11,470
70. Wilhelm Hochberg—Goraj/Czarnków 11,410
71. Hieronim Tarnowski—Rudnik/Nisko 11,370
72. Maria Drucka-Lubecka, née Zamoyska—Szczuczyn/
    Lida 11,330
73. Kazimierz Kwilecki—Gosławice, Pątnów/Konin 11,330
74. Róża Radziwiłł, née Potocka—Łubnice,
    Karsy, Pacanów Stopnica, Rytwiany/
    Sandomierz 11,310
75. Adam Ronikier—Domaczów/Brześć 11,270
76. Hipolit Młodzianowski—Tymne/Sarny 11,180
77. Janina Potocka, née Zamoyska—Koryciny and Rudka/
    Bielsk Podlaski 11,130
78. Ignacy Mielżynski—Iwno Środa, Chobienice/
    Wolsztyn 10,970
79. Grzegorz Canko-Kilczyk—Niemowicze and Czudel/Sarny 10,950
80. Stefan Hulanicki—Mulsk and Nowosiółki/Zdołburów
    Wiśniowiec Stary/Krzemieniec 10,880
81. Jerzy Tyszkiewicz—Werynia/Mielec 10,870
82. Roger Raczyński—Dębica/Ropczyce, Łęg/ Śrem 10,680
83. Leon Sapieha—Krasiczyn/Przemyś 10,550
84. Paweł Stecki—Międzyrzecz/Równe 10,550
85. Jan Goetz-Okocimski—Okocim/Brzesko, Skowierzyn/
    Tarnobrzeg 10,530
86. Stanisław Badeni-Radziechów/Kamionka
    Strumiłowa 10,500
87. Ludwik Kraków—part of Lubań/Wilejka 10,400
88. Aleksander Lubański—part of Lubań/Wilejka 10,400
89. Maria Lubomirska, née Zamoyska—Jeziorany/Łuck,
    Stężyca/Korytnica, Zaleszczyki/
    Zaleszczyki 10,380
90. Władysław Zamoyski—Kórnik/Śrem, Zakopane/Nowy
    Targ 10,330

91. Klaus Thiele Winkler—Mysłowice/Katowice   10,320
92. Jerzy Osmołowski—Sieliszcze/Pińsk   10,220
93. Władysław Szyczewski—Lady/Sarny   10,210
94. Maria Plater-Zyberk—Horodziec/Dzisna, Sawczyn/
    Sokal   10,000
95. Albina Włodek, née Goetz-Okocimska—Tuszów/
    Mielec   10,000
96. Henryk Kolischer—Bilcze/Drohobycz, Przyłęk/
    Kolbuszowa   9,990
97. Vanda Plemannikov—Górki/Drohiczyn   9,880
98. Stanisław Tyszkiewicz—Lelechówka/Grłodek   9,800
99. Jadwig—a Rzyszczewska, née Gorayska—Podmon-
    asterek/ Kamionka Strumiłowa,
    Ratniów/Łuck   9,800
100. Paweł Sapieha—Siedlisko/Rawa Ruska, Borszców/
     Borszczów   9,750
101. Maria Krasicka, née Lach Szyrma—Sporów/Kosów
     Poleski   9,750
102. Adam Lubomirski—Miżyniec entail/Przemyśl,
     Górka and Tynne/Równe   9,730
103. Agenor Gołuchowski—Skała entail/Borszczów,
     Lubaczów/Cieszanów   9,530
104. Adam Branicki—Roś entail/Wołkowysk   9,510
105. Jan Drucki-Lubecki—Pohost Zahorodny/Pińsk,
     etc.   9,500
106. Zygmunt Zamoyski—Wysock/Jarosław   9,490
107. Karol Tołłoczko—Bielin and Wołowiel/Drohiczyn   9,450
108. Antoni Jundziłł—Hrudopol and Dobromśl/
     Baronowicze   9,450
109. Jan Oskierka—Budsław/Wilejka, Czerenka/Dzisna   9,290
110. JaninaMilewska, née Umiastowska—Klewica, etc. /
     Oszmiana, Puziniewicze/Stołpce   9,270
111. Elizabeta Shuvalova—Pełcza and Dubno forests/
     Dubno   9,230
112. Krystyn Ostrowski—Korczew/Sokołów, Miedzna/
     Węgrów   9,080
113. Włodzimierz Czetwertynski—Woronczyn/Horochów,
     Rudzieniec, etc./Radzyń   9,060
114. Zofia Stanek—Wiszenka/Gródek, Krechów/
     Żołkiew   9,000

115. Antoni Sobański—Bolimów/Łowicz, Guzów/
     Błonie   8,890
116. Mikhail Slezkin—Karasin/Kowel   8,830
117. Wojciech Zatwarnicki—Wysock/Brześć   8,820
118. Stanisław Stępkowski—Planta/Słonim   8,750
119. Jerzy Jezierski—Zawierowo and Kotów/Łuck   8,620
120. Andrzej Lubomirski—Przeworsk entail/Przeworsk   8,560
121. Dawid Lindenbaum—Kropiwnik, etc., Dobromil   8,850
122. Edward Krasiński—Opinogóra entail/Ciechanów   8,480
123. Andrzej Zamoyski—Podzamcze, etc./Garwolin   8, 440
124. Kamil Pourbaix—Antonówka and Horodno/Sarny   8,420
125. Aleksander Wielopolski—Chroberz/Pinczów   8,400
126. Aleksey Kaufman–Turkestansky—Milacze/Stolin,
     Hulewicze/Gródek   8,300
127. Mieczysław Bohdanowicz—Obwodowce and Rajówka/
     Wilejka   8,000
128. Józef Tyszkiewicz—Zatrocze entail, Duniłowicze/
     Postawy   8,000
129. Władysław Jaroszyński—Kołki/Łuck   7,980
130. Tomasz Zamoyski—Iwje/Oszmiana, etc.   7,930
131. Feliks Szańkowski—Ołtusz Leśny/Brześć,
     Stepanogrod/Sarny   7,920
132. Jan bisping–Gallen—Massalany entail, Brzostowiec/
     Grodno, Kuźnica/Wołkowysk   7,900
133. Henryk Dolański—Radłow/Brzesko   7,900
134. Kazimierz Czartoryski—Żurawne/Żydaczów   7,880
135. Stanisław Judndziłł—Reginów/Baranowicze,
     Sienierzyce/Nowogródek   7,860
136. Rudolf Baworowski—Niżbork entail, Czabarówka/
     Husiatyn   7,850
137. Maurycy Potocki—Jabłonna/Warsaw   7,840
138. Ludwika Czartoryska, née Krasińska—Przystań/
     Maków Mazowiecki, Gułow, etc.
     /Ciechanów   7,830
139. Jadwiga Bnińska, née Tarnowska—Szelągówka/
     Białystok   7,790
140. Gipolit Vorontsov–Dashkov—Majdan/Zdołbunów,
     Obhów/Dubno   7,750
141. Andrzej Potocki—Dołhołęka, Tuliłów, etc./
     Radzyń   7,750

142. Stanisław Czacki—Poryck, etc./Włodziemierz
     Wołyński   7,700
143. Eustachy Sapieh—Spusza/Lida, Jelna/Grodno   7,700
144. Helena Czartoryska, née Skrzyńska—Wiry, etc./
     Poznań, Żydaczow/Żydaczów   7,650
145. Adam Zamoyski—Kozłówa entail/Lubartoów   7,650
146. Mieczysław Chodkiewicz—Młynów/Dubno, Antonowce/
     Krzemieniec   7,640
147. Seweryn Dolański—Gręhów/Tarnobrzeg   7,610
148. Maria Dembińska—Witkowo and Czarna/Ropczyce,
     Borkowice/Końskie   7,600
149. Maria Niemojowska—Lubstów/Kolo, Miastków/
     Garwolin   7,590
150. Basily Radionov—Ołtusz/Brzećć   7,590
151. August Potocki—Moskorzew/Włoszczowa, Praszka/
     Wieluń   7,580
152. Zdzisław Lubomirski—Werba/Dubno, Kohilno/
     Włodzimierz Wołyński   7,560
152. Zdzisław Lubomirski—Werba/Dubno, Kohilno/
     Włodzimierz Wołyński   7,560
153. Zygmunt Broel-Plater—Białaczów/Opoczno,
     Blizin/Końskie   7,550
154. Agnes von Diergardt—Kuźnica Sośnieńska   7,450
155. Stanisław Stadnicki—Krysowice/Mościska   7,410
156. aniela Potulicka—Potulice and Ślesin/Bydgoszcz 7,410
157. Leontyna Młodzianowska—Soszyczno/Kamień
     Koszyrski   7,400
158. Hans Hugo von Radolin—Jarocin/Jarocin   7,340
159. Edward Jankowski—Miedziera, etc./Końskie   7,280
160. Genowefa Broel-Plater, née Pusłowska—Dobra Wola/
     Pińsk   7.260
161. Leon Lipszyc—Bielczaki andHłużowo/
     Kostopol   7,250
162. Juliusz Vielski—Roszniów/Tłumacz   7,220
163. Heinrich von Reuss—Baszków and Kobylin/
     Krotoszyn   7,190
164. Julia Paszkowska—Ostrów and Wianuża/Dzisna   7,190
165. Józef Uznański—Terebieżów/Stolin, Poronin/
     Nowy Targ (joint ownership)   7,160
166. Jerzy Uznański—Terebieżów/Stolin, Poronin/

Nowy Targ (joint ownership) 7,130
167. Otto Jouanne–Klęka and Boguszyn/Jarocin,
    Murzynówa/Środa 7,130
168. Aleksander Ledóchowski—Smordwa and Berehy/
    Dubno 7,130
169. Antoni Zamoyski–Chorostów/Łuniniec 7,120
170. Michal Leliwa–Bajer—Strzelce Wielkie/Brzesko,
    Partyń/Mielec 7,110
171. Władysław Tyszkiewicz—part of Wołczyn/
    Wołożyn 7,070
172. Heinrich Keyserlingk—Wejherowo/Wejherowo 7,060
173. Stefan Badeni—Koropiec/Buczacz, Znosiecze/Sarny 7,000
174. Stanisław Niezabytowski—Uherce/Gródek,
    Butyny/Żółkiew 7,000
175. stanisław Mańkowski—Kazimierz Biskupi/Konin 7,000
176. Mordech Rymar—Struga/Stolin 6,900
177. Stanisław Komorowski—Bojanów/Nisko, Gwoździec/
    Kołomyja 6,980
178. Włodzimierz Karski–Nieznanowice/Włoszczowa,
    Nawodzice/Sandomierz, etc. 6,950
179. Georgi Davidov—Wólka/Łuniniec 6,940
180. Stanisław Findeisen—Doboje/Stolin 6,940
181. Jan Nowicki—Rudnia, etc./ Baranowicze 6,930
182. Jan Madeyski—Parchacz/Sokal, Gaje Hołoskowieckie/
    Brody 6,920
183. Stanisław Siemie nski-Lewicki—Chorostków
    entail 6,920
184. Ignacy Krasicki—Lesko/Lisko 6,900
185. Henryk Potocki—Chrząstów/Włoszczowa, Koniecpol/
    Radomsko 6,850
186. Feliks Broel–Plater—Belmont/Brasław 6,780
187. Leopold Kronenberg—Wieniec/Włocławek,
    Łękińsko/Piotrków 6,750
188. Michał Światopełk–Mirski—Mir/Stołpce, Wielki
    Dwów/Nieśwież 6,750
189. Piotr Zapolski—Buchowo/Pińsk 6,740
190. Maria Słotwińska—Paafianowo and Zacisze/
    Dzisna 6,730
191. Hedwig Jouanne, née Kennemann—Rożnów/
    Oborniki, Jerziory/Środa 6,700

192. Helena Gąsiorowska—Balin/Inowrocław, Bytyń/
     Szamotuły   6,660
193. Roman Skirmuntt—Porzecze/Pińsk   6,640
194. Anfisa Białowąsowicz—Woronki and Łuka/Sarny   6,640
195. Stanisław Rey—Przecław/Mielec, Sieciechowice/
     Olkusz, etc.   6,620
196. Adam Ledóchowski—Kisielin/Horochów, Berezowicz/
     Włodziemierz Wołyński   6,600
197. Aleksander Drucki-Lubecki—Bałtów/Iłża,
     Ruda Kościelna/Opatów   6,550
198. Anna Tuszowska—Lubieszów/Pińsk, Kołki/
     Sarny   6,530
199. Zofia Ruediger—Sobolewo and Olmond/Białystok   6,490
200. Mikoĺaj Birar—Maniewicze and Smołodówka/
     Kowel   6,480

Source: *Księga adresowa obywataeli ziemskich Rzeczypospolitej oraz
kółek rolniczych, syndykatów, stowarzyszeń i kooperatyw z działem
handlowo-przemysłowym b. Kongresówki i Kresów 1922/23 (Address
Book of Landowners of the Polish Republic, Farmers Circles Syndicates, Societies, and Cooperatives with a Commercial Section for the
Former Kingdom of Poland and the Eastern Borderland 1922/23),*
Warsaw, no date; *Księga adresowa obywateli ziemskich Rzeczypospolitej Polskiej oraz spis kółek rolniczych z działem handlowo-przemysłowym Wielkopolski i Pomorza (Address Book of Commercial Section
for Greater Poland and Pomerania),* Warsaw 1923; *Księga adresowa
obywateli ziemskich R. P. Małopolska, rok 1928/29 (Address Book of
Landowners of the Polish Republic, Lesser Poland, 1928/29),* Warsaw, no date; *Księga adresowa Polski (wraz z W. M. Gda nskiem)
dia handlu, przemsłu, rzemiosła rolnictwa (Address Book of Poland
with the Free Town of Gdańsk for Trade, Industry, Handicraft, and
Agriculture),* Warsaw 1926; *Ilustrowana Encyklopedia Trzaski, Everta i Michalskiego (Illustrated Encyclopedia of Trzaska, Evert, and
Michalski),* Vol. 3, pp. 990–991; Serafin, F., *Wieś śląska w latach
międzywojennych (The Silesian Countryside in the Interwar Years),*
Katowice 1977, pp. 27, 32; Letter by Juliusz Ostrowski of 3 April
1985.

BIBLIOGRAPHY

1. Archives

Archive of Modern Records (Archiwum Akt Nowych), Warsaw, Sets of documents:
Biuro Sejmu, Centralne Towarzystwo Rolnicze, Artur Dobiecki, Stanisław Dzierzbicki, Fundacja im. J. hr. Potockiego, Ministerstwo Rolnictwa i Reform Rolnych, Ministerstwo Skarbu Obóz Zjednoczenia Narodowego, Państwowy Bank Rolny, Józef Poniatowski, Władysław Sikorski, Towarzystwo Straży Kresowej, Zjednoczony Bank Ziemiański S. A., Lucjan Żeligowski.

Archive of Old Records (Archiwum Główne Akt Dawnych), Warsaw
Sets of documents:
Lubieński Archive, Niemojewski Archive, Niemojewski of Marchwacz Archive, Popiel of Turna Archive, Potocki of Jabłonna Archive, Potocki of Łańcut Archive, Radziwiłł Archive Section XL, Radziwiłł of Nieborów Archive, Zamoyski Archive.

Central Archive of the Chief Census Bureau (Główny Urząd Statystyczny), Warsaw
Wydział Statystyki Rolnictwa, File 317, 502–828.

Library of the Catholic University of Lublin (Katolicki Uniwersytet Lubelski) Lublin. Sets of documents:
Jan Stecki Archive, Memoirs of Leon Białkowski, Jadwiga Skirmunt, and Konstanty Skirmuntt.

Library of the Central School of Planning and Statistics (Szkoła Główna Planowania i Statystyki), Warsaw
Manuscripts of Ph.D. and M.Sc. theses.

Library of the Central School of Rural Economy (Szkoła Główna Bospodarstwa Wiejskiego), Warsaw
Manuscripts of Ph.D. and M.Sc. theses.

2. Periodicals

Agronomia Społeczna (1934–39), *Drogj Naprawy* (1926–27), *Drogi Polski* (1922–24), *Dzień Polski* (1928), *Echa Leśne* (1929–30), *Ekonomista* (1909–39), *Gazeta Rolnicza* (1918–39, *Głos Ziemi* (1937–39), *Głos Ziemiański* (1920), *Kwartaln ik Statystyczny* (1924–34), *Las Polski* (1921–39), *Miesięcznik Statystyczny* (1928–33), *Monarchia Narodowa* (1938–39), *Myśl Narodowa* (1921–39), *Polesie* (1929), *Polska Gospodarcza* (1930–39), *Prace Instytutu Badania Stanu Gospodarczego Ziem Wschodnich* (1927–28), *Przegląd Dyplomatyczny* (1919), *Przegled Historyczny* (1958–83), *Przegląd Rybacki* (1919, 1921), *Przegląd Powszechny* (1918–39), *Przegląd Rybacki* (1928, 1930–39), *Przegląd Statystyczny* (1938–39), *Przegląd Współczesny* (1922–39), *Przechpolski* (1922–26), *Przegled Zie- miański* (1922–23), *Roczniki Dziejów Ruchi Ludowego* (1959–68), *Roczniki Dziejów Społecznych i Gospodarczych* (1931–84), *Roczniki Nauk Rolniczych i Leśnych* (1923–39), *Rolnictwo* (1928–39), *Rolnik* (1923–27), *Rolnik Ekonomista* (1925–36), *Rolnik Pomorski* (1930–31), *Rolnik Żydowski* (1933-39), *Słowo* (1926–27, 1935–36), *Sprawa Rolna* (1919–21), *Statystyka Pracy* (1929–38), *Statystyka Rolnicza* (1931–38), *Studia z Dziejćw Gospodarstwa Wiejskiego* (1957–70), *Tygodnik Rolniczy* (1922, 1928–29, 1938–39), *Wiadomości Statystyczne* (1923–39), *Wieś i Państwo* (1938–39), *Włóczęga* (1932–36), *Wschód Polski* (1920–22), *Zaczyn* (1936–39), *Ziemia* (1920–39), *Ziemia i Naród* (1938–39), *Ziemia Wołyńska* (1928–32), *Ziemianin* (1918–19, 1930), *Ziemianka* (1918–20), *Ziemianka Polska* (1925–29), *Zycie obotnika Rolnego* (1934–39), *Zycie Rolnicze* (1936–39).

Official Sources

Adresy obywateli ziemskich Królestwa Polskiego, Litwy i Rusi (Addresses of Landowners of the Kingdom of Poland, Lituhuania, and Ruthenia), Warsaw 1913.

Annuaire International de Statistique Agricole 1939/40, Rome 1940.

Dziennik Ustaw R. P. (Official Gazette of the Polish Republic) 1918–1939.

Kalendarz Ludowy Towarzystwa Straży Kresowej (Popular Calendar of the Society of the Borderland Guard) 1920, 1921.

S. Kasztelewicz, *Spis ziemian ziemi kaliskiej, kieleckiej, łonżynskiej, piotrkowskiej, płockiej, radomskiej, siedleckiej suwalskiej i warsza-*

wskiej *(List of Landowners of the Kalisz, Kielce, Lomża, Pi-ortrkow, Płock, Radom,. Siedice, Suwalki, and Warsaw Lands)*, Warsaw 1919.

Księga adresowa obywateli ziemskich Rzeczypospolitej oraz kółek rolniczych, syndykatów, stowarzyszeń i kooperatyw z działem handlowo-przemysłowym b. Kongresówi i Kresów 1922/23 (Address Book of Landowners of the Polish Republic. Farmers Circles, Syndicates, Societies, and Cooperatives with a Commercial Section, for the Former Kingdom of Poland and the Eastern Borderland 1922/23), Warsaw, no date.

Księga adresowa obywateli ziemskich Rzeczypospolitej Polskiej oraz spis kółek Rolniczych z dziełem handlowo-przemyłowym Wielkopski i Pomorza (Address Book of Landowners of the Polish Republic and Farmers Circles with a Commercial Section for Greater Poland and Pomerania), Warsaw 1928.

Księga adresowa obywateli ziemskich R. P. t. Małopolska, rok 1928/29 (Address Book of Landowners of the Polish Republic, Lesser Poland, Year 1928/29), Warsaw, no date.

Kséga adresowa Polski (wraz z W. M. Gdańskiem) dla handlu, przemyłu, rzemioła i rolnictwa (Address Book of Poland with the Free Town of Gdańsk for Trade, Industry, Handicraft, and Agriculture), Warsaw 1926.

Mały Rocznik Statystyczny (Concise Statistical Yearbook) 1931–39.

Obciążenie państwowymi podatkami pośrednimi w roku 1928 (Direct State Tax Burden in 1928), Warsaw 1930.

Rocznik informacyjny o spółkach akcyjnych w Polsce (Information Yearbook of Stock Companies in Poland), Warsaw 1930.

Rocznik Statystyczny R. P. (Statistical Yearbook of the Polish Republic) 1920/21–30.

Statystyka Polski, T. V. Wielka własność ziemska (Statistics of Poland, Vol. 5, Large Landed Property), Warsaw 1925.

Interviews

Dezydery Chłapowski, 8 February 1984
Teresa Czartoryska-Rostworowska, 14 March 1981
Stefan Hubert, 7 March 1981
Jerzy Kostrowicki, 10 December 1980
Stanisław Lipkowski-Milewski, 18 October 1983
Andrzej Niegolewski, 4 October 1983
Zofia Tyszkiewicz-Potocka, 29 May 1982

Izabela Radziwił ł , 7 and 10 October 1083
Jan Serwatowski, 1 June 1984
Jan Zamoyski, 7 March 1981

5. Memoirs

Badeni, Stanisław, *Wczoraj i przedwczoraj (Yesterday and the Day Before Yesterday)*, London 1963.

Broel–Plater, Ludwik, *Dookoła wspomnień (All-Around Memoirs)*, London, no date.

Czarkowski–Golejewski, Cyryl, *Wspomnienia z rykowisk (Memoirs from the Rutting Grounds)*, Lwow 1927.

Dorożynska–Zaleska, Elżbieta, *Na ostatniej placówce. Dziennik z życia wsi podolskiej w latach 1917-1921 (At the Last Outpost Diary from the Podolian Countryside, 1917-21)*, Warsaw 1925.

Dowbór–Muśnicki, Józef, *Moje wspomnienia (My Memoirs)*, Warsaw 1935.

Drohojowski, Jan, *Wspomnienia dyplomatyczne (Diplomatic Memoirs)*, Cracow 1969.

Dunin–Kozicka, Maria, *Burza od wschodu (Tempest from the East)*, Cracow 1925.

Gawroński, Jan, *Dyplomatyczne wagary (Playing Diplomatic Truant)*, Warsaw 1965.

Ginter, Maria, *Galopem na przełaj (Cross-Country Galloping)*, Warsaw 1983.

Glinka, Władysław, *Pamiętnik z wielkiej wojny (Diary from the Great War)*, vols. 1–4, Warsaw 1927–28.

Gombrowicz, Witold, *Wspomnienia polskie (Polish Memoirs)*, Paris 1977.

Hulewicz, Bohdan, *Wielkie wczoraj w małym kręgu (Great Yesterday in a Small Circle)*, Warsaw 1973.

Hupka, Jan, *Z czasów wielkiej wojny (During the Great War)*, Lwow 1937.

Hutten–Czapski, Bogdan, *60 lat życia publicznego towarzyskiego (Sixty Years of Public and Social Life)*, Warsaw 1968.

Iwański, August, *Pamiętniki 1832-1876 (Memoirs, 1932-76)*; August Iwaśki, Jr., *Wspomnienia 1881-1939 (Memoirs, 1881-1939)*, Warsaw 1968.

Korwin–Milewski, Hipolit, *Siedemdziesiąt lat wspomnień 1855-1925 (Seventy Years of Memoirs, 1855-1925)*, Poznań 1930.

Kossak, Zofia, *Pożoga (Ravage)*, Warsaw 1935.

References 183

Laroche, Jules, *Polska lat 1926-1935 (Poland of the Years 1926-1935)*, Warsaw 1966.

Lednicki, Eacław, *20 lat w wolnej Polsce (Twenty Years in Free Poland)*, Warsaw no date.

Longchamps de Berier, Bogusław, *Ochrzczony na szablach powstańczych (Baptized by the Sabres of the Insurgents)*, Wrocław 1983.

Meysztowicz, Walerian, *Gawędy o czasach i ludziach (Tales About Times and People)*, London 1983.

Morawski, Krzysztof, *Wspomnienia z Turwi (Memoirs of Turew)*, Cracow 1981.

Potocka–Działynska, Anna, *Mó Pamietnik (My Diary)*, Warsaw 1973.

Potocki, Alfred, *Master of Łaćut*, London 1959.

Potocki, Jerzy, *Na wojnie i na łowach (At War and at the Hung)*, Warsaw 1932.

Regulski, Janusz, *Blaski i cienie długiego życia (Ups and Downs of a Long Life)*, Warsaw 1980.

Słomka, Jan, *From Serfdom to Self-Government. Memoirs of a Polish Village Mayor, 1842-1927*, London 1941.

Spiss, Tadeusz, *Ze wspomnień c. k. urzédnika politycznego (Memoirs of the Royal–Imperial Political Official)*, Rzeszów 1936.

Wańkowicz, Melchior, *Czerwień i amarant (Red and Amaranth)*, Warsaw 1974.

Wieloplska–Jehanne, Maria, *Gontowszczyzna Wspomnienia z rebelii ukraińskiej w Małopolsce Wschodniej (Gontowszozyzna. Memoirs of the Ukrainian Rebellion in Eastern Galicia)*, Poznań 1925.

Wierzbicki, Andrzej, *Wspomnienia i dokumenty 1877-1920 (Memoirs and Documents, 1877-1920)*, Warsaw 1957.

Witos, Wincenty, *Moje wspomnienia (My Memoirs)*, vols. 1–3, Paris 1964–65.

Woyniłłowicz, Edward, *Wspomnienia 1947-1928 (Memoirs, 1847-1928)*, Wilno 1932.

Books and Articles

Ajnenkiel, Andrzej, *Położenie prawne robotników rolnych w Polsce 1918-1939 (The Legal Situation of Farm Workers in Poland, 1918-39)*, Warsaw 1962.

Ajnenkiel, Andrzej, "Zbiorowe umowy pracy w rolnictwie w Polsce w latach 1918-1926" ("Collective Labor Contracts in Polish Agriculture, 1918-1926"), *Czasopismo Prawno-Historyczne*, 1957, no. 2, 1929, no. 11.

Antoniewski, Stanisław, "Dochodowość dużych i małych gospodarstw" ("Profitability of Large and Small Farms"), *Przemysł i Handel,* 1929, no. 11.

Antoniewski, Stanisław, *Z ekonomiki gospodarstwo dużych i małych (Economics of Large and Small Farms),* Warsaw 1938.

Babiński, Witold, "Kazimierz Fudakowski," *Zeszyty Historyczne,* 1966, no. 9.

Babiński, Witold, "Nowelizacja prawa leśnego" ("Amendment to the Forest Law"), *Rolnik Ekonomista,* 1933, no. 1.

Babiński, Witold, *Zagadnienia leśne i drzewne w Polsce (Forest and Timber Problems in Poland),* Warsaw 1937.

Barński, Władysław, *Kwestia drzewna w Polsce (The Timber Question in Poland),* Warsaw 1928.

Bardach, Juliusz, "Z dziejów mentalonosci feudalno–konserwatynej" ("History of the Feudal Conservative Mentality"), *Przegląd Historyczny,* 1977, no. 1.

Bartoszewicz, Joachim, *Na Rusi. Polski stan posiadania (In Ruthenia. The Range of Polish Property),* Kiev 1912.

Bartoszewicz, K., *Radziwiłł owie (The Radziwiłłs),* Cracow 1928.

Biegeleisen, Leon W., *Reforma rolna głównych państw europejskich (Land Reform of the Major European Countries),* vols. 1–2, Warsaw 1924–26.

Biegeleisen, Leon W., *Teoria małej i wielkiej własności ziemskiej (Theory of Small and Large Landed Property),* Cracow 1918.

Bilans gospodaraczy dziesięciolecia Polski Odrodzonej (The Balance Sheet of Ten Years of Independent Poland), vols. 1–2, Poznań 1929.

Bocheński, Aleksander, "O przyszłość młodych ziemian" ("The Future of Young Landed Gentry") *Słowo,* 26 January 1936.

Bogusławski, F., "Ekstensyfikacja rolnictwa polskiego" ("Extension of Polish Agriculture"), *Życie Rolnicze,* 1939, no. 17.

Borowski, W., *Kredyt rolniczy w Polsce (Agricultural Credit in Poland),* Warsaw 1927.

Brzeski, Tadeusz, *Materiały statystyczne do sprawy rolnej (Statistical Evidence on the Agrarian Question),* Warsaw 1919.

Brzeski, Tadeusz, "Przyszłość reformy rolnej w Polsce" ("The Future of the Land Reform in Poland"), *Sprawa Rolna,* 1921, no. 8.

Brzeski, Tadeusz, *Uwagi o reformie stosunków rolnych w Polsce (Remarks on the Reform of Agrarian Relations in Poland),* Warsaw 1929.

Bujak, Franciszek, *O naaprawie ustroju rolnego w Polsce (On Improvement of the Agrarian System in Poland)*, Warsaw, no date.

Bujak, Franciszek, *O podziale ziemi i reformie rolnej (On Distribution of Land and Land Reform)*, Warsaw 1920.

Bujak, Franciszek, *Uwagi krytyczne o naszej reformie rolnej (Critical Remarks on Our Land Reform)*, Warsaw 1921.

Buławski, Rajmund, "Warstwy społeczne" ("Social Strata"), *Kwartalnik Statystyczny*, 1932, no. 3.

Buławski, Rajmund, *W sprawie ośmiu milionów osiemset tysięcy "zbędnej" ludności rolniczej w Polsce (On the Eight Million Eight Hundred Thousand "Redundant" Agrarian Population in Poland)*, Katowice 1936.

Caspari, Emil, "Polska wielka własność ziemska w Wielkim Księstwie Poznańskim" ("Polish Large Estates in the Grand Duchy of Poznania"), *Ekonomista*, 1909, no. 1.

Caspari, Emil, "Wielka własność ziemska w polskich powiatach Górnego Śięka" ("Large Estates in the Polish Counties of Upper Silesia"), *Ekonomista*, 1911, no. 3.

Chlebowski, B., *Zamość, ordynacia Zamoyskich i powiat zamojski (Zamość, the Zamoyski Entail, and Zamoćć County)*, Zamość, no date.

Chłapowski, Alfred, *Cukrownictwo Polski a eksport cukru (Sugar Refining in Poland and the Sugar Exports)*, no place, no date.

Chojecki, Z., *Produkcja rolnoza i przemysł rolniczy w Polsce współczesnej (Agricultural Output and Industry in Contemporary Poland)*, Warsaw 1937.

Chojecki, Z., *Społeczeństwo polskie na Rusi (Polish Society in Ruthenia)*, Warsaw 1937.

Ciechomski, Jerzy, *Produkeja mniejszej i większej włesności ziemskiej w Polsce (Output of Small and Large Farms in Poland)*, Warsaw 1937.

Ciepielewski, Jerzy, *Polityka agrarna rządu polekiego w latach 1929–1935 (The Agrarian Policy of the Polish Government, 1929-35)*, Warsaw 1968.

Ciepielewski, Jerzy, *Wieś polska w latach wielkiego kryzysu 1929–1935. Materiały i dokumentary (The Polish Countryside during the Great Depression, 1929-35. Materials and Documents)*, Warsaw 1968.

Cieszewski, J., *Uwagi o opodatkowaniu rolnictwa (Remarks on Agricultural Taxation)*, Warsaw 1926.

Cieszewski, J., Englicht, W., *Obciążenia podatkowa (Tax Burden)*, Warsaw 1926.

Cieśiak, T., *Szlachta zagrodowa województwa stanisławowskiego (Petty Nobles of Stanisławów Province)*, Warsaw 1938.

Czerniewska, Maria, "Gruntu orne, struktura zasiewów i plony w latach 1928–1937" ("The Arable Land, Crop Structure, and Yields in the Years 1928–37"), *Statystyka Rolnicza*, 1937.

Czerniewski, K., *Struktura społeczna wsi polskiej (The Social Structure of the Polish Countryside)*, Warsaw 1937.

Czerniewski, K., *Zagadnienie struktury agrarnej (The Question of the Agrarian Structure)*, Warsaw 1937.

Czerwijowski, Z., *Zarys stosunków rolniczo-ekonomicznych na Wołyniu, 1919–1924 rok (Outline of Agricultural and Economic Relations in Volhynia, 1919–24)*, Luck 1924.

Czubiński, A., Skrzek, M., *Strajki rolne w Wielkopolsce 1919–1922 (Agricultural Strikes in Greater Poland, 1919–22)*, Warsaw 1959.

Dąbkowski, P., *Szlachta zaściankowa w Korczynie i Kruszelnicy nad Stryjem (Noble Villages in Korczyn and Kruszelnica on the Stryj)*, Lwow 1936.

Dć abrowska, Maria, *Rozdroża (Crossroads)*, Warsaw 1937.

Dederko, Bohdan, *Majątek narodowy Polski (The National Property of Poland)*, Warsaw 1930.

Dederko, Bohdan, *Najkorzystniejszy rozmiar gospodarstw wiejskich (The Optimum Size of Farms)*, Warsaw 1925.

Dederko, Bohdan, *Zdolność płatnicza podatkowa rolnictwa (The Tax Payment Capacity of Agriculture)*, Warsaw 1930.

"Deklaracja Rady Społecznej przy Prymasie Polski" ("Declaration by the Social Council of the Primate of Poland"), *Przegląd Ekonomiczny*, 1938, vol. 21.

Dowgiałło, W., "Inflanty Polskie" ("Polish Latgalia"), *Przegląd Dyplomatyczny*, 1919, no. 1.

Dunin, Rodryz, "Znaczenie mniejszej i większej własności rolnej w gospodarstwie społeczny" ("Importance of Small and Large Farms for the National Economy"), *Sprawa Rolna*, 1919, vol. 1.

Dworakowski, S., *Szlachta zagrodowa we wschodnich powiatach Wołynia i Polesia (Noble Villages in the Eastern Counties of Volhynia and Polesia)*, Warsaw 1939.

Dworzaczek, Włodzimierz, *Genealogia (Geneology)*, Warsaw 1956.

Dziadulewicz, Stanisław, *Herbarz rodzin tatarskich w Polsce (Armorial of Tatar Families in Poland)*, Wilno 1929.

Dzieje lasów, leśnictwa i drzewnictwa w Polsce (History of Forests, Forestry, and Timber Industry in Poland), Warsaw 1965.

Dzieje wsi wielkopolskiej (History of the Great Polish Countryside), Poznań 1959.

Dziesięciolecie Polski Odrodzonej (Ten Years of Reborn Poland), Cracow 1928.

Dzik, A., *Młynarstwo w Polsce (Flour Milling in Poland)*, Warsaw 1928.

Dzikowski, Stanisław, *Egzotyczna Polska (Exotic Poland)*, Warsaw 1931.

E. A. M., *Na marginesie projektu ustawy o zniesieniu ordynacji (Sidenote to the Draft Law on the Liquidation of Entails)*, Warsaw 1936.

The Eckert, Marian, *Przemysł rolno-spożywczy w Polsce 1918–1939 (The Food Processing Industry in Poland, 1918–19)*, Poznań 1974.

Encyklopedia podręczna polskiego rolnictwa, przemsłu, handlu i finansów (Handy Encyclopedia of Polish Agriculture, Industry, Trade, and Finance), Warsaw 1929.

Englicht, W., "Obciążenie podatkami bezpośrednimi gospodarstw rolnych w Polsce" ("The Direct Tax Burden of Farms in Poland"), *Rolnik Ekonomista*, 1926, no. 12.

Estreicher, Stanisław, *Konserwatyzm (Conservatism)*, Warsaw 1928.

Estreicherówna, E., "Płace robotników dniówkowych niestałych w rolnictwie w roku 1928" ("Wages of Seasonal Day Laborers in Agriculture in 1928"), *Satystyka Pracy*, 1929.

Estericherówna, E., "Płace stałych robotników rolnych na podstawie umów zbiorowych w latach 1927/28 i 1928/29" ("Wages of Permanent Farm Workers on the Basis of Collective Contracts in the Years 1927/28 and 1928/29"), *Statystyka Pracy*, 1929.

Frankowski, Jan, *Zadłużenie gospodarstw rolnych woj. pomorskiego w latach 1930–1936 (Indebtedness of Farms in Pomeranian Province, 1930–36)*, Lublin 1937.

Frankowski, Jan, *Zadłużenie gospodarstw rolnych w woj. poznańskim w latach 1932–36 (Indebtedness of Farms in Poznań Province, 1932–36)*, Poznań 1938.

Frycz, Karol S., "Ziemiaństwo" ("Landed Gentry"), *Myśl Narodowa*, 28 April 1935.

Fudakowska, Anna, "Zadania ziemianek w chwili obecnej" ("Present Tasks of Landladies"), *Głos Ziemiański*, 1920, no. 6.

Gajownieczek, W., *Statystka porównawcza dochodów i rozchodów gospo-*

darstw folwarcznych w powiatach włoławskim, nieszawskim i lip-
nowskim za lata gospodarcze 1930/31, 1931/32 i 1932/33 (Comparative Statistics of Returns and Expenditures of Estates in Włocławek, Nieszawa, and Lipno Counties for the Economic Years
1930/31, 1931/32, and 1932/33.), Włocławek 1935.

Gerlicz, R., Praca najemna na roli w większej własnośći ziemskiej
(Hired Labor on Large Estates), Warsaw 1929.

Glinka, Władysław, Bolszewizm a sprawa agrarna w Polsce (Bolshe-
vism and the Agrarian Question in Poland), Warsaw 1918.

Głos wolny o Związku Ziemian (Free Voice About the Landowners'
Society), Warsaw 1920.

Gójski, J., 40 lat Związku Zawodowego Robotników Rolnych (Forty
Years of the Trade Union of Farm Workers), Warsaw 1960.

Górski, Ludwik, W sprawie reformy rolnej w Polsce (On the Land
Reform in Poland), Warsaw 1919.

Górski, Ludwik, Wytyczne programn wiejskiego w świetle zased ka-
tolickich (Guidelines for the Countryside Program in the Light
of Catholic Principles), Lublin 1937.

Górski, Ludwik, Wywłaszczenie ziemi (Expropriation of Land), Warsaw 1918.

Grabowski, J., Warunki, Rozmieszczenie typów, poziom i okręgi hodowli koni w Polsce (Conditions, Distribution, Standards, and Regions of Horse Breeding in Poland), no place, 1933.

Grabski, Władysław, Idea Polski (The Idea of Poland), Warsaw 1935.

Grabski, Władysław, Kryzys rolniczy. Memoriałna I Zjazd Ekonomis-
tow Polskich w Poznaniu w maju 1929 r. (Agricultural Depression. Report to the First Congress of Polish Economists in
Poznań in May 1929), Warsaw 1929.

Grabski, Władysław, "Parcelacja agrarna wobec struktury koniuntury
i chwili dziejowej Polski" ("Land Parcelling in View of the Structure, Market Situation, and the Historical Moment in Poland"),
Ekonomista, 1938, no. 4.

Grabski, Władysław, Społeczne gospodarstwo agrarne (The Social Economy in Agriculture), Warsaw 1923.

Grabski, Władysław, Wieś i folwark (The Village and the Manor),
Warsaw 1930.

Gr(yziewicz), S(tanisław), "Próba szacunku spożycia środków żywno-
ści przez ludość rolniczą" ("Attempt to Estimate Food Consumption by Agricultural Population"), Rolnik Ekonomista, 1936.

Von Hernier, Alexander, Entwicklung und Ergebnisse der Agrarreform *in Polen*, Danzig 1931.

Hedemann, O., *Historia powiatu brasławskiego (History of Brasław County)*, Wilno 1930.

Hodoly, A., Jastrzębowski, W., *Handel wiejski w Polsce międzywojennej (Countryside Trade in Interwar Poland)*, Warsaw 1957.

Hołówko, Tadeusz, *Ziemianie (Landowners)*, Warsaw 1919.

Horoszkiewicz, R., *Pińsk i jego okolice (Pińsk and Its Neighborhood)*, Pińsk 1926.

Horoszkiewicz, R., *Powiat stoliński (Stolin County)*, Brześć na Bugiem 1930.

Horoszkiewicz, R., *Tradycje ziemi pińskiej (Traditions of the Pińsk Land)*, Warsaw 1935.

Humnicki, Stefan, *Stan posiadania. Reforma rolna (Land Possessions. Land Reform)*, Warsaw 1929.

Hupka, Jan *W sprawie reformy agrarnej (On the Agrarian Reform)*, Cracow 1919.

Ihnatowicz, S., "Likwidacja lasów woj, nowogródzkiego" ("Liquidation of Forests in Nowogrodek Province"), *Las Polski*, 1928.

Iwasiewicz, J., *Znaczenie cukrownictwa dla życia gospodarczego Polski (The Importance of Sugar Refining for the Economic Life of Poland)*, Warsaw 1938.

Iwaszkiewicz, J., "Ofiarność ziemian na cele cświatowo–kulturalne 1800–1929" ("Generosity of Landowners in Education and Culture, 1800–1929"), in *Ziemiaństwo i większa własność rolna (The Landed Gentry and Large Estates)*, Poznań 1929.

Jałowiecki, M., *Po dworach i wsi litewskiej (In Lithuanian Manors and Villages)*, Kamień 1928.

Janikowski, T., "Zarys stanu rolnictwa ziemi nowogróckiej" ("Outline of the Agricultural Conditions in the Nowogródek Land"), *Prace Instytutu Badania Stanu Gospodarczego Ziem Wschodnich*, 1927, vol. 1.

Jankowski, Czesław, *Powiat oszmiański (Oszmiana County)*, vols. 1–3, Petersburg 1898.

Jaruzelski, Jerzy, *Mackiewicz i konserwatyści (Mackiewicz and the Conservatives)*, Warsaw 1976.

Jasnorzewski, S., *Statystyka porównawcza dochodów i rozchodów gospodarstw wielkorolnych 1926/27–1929/30 (Comparative Statistics of Returns and Expenditures of Large Estates, 1926/27–1929/30)*, Poznań 1928–31.

Jassem, Grażyna, *Majątek smogulecki w latach 1918–1937 (The Smog-*

ulec Estate, 1918-37, Poznań 1976.

Jastrzębski, W., *Przymusowa parcelacja w świetle katolickiej zasady (Forced Parcelling in the Light of Catholic Principles)*, Warsaw 1938.

Jundziłł, Antoni, *Nowe ustawodawstwo oddłużeniowe w rolnictwie (New Agricultural Debt Clearance Legislation)*, Warsaw 1934.

Kaczkowski, J., *Antyteza stosunków agrarnych w Polsce i w Rosji (Opposite Agrarian Relations in Poland and Russia)*, Warsaw 1918.

Kaczkowski, J., *Ordynacje w Królestwie Polskim (Entails in the Kingdom of Poland)*, Warsaw 1917.

Karwowski, Stanisław, *Jarocin i jego dziedzice (Jarocin and Its Heirs)*, Poznań 1902.

Kaszuba, W., "Zagadnienie rolnictwa na tle akcji parcelacyjnej" ("The Agrarian Question in View of Parcelling"), *Drogi Polski*, 1939, no. 3.

Kiniorski, Marian, *W służbie ziemi (In the Service of the Land)*, Warsaw 1929.

Klarner, Czesław, *Dochód społeczny wsi i miast w okresie przesilenia gospodarczego 1929-1936 (The Social Income of the Countryside and Towns during the Depression of 1929-36)*, Lwow 1937.

Kloska, J., "Lasy prywatne w pierwszym dziesięcioleciu Polski Odrodzonej" ("Private Forests in the First Twenty Years of Reborn Poland"), *Las Polski*, 1939.

Kłoczowski, Eugeniusz, *Drogi rozwoju wsi polskiej (Ways of Development of the Polish Countryside)*, Płock, 1936.

Kłoczowski, Eugeniusz, *Obecne prądy społeczne i gospodarcze nurtujące wieś polską. Problem agrarny w Polsce (Present Social and Economic Currents in the Polish Countryside. The Agrarian Question in Poland)*, Płock 1937.

Kobylański, A., *Oświetlenia do programu gospodarczego i zmiany ustroju rolnego w Polsce (Explanation of the Economic Program of the Reform of the Agrarian System in Poland)*, Cracow 1937.

Kohutek, L., *Dobra Wielkie Soleczniki (The Wielkie Soleczniki Estate)*, Wilno 1934.

Konarski, Szymon, *Szlachta kalwińska w Polsce (The Calvinist Nobility in Poland)*, Warsaw 1936.

Konopiński, T., *Cele i zadania produkcji zwierzęcej w Polsce (Objectives and Tasks of Animal Production in Poland)*, Poznań 1937.

Koprukowniak, Albin, "Likwidacja serwitutów w Ordynacji zamojskiej (1920–1932)" ("Liquidation of Easements in the Zamość Entail, 1920–32"), *Rocznik Lubelski*, 1960, no. 3.

Korowicz Henryk, *Polityka agrarna w zarysie (Outline of Agrarian Policy)*, Lwow 1933.

Korwin, L., *Ormiańskie rody szlacheckie (Armenian Noble Families)*, Cracow 1934.

Korwin, L., *Szlachta mojżeszowa (Judaic Nobility)*, Cracow 1938.

Korwin, L., *Szlachta neoficka (Convert Nobility)*, Cracow 1939.

Koszutski, Stanisław, *Geografia gospodarcza Polski (Economic Geography of Poland)*, Warsaw 1918.

Kowal, S., *Struktura społeczna Wielkopolski w międzywojennym dwudziestoleciu 1919–1939 (The Social Structure of Greater Poland in the Twenty Interwar Years, 1919–39)*, Poznań 1974.

Kowalski, K., *Katolickie plany reformy społecznej a ustrój rolny w Polsce (Catholic Plans for Social Reform and the Agrarian System in Poland)*, Poznań 1938.

Kresy litewsko-białoruskie Rzeczypospolitej Polskiej (Lithuanian and Byelorussian Borderlands of the Polish Republic), Warsaw 1919.

Kruk, S., *Problem drzewny w Polsce (The Timber Question in Poland)*, Warsaw 1926.

Kruk, W., *Zestawienie porównawcze wyników gospodarstw rolnych za rok 1926/27 (Comparative Statement of Farm Accountacy for the Years 1926/27)*, Cracow, no date.

Krycznyński, S., *Tatarzy litewscy (Lithuanian Tatars)*, Warsaw 1938.

Kryczyński, Ludwik, *Kwestia rolna (The Agrarian Question)*, Warsaw 1903.

Księga pamiątkowa na dziewięćdziesiolecie dziennika Czas *1848–1938 (The Nineteenth Anniversary Book of* Czas *1848–1938)*, Warsaw 1938.

Księga pamiątkowa na 75-lecie Gazety Rolnieczej *(The Seventy–Fifth Anniversary Book of* Gazeta Rolnicza*)*, vols. 1–2, Warsaw 1938.

Landau, Ludwik "Skład azwodowy ludnośći Polski jako podstwa badania struktury gospodarczej" ("The Occupational Structure of the Polish Population as the Basis for Studies on the Economic Structure") in *Wybśr pism (Selected Works)*, Warsaw 1957.

Landau, Zbigniew, "Oligarchia finansowa II Rzeczypospolitej" ("The Financial Oligarchy of the Second Polish Republic") *Przegląd Historyczny*, 1971, no. 1.

Landau, Zbieniew, Tomaszewski, Jerzy, *Gospodarka Polski międzywojennej (The Economy of Interwar Poland)*, vols. 1–3, Warsaw

1967-82.

Leszczyński, W., "Nasze większe gospodarstwa w świetle cyfr" ("Our Large Estates in the Light of Figures"), *Gazeta Rolnicza*, 19 March 1920.

Ludkiewicz, W., *Kwestia robotnika rolnego na Wileńszczyźnie (The Question of Farm Hands in the Wilno Region)*, Warsaw 1927.

Ludkiewciz, Zdzisław, *Rozmieszczenie własności ziemskiej gospodarstw wiejskich w Polsce (Distribution of Large Estates and Peasant Farms in Poland)*, Warsaw 1923.

Ludkiewicz, Zdzisław, *Struktura agrarna Pomorza (The Agrarian Structure in Pomerania)*, Toruń 1934.

Ludkiewicz, Zdzisław, *Ustrój rolny w Polsce i jego niedomagania (The Agrarian System in Poland and Its Shortcomings)*, Warsaw 1935.

Ludkiewicz, Zdzisław, "Ziemia i ludność rolnicza" ("The Land and the Agrarian Population") in *Dzieje gospodarcze Polski porozbiorowej (The Economic History of Poland After the Partitions)*, vol. 2, Warsaw 1922.

Ludkiewicz, Zdzisław, *Źródła i istota kwestii agrarnej na Litwie, Białej Rusi i Wołyniu (The Origin and Essence of the Agrarian Question in Lithuania, Byelorussia, and Volhynia)*, Warsaw 1921.

Lutosławski, Jan, *O katolicką politykę agrarną (On the Catholic Agrarian Policy)*, Warsaw 1938.

Lutosławski, Jan, *O upadku kultury rolniczej w Polsce (On the Decline of Agriculture in Poland)*, Warsaw 1930.

Lutosławski, Jan, *Sprawa rolna jako problemat Polski (The Agrarian Question as the Polish Problem)*, Warsaw 1919.

Łańcucka, G., *Aniela hr. Potulicka (Countess Aniela Potulicka)*, Potulice 1939.

Łęczycki, S., Żemoytel, T., *Przebudowa ustroju rolnego w ziemi wileńskiej (The Transformation of the Agrarian System in the Wilno Land)*, Wilno 1927.

Łubieński, Tadeusz, *Parę myśli w sprawie rozsądnego organizowania się społeczeństwa (Some Thoughts on a Reasonable Organization of the Society)*, Cracow 1927.

Łubieński, Tadeusz, *Przewrót ustroju polskiej wsi (Revolution in the Polish Countryside)*, Cracow 1936.

Machay, Ferdynand, *Problem wsi polskiej jako zagadnienie społeczne (The Polish Countryside as a Social Problem)*, Poznań 1937.

Mackiewicz, Stanisláw, *Dziś i jutro (Today and Tomorrow)*, Wilno 1929.

Madajczyk, Czesław, *Burżuazy jno-obszanrnicza reforma rolna w Polsce (1918–1939) (Bourgeois–Landowner Land Reform in Poland, 1918–1939)*, Warsaw 1956.

Maliszewski, Edward, *Białoruś w cyfrach i faktach (Byelorussia in Figures and Facts)*, Piotrków 1918.

Maliszewski, Edward, *Polacy na Litwie (Poles in Lithuania)*, Warsaw 1918.

Maliszewski, Edward, *Polacy na Łotwie (Poles in Latvia)*, Warsaw 1922.

Maliszewski, Edward, *Przewodnik po ziemi grodzieńskiej (Guide to the Grodo Land)*, Warsaw 1919.

Maliszewski, Edward, *Przewodnik po guberni mińskiej (Guide to the Minsk Guvernia)*, Warsaw 1919.

Manteuffel, Gustaw, *O starodawnej szlachcie krzyżacko–rycerskiej na kresach inflanckich (On Old–Time Teutonic Nobility of the Latgalian Borderland)*, Lwow 1912.

Marchlewski, Julian, "O nowy ład na wsi" ("On the New Deal in the Countryside"), *Goniec Czerwony*, 14 August 1920.

Marczak, M., *Przewodnik po Polesiu (Polesie Guide)*, Brześć nad Bugiem 1935.

Materiały do biografii, genealogii i heraldyki polskiej (Materials on Polish Biography, Geneology, and Heraldry), Konarski Szymon, ed., vols. 1–6, Paris–Buenos Aires 1963–72.

Mełeń, A., "Ordynacje w dawnej Polsce" ("Entails in Old Poland"), *Pamiętnik Historyczno–Prawny*, vol. 7, Lwow 1929.

Memorandum w sprawie szlachty zagrodowej na wschodzie Polski (Memorandum on the Village Nobility in Eastern Poland), Warsaw 1938.

Mieszczankowski, Mieczysław, *Rolnictwo II Rzeczypospolitej (Agriculture of the Polish Second Republic)*, Warsaw 1983.

Mieszczankowski, Mieczysław, *Struktura agrarna Polski międzywojennej (Agrarian Structure of Interwar Poland)*, Warsaw 1960.

Miklaszewski, J., *Lasy i leśnictwo w Polsce (Forests and Forestry in Poland)*, Warsaw 1928.

Miklaszewski, J., *Lasy na ziemiach polskich i ich los podczas inwazji (Forests in Polish Territories and Their Fate During the Invasion)*, Lwow 1917.

Miklaszewski, S., *Izby rolnicze (Agricultural Chambers)*, Warsaw 1935.

Mondalski, W., *Polesie*, Brześć nad Bugiem 1927.

Nowacki, B., *Ochrona lasów prywatnych w Polsce (Protection of Pri-*

vate Forests in Poland), Warsaw 1935.

Nowakowski, Stanisław, *Geografia gospodarcza Polski Zachodniej (Economic Geography of Western Poland)*, vols. 1–2, Poznań 1929.

Obrębski, Józef, *Problem etniczny Polesia (The Ethnic Problem in Polesia)*, Warsaw 1936.

Obst, J., *Nasze dwory wiejskie (Our Country Manors)*, Wilno 1919.

Obst, J., *Obwieczny spór Polski z Moskwą o Litwę (The Traditional Conflict Between Poland and Muscovy over Lithuania)*, Warsaw 1919.

Odanicki–Poczobutt, S., *Województwo nowogrłodzkie (Nowogródek Province)*, Wilno 1936.

Okołowicz, Alfred, "Perspektywy reformy rolnej na Śląsku" ("Perspectives on Land Reform in Silesia"), *Polska Gospodarcza*, 1938, no. 36.

Okołowicz, Alfred, "Regulacje rolne" ("Agrarian Regulations"), *Polska Gospodarcza*, 1938, no. 24.

Okoń, Eugeniusz, *Mowa w sprawie rolnej (A Speech on the Agrarian Question)*, Warsaw 1919.

"Okólniki Związku Ziemian z lat 1926–1928" ("Circulars of the Landowners' Society, 1926–28"), Madajczyk, Czesław, Ajnenkiel, Andrzej, eds., *Dzieje Najnowsze*, 1970, no. 3.

Opłacalność i oddłużenie w rolnictwie. Memoriał sochaczewskiego oddziału Związku Ziemian (Profitability and Debt Clearance. Memorandum of the Sochaszew Branch of the Landowners Society), Warsaw 1933.

Orczyk, Józef, *Produkcja rolna Polski w latach wielkiego kryzysu gospodarczego 1929–1935 (Agricultural Output in Poland During the Great Depression, 1929–35*, Poznań 1971.

Orczyk, Józef, *Studia nad opłacalnością gospodarstw rolnych w Polsce w latach 1929–1938 (Studies on Profitability of Farms in Poland, 1929–38)*, Warsaw 1981.

Organicacje ziemiańskie na ziemiach polskich (Landowners' Organizations in Polish Territories), Warsaw 1929.

Ormicki, Wiktor, *Sprawa reformy rolnej na Śląsku (The Land Reform Question in Silesia)*, Poznań 1937.

Ormicki, Wiktor, *Życie gospodarcze Kresów Wschodnich R. P. (Economic Life of the Eastern Borderland of the Polish Republic)*, Cracow 1929.

Orobkiewicz, W., *Z dziejów walk i cierpień na Kresach (From the History of Struggle and Suffering in the Eastern Borderland)*,

Warsaw 1919.

Pamiętnik I Walnego Zjazdu Zrzeszonego Ziemiaństwa Polskiego (Diary of the First Congress of Organized Polish Landowners), Warsaw 1925.

Pampuch, Piotr, "Reforma rolna w głornośleęskiej częsci województwa śląskiego" ("Land Reform in the Upper Silesian Part of the Silesian Province"), in *Pisma Piotra Pampuch (Works of Piotr Pampuch)*, Katowice 1955.

Parcelacja prywatna (Private Parcelling), Warsaw 1933.

Pawłowski, K., "Niektóre dane statystyczne dotyczące wielkorolnych gospodarstw województwa poznańskrego" ("Some Data Concerning Large Estates of Poznań Province"), *Roczniki Nauk Rolniczych i Leśnych*, 1935, vol. 35.

Pawłowski, S., *Wielka własność w byłej Galicji Wschodniej (Large Estates in Former Eastern Galicia)*, Lwow 1921.

Pic de Replonge, Jan, *Kredyt a oddłużenie rolnictwa (Credits and Debt Clearance in Agriculture)*, Warsaw 1939.

Pietkiewicz, Zenon, *Reforma rolna na ziemiach narodów odrodzonych (Land Reforms in the Reborn States)*, Warsaw 1921.

Pitowarczyk, Jan. *Katolicyzm i reforma rolna (Catholicism and the Land Reform)*, Warsaw 1938.

Plater, Zygmunt, *Lasy polskie przad, podczas i po wojnie (Polish Forests Before, During, and After the War)*, Warsaw 1918.

Polesie ilustrowane (Polesie Illustrated), Braześć nad Bugiem, 1923.

Poniatowski, Juliusz, *Cele i założenia reformy rolnej w dwudziestoleciu niepodległości (Objectives and Foundations of the Land Reform During the Twenty Years of Independence)*, London 1951.

Poniatowski, Juliusz. *Przeludnienie wsi i rolnictwa (Overpopulation of the Countryside and Agriculture)*, Warsaw, no date.

Ponikowski, Wacław, "Badanie porównawcze gospodarstw wiejskich rozmaitych wielkości lub rozmaitych typów pracy" ("Comparative Study of Farms of Various Size and Various Types of Labor"), *Roczniki Nauk Rolniczych i Leśnych*, 1934, vol. 33.

Ponikowski, Wacław, "Materiały rachunkowe Wydziału Ekonomiki Rolnej Drobnych Gospodarstw Wiejskich Instytut Naukowego Puławach jako podstawa badania życia gospodarczego wsi" ("Book Institute of Puławy As a Basis for Studies in the Economic Life of the Countryside"), *Roczniki Nauk Rolniczych i Leśnych*, 1937, vol. 40.

Ponikowski, Wacław, *Gospodarstwa włościanskie i folwarczne (Peasant*

Farms and Large Estates), Warsaw 1935.

Ponikowski, Wacław, "Próba obliczenia wartości produkcji rolnicz- ej w Polsce w roku gospodarczym 1927/28" ("Attempt to Calculate the Value of Agricultural Output in Poland in the Economic Year 1927/28"), *Rolnik Ekonomista*, 1929, no. 13/14.

Ponikowski, Wadław, "Próba obliczenia wartości wytwórczości roślinnej i zwierzęcej w Polsce" ("Attempt to Calculate the Value of Plant and Animal Production in Poland"), *Rolnik Ekonomista*, 1926, no. 7.

Potocki, S., *Położenie mniejszości niemieckiej w Polsce 1918–1939 (The Situation of the German Minority in Poland, 1918–39)*, Gdańsk 1969.

Potworowski, Edward, *Majętność Gola (The Gola Estate)*, Poznań 1929.

Powierza, B., *Melioracje w świetle statystyki (Land Drainage in the Light of Statistics)*, Warsaw 1929.

Roszkowski, Wojeich, *Gospodarcza rola większej prywatnej własności ziemskiej w Polsce 1918–1939, (Economic Role of Large Private Estates in Poland, 1918–39)*, Warsaw 1986.

Roszkowski, Wojciech, "Large Estates and Small Farms in the Polish Agrarian Economy Between the Wars (1918–1938)," *The Journal of European Economic History*, 1987, no. 1.

Roszkowski, Wojciech, "Stan posiadania ziemiaństwa polskiego do 1939 r." ("The Landed Property of Polish Landowners Before 1939") in *Najnowsza historia gospodarcza Polski (Modern Economic History of Poland)*, vol. 4, Warsaw 1985.

Rościszewska, M., "Próba porównania płac robotników rolnych" ("Attempt to Compare the Wages of Farm Hands"), *Statystyka Pracy*, 1935.

Rotkel, K., "Byt robotnika rolnego w świletle liczb" ("The Existence of Farm Workers in the Light of Figures"), *Przegląd Ziemiański*, 1922, no. 2.

Rouba, N., *Przewodnik po Litwie i Białej Rusi (Guide to Lithuania and Byelorussia)*, Wilno, no date.

Rozanów, M., *Powiat prużański (Prużana County)*, Prużana 1935.

Rudnicki, Szymon, *Działalność polityczna polskich konserwatystów 1918–1926 (Political Activities of Polish Conservatives, 1918–26)*, Wrocław 1918.

Ruśkiewicz, S. *Zmniejszanie się powierzchni leśnej w Polsce (The Decline of Forest Area in Poland)*, Warsaw 1930.

Rutkowski, Jan, *l asność taburlarna Galicji według stanu z końca 1912 r.* *(Large Landed Property in Galicia at the End of 1912)*, Lwow 1916.

Rychlikowa, Irena, "Dzieje ziemiaństwa polskiego w latach 1795–1945" ("History of Polish Landowners, 1795–1945"), *Dzieje Najonowsze*, 1976, no. 1.

Rychlikowa, Irena, *Gospodarka panów na Łańcucie (The Economy on the Masters of Łańcut*, Łańcut 1971.

Rylski, Eustachy, "Produkcja zbożowa w Polsce w dobie kryzysu" ("Grain Output in Poland During the Depression"), *Życie Rolnicze*, 1937, no. 32.

Ryz, Jerzy, *Kredyt dla większej własności w latach od 1927 do 1930 ruku (Credits for Large Landowners Between 1927 and 1930)*, Lwow 1931.

Sas–Jaworski, Tadeusz, "Bilans własności ziemskiej" ("The Balance Sheet of Landed Property"), *Ziemia Wołyńska*, 1931, no. 45.

Sas–Jaworski, Tadeusz, "Dziwna kalkulacj" ("Strange Calculation"), *Gazeta Rolnicza*, 6 November 1936.

Sas–Jaworski, Tadeusz, "Rolnictwo w obronie państwa" ("Agriculture in the Defense of the Nation"), *Gazeta Rolnicza*, 26 June 1936.

Schmidt, Stefan, "Problemy związane z napawą ustroju rolnego" ("Problems Concerning Improvement of the Agrarian System"), *Ekono- mista*, 1938, no. 2.

Schmidt, Stefan, *Stan i kierunki rozwoju rolnictwa w Polsce (The State and Directions of Development of Agriculture in Poland)*, Cracow 1928.

Schmidt, Stefan, *Własność folwarczna Zachodniej Małopolski w chwili wskrzeszenia państwa polskiego (Large Estates of Western Lesser Poland by the Resurrection of the Polish Statehood)*, Cracow 1924.

Schramm, Wiktor, "Ceny sprzedażne większych majątków ziemskich w zachodnich województwach Polski w pierwszych latach powojennych" ("Prices of Large Estates in Western Poland in the First Postwar Years"), *Roczniki Nauk Rolniczych i Leśnych*, 1925, vol. 13.

Schramm, Wiktor, *Koszta robocizny gospodarstw folwarcznych zachodniej Polski w okresie dewaluacji pieniądza 1911/12–1922/23 (Labor Costs of Large Estates in Western Poland During the Devaluation of Currency 1911/12–1922/23)*, Poznań 1925.

Schramm, Wiktor, "Problem poznawania organizacji gospodarstwa ziemskiego" ("The Question of Exploration of Large Estate Organization"), *Roczniki Nauk Rolniczych i Leśnych*, 1939, vol. 47.

Schramm, W., Kubera, J., *Ilość i wartość inwentarzy w wielkorolnych gospodarstwach województwa poznańskiego (The Quantity
and Quality of Stocks on Large Estates in Poznań Province)*,
Poznań 1931.

Serafin, F., *Wieś śląska w latach międzywojennych (The Silesian Countryside in the Interwar Years)*, Katowice 1977.

Skarbek–Kruszewska, Janina, "Dwór wiejski" ("The Country Manor
House"), *Ziemianka Polska,* 1930, no. 11.

Skwarczyńmski, Stanisław, *Czynniki wzrostu produkcji w rolnictwie
(Factors of Output Growth in Agriculture)*, Warsaw 1939.

Stan posiadania ziemi na Pomorzu (Possession of Land in Pomerania), vol. 2, Toruń 1935.

Staniszkis, Witold, *Sprawa rolna (The Agrarian Question)*, Warsaw
1918.

Staniszkis, Witold, *Dwa lata dalszej pracy nad przebudową ustroju rolnego w Polsce (1928–1929) (Two Further Years of Work on Reconstruction of the Agrarian System in Poland, 1928–29)*, Warsaw 1930.

Staniszkis, Witold, *O program agrarny w Polsce (For an Agrarian
Program in Poland)*, Warsaw 1928.

Staniszkis, Witold, "Reforma rolna w wytwórczość rolnicza" ("Land
Reform and Agricultural Output"), *Rolnictwo*, 1928, no. 10.

Staniszkis, Witold, *Zmiany w strukturze agrarnej Polski (Changes in
the Agrarian Structure of Poland)*, Poznań 1936.

Stankiewicz, Witold, *Konflikty społeczne na wsi polskiej 1918–1920
(Social Conflicts in the Polish Countryside, 1919–1920*, Warsaw
1963.

Staniewicz, Witold, "Pakt lanckoroński" ("The Lanckorona Agreement"), *Roczniki Dziejów Ruchu Ludowego*, 1959, no. 1.

Stark, H., Stein, E., *Reforma rolna (The Land Reform)*, Cracow 1939.

Stecki, Jan, "Obdłużenie większej własności ziemskiej" ("Indebtedness of Large Estates"), *Rolnik Ekonimista*, 1926, no. 6.

Stecki, Jan, "Podatki i opłaty publiczne a własność ziemska w b Kongresówce" ("Taxes and Public Burdens in Relation to Landed
Property in the Former Kingdom of Poland"), *Przegląd Ziemiański*, 1923, no. 11.

Stecki, Jan, "Reforma rolna a kapitalizacja" ("The Land Reform and
Capital Formation"), *Przegląd Ekonomiczny*, 1937, vol. 18.

References 199

Stecki, Jan, *Wartość i ceny ziemi (The Value and Prices of Land)*, Warsaw 1937.

Stecki, Jan, *Zagadnienie rozwoju gospodarczego wsi polskiej (The Question of Economic Devleopment of the Polish Countryside)*, Warsaw 1938.

Stosunki rolnicze Królestwa Polskiego (Agricultural Relations in the Kingdom of Poland), Warsaw 1918.

Stosunki rolnicze Rzeczypospolitej Polskiej (Agricultural Relations in the Polish Republic), vols. 1–2, Warsaw 1925.

Strajk chłopski w 1937 r. (The Peasant Strike of 1937), vols. 1–2, Warsaw 1960.

Struktura społeczna wsi polskiej (The Social Structure of the Polish Countryside), Warsaw 1937.

Studniarski, S., *Podstwy i zadania polityki leśnej (Foundations and Goals of the Forest Policy)*, Poznań 1937.

Studnicki, Władysław, *Przewroty i reformy agrarne Europy powojennej i Polski (Agrarian Upheavals and Reforms in Postwar Europe and Poland)*, Warsaw 1927.

Studnicki, Władysław, *Ziemie wschodnie (The Eastern Territories)*, Warsaw 1929.

Suchodolski, Bohdan, "Indywidualizm szlachecki" ("Noble Individualism"), *Roczniki Towarzystwa Przyjackiół Nauki na śięsku*, vol. 3, Katowice 1931.

Suhanek, W., "Spoŕ o dobra cieszyńskie" ("The Teschen Domain Conflict"), *Roczniki Towarzystwa Przyjackiøł Nauki na śięsku*, vol. 3, Katowice 1931.

Sukiennicki, Wiktor, *Pruska polityka kolonizacyjna na ziemiach polskich 1886–1919 (Prussian Colonization Policies in Polish Territories, 1886–1919)*, Warsaw 1931.

Symonowicz, S. "Zadłużenie większych gospodarstwo rolnych województwa wileńskiego i nowogródzkiego" ("Indebtedness of Large Estates in the Wilno and Nowogródek Provinces"), *Roczniki Nauk Rolniczych i Leśnych*, 1937, vol. 40.

Szczawiński, Z., *Likwidacja majątków niemieckich w Polsce (Liquidation of German Estates in Poland)*, Warsaw 1923.

Szemraj, Piotr, "Stopa życiowa wsi na tle dochodu" ("The Standard of Living in the Countryside in Light of Incomes"), *Życie Rolnicze*, 1938, no. 28.

Szewczyk, Wilhelm, *Skarb Donnersmarcków (Treasury of the Donnersmarcks)*, Katowice 1973.

Szymaczak, Z., *Działalność Banku Cukrownictwa w Poznaniu na rzecz skartelizowanego przemysłu cukrowniczego w Polsce (Activities of the Bank Cukrownictwa of Poznań in Favor of the Sugar Cartel in Poland)*, Poznań 1964.

Śląski, Jan, "Organizacja gospodarstw po przesileniu w rolnictwie" ("Organization of Estates After the Agricultural Depression"), *Gazeta Rolnicza*, 30 November 1928.

Świeżyński, W., *Organizacje ogólno-rolnicze (General Agricultural Organizations)*, Warsaw 1935.

Talko-Hryncewicz, J., *Muślimowie czylie tak zwani Tatarzy litewscy (Muslims, or the So-Called Lithuanian Tatars)*, Cracow 1907.

Tarnowski, T., "Praca kulturalno-oświatowa, wśród służby folwarczne (Education and Cultural Work Among Farm Hands"), *Gazeta Rolnicza*, 25 November 1938.

Tilgner, Władysław, *Analiza liczhowa wyhików rachunkowości wielkiej i małej własności województwa poznaniskiego (Numerical Analysis of Accounting on Large and Small Farms of Poznań Province)*, Poznań 1937.

Tilgner, W., Zeyland, M., Biliński, O., Gertner, C., *Statystyka porównawcza dochodów i rozchodów gospodarstw wielkorolnych i małbrolnych województwa poznańskiego za sześciolecie 1930/31 do 1935/36 (Comparative Statitistics of Returns and Expenditaures of Large and Small Farms of Poznań Province for the Six Years Between 1930/31 and 1935/36)*, Poznań 1938.

Tochtermann, J. J., *Lasy i gospodark drzewna Ziem Północno-Wschodinich (Forests and Timber Industry of the Northeastern Region)*, Wilno 1938.

Tomaszewski, T., *Badania wykresowe nad organizacją pracy w gospodarstwach wiejskich (Graph Studies in Organization of Farm Work)*, Warsaw 1938.

Trojanowski, M., *Analiza trzech wołyńskich gospodarstw folwarcznych (Analysis of Three Volhynian Large Estates)*, Łuck 1936.

Tuhan-Taurogiński, B., *Nieświeża (From the History of Nieśwież)*, Warsaw 1937.

Turowski, Grzegorz, *Warunki i drogi rozwoju gospodarczego wsi polskiej (Conditions and Ways of Development of the Polish Countryside)*, Warsaw, no date.

Tuskiewicz, O., *Przesilenie zbożowe w Polsce (The Grain Depression in Poland)*, Poznań 1934.

Udział ziemian w rozwoju kultury rolniczej w Polsce (Participation of Landowners in the Development of Agriculture in Poland), Warsaw 1929.

Urbański, A., *Memento kresowe (Eastern Borderland Memento)*, Warsaw 1929.

Urbański, A., *Podzwonne na zgliszczach Litwy i Rusi (The Death Knell for the Ruins of Lithuania and Ruthenia)*, Warsaw, no date.

Urbański, A., *Pro memoria*, Warsaw, no date.

Urbański, A., *Z czarnego szlaku i tamtych rubieży (From the Black Trail and Those Borderlands)*, Warsaw 1987.

Uziembło, Henryk, *Radziwiłł owska puszcza (The Radziwiłł Forest)*, Cracow 1934.

Walicki, J., "Na temat opłacalncśc gospodarstw forwarcznych w r. 1932/33" ("On the Profitability of Large Estates in 1932/33"), *Gazeta Rolnicza.* 6 October 1933.

Wapiński, Roman, "Problemy kształtowania sięelit politycznych II Rzeczypospolitej" ("Problems of Formation of Political Elites in the Polish Second Republic" in *Społeczeństwo polskie XVIII i XIX wieku (The Polish Society in the 18th and 19th Centuries)*, vol. 7, Warsaw 1982.

Warkoczewski, Stanisław, *Położenie robotników rolnych w Wielkopolsce w latach 1929-1939 (The Situation of Farm Workers in Greater Poland in the Years 1929-39)*, Warsaw 1965.

Weryha–Darowski, Aleksander, *Kresy ruskie Rzeczypospolitej (The Ruthenian Borderland of the Res Republica)*, Warsaw 1919.

Wize, Kazimierz, *Położenie robotników rolnych w Poznańskiem po wojnie (1919-1923) (The Situation of Farm Workers in Poznania After the War, 1919-23)*, Poznań 1925.

Władyka, Wiesław, *Działność polityczna polskich stronnictw konserwatywnych w latach 1926-1935 (Political Activities of the Polish Conservative Parties in the Years 1926-35)*, Wrocław 1977.

Województwo tarnopolskie (Tarnopol Province), Tarnopol 1931.

Wolff, Jozef, *Kniaziowie litewsko-ruscy (The Lithuanian-Ruthenian Princes)*, Warsaw 1895.

Wołłosowicz, S., *Ziemia wileńska (The Wilno Land)*, Cracow 1925.

Wrzos, Konrad, *Oko we oko z kryzysem (Face to Face with the Depression)*, Warsaw 1933.

Wrzosek, A., Zwierz, S., *Stosunki narodowcściowe w rolnictwie pomorskim (Nationality Relations in Pomeanian Agriculture)*, Gdynia–Toruń 1937.

Wydżga, Wojciech, *Z wycieczki na Kresy (An Excursion to the East-ern Borderland)*, Warsaw 1923.

Wydżga, Wojciech, "Ziemiaństwo i polityka" ("The Landed Gentry and Politics"), *Przegląd Ziemiański*, 1923, no. 51.

Wykresy stanu i rozwoju gospodarki leśnej w Polsce w latach 1919–1935 (Graphs Illustrating the State and Development of the Pol-ish Forest Economy), Warsaw, no date.

Wysocka, Barbara, "Elify społeczne Wielkopolski w II Rzeczypospo-litej" ("Social Elites of Greater Poland in the Second Republic"), *Studia i materiały do Dziejów Wielkopolski i Pomorza*, vol. 11, no. 2.

Zadania i owowiąski ziemiaństwa (Tasks and Duties of the Landed Gentry), Warsaw 1921.

Zagadnienia wytwóroczości zwierzęcej w Polsce (Problems of Animal Husbandry in Poland), Warsaw 1938.

Zaklika, Walerian, *Bilans obrotów gotówkowych rolnictwa polskiego (The Balance Sheet of Cash Turnover in Polish Agriculture)*, Lwow 1938.

Zalewski, S., *Ewolucja kredytu długoterminowego ziemskiego w Polsce (Evolution of Long-Term Land Credits in Poland)*, Warsaw 1938.

Zarys historii gospodarstwa wiejskiego w Polsce (Outline of History of the Rural Economy in Poland), vol. 3, Warsaw 1970.

Zasady współpracy stronnictw polskiej wić ekszości parlamentarnej w Sejmie w 1923 (Principles of Cooperation by the Polish Majority Parties in the Sejm in 1923), Warsaw 1923.

Ziemiaństwo i większa własność rolna (The Landed Gentry with Large Estates), WArsaw 1929.

Ziemiaństwo, rolnictwo i samorządy województwa Łódzkiego (The Landed Gentry, Agriculture, and Self-Government in Łódź Province), Łódź 1928.

Ziemiaństwo w pracy społecznej (The Landed Gentry in Social Work), Warsaw 1929.

Zjazd przedstawicieli pracy narodowej na wsi (The Congress of Repre-sentatives of National Labor in the Countryside), Warsaw 1937.

Złota księga ziemiaństwa polskiego. Wielkopolska (The Golden Book of the Polish Landed Gentry. Greater Poland), Warsaw 1929.

Żabko-Potopowicz, Antoni, *Rolnictwo w Polsce (Agriculture in Poland)*, Warsaw 1938.

Żabko-Potopowicz, Antoni. *Stulecie działnosci ziemieństwa polskiego 1814-1914 (The Hundred Years of Activity of the Polish Landed*

Gentry, 1814–1914), Warsaw 1929.

Żabko–Potopowicz, Antoni, "Zagadnienie najokorzystniejszego stosunku między gospodarstwami wiejskimi różnych rozmiarów w polskiej literaturz naukowej" ("The Question of the Optimum Relation Between Farms of Various Size in Polish Scholarly Literature"), *Ekonomista*, 1937, no. 3.

Żarnowski, Janusz, *Społeczenstwo Drugiej Rzeczypospolitej (The Society of the Polish Second Republic)*, Warsaw 1973.

Żmigrodzki, J., *Nowogródek i okolice (Nowogródek and Its Neighborhood)*, Nowogródek, 1927.

Żmigrodzki, K., *Powiat złoczowski (Złoczów County)*, Złoczów 1927.

Żychliński, Teodor, *Złota księga szlachty polskiej (The Golden Book of Polish Nobility)*, vols. 1–31, Poznań 1879–1908.

"Żydowskie gospodarstwa rolne w Polsce" ("The Jewish Farms in Poland"), *Rolnik Żydowski*, 1937, no. 9.

LIBRARY OF DAVIDSON COLLEGE